SURVIVAL THEMES
in Fiction for Children and Young People

by
BINNIE TATE WILKIN

with a Foreword
by
Jerome Cushman

The Scarecrow Press, Inc.
Metuchen, N.J. & London
1978

Library of Congress Cataloging in Publication Data

Wilkin, Binnie Tate, 1933-
    Survival themes in fiction for children and young people.

    Includes index.
    1. Children's literature--Bibliography.
2. Children's literature--History and criticism.
I. Title.
Z1037.W67   028.52   77-14295
ISBN 0-8108-1048-4

Copyright © 1978 by Binnie Tate Wilkin

Manufactured in the United States of America

CONTENTS

FOREWORD, by Jerome Cushman — v

INTRODUCTION — 1
    Historical Outline — 5

I. THE INDIVIDUAL — 25
    Aloneness and Loneliness — 28
    Feelings — 39
    Sexuality — 51
    Images — 79

II. PAIRINGS AND GROUPINGS — 90
    Friendship; Peer Pressures — 91
    Families — 107

III. VIEWS OF THE WORLD — 125
    Man and the Environment — 128
    Religion and Politics — 137
    War and Peace — 148
    Celebration of Life and Death — 174

IV. SOURCES AND NOTES — 185

INDEX — 227

FOREWORD

The survival of children in an uncertain world is the name of the game for Binnie Tate Wilkin and she exerts considerable expertise in helping them discover and exploit their life space. When she was on the staff of the Los Angeles Public Library a leadership syndrome gravitated toward her because her colleagues often waited to check out her opinion on a book or a program. She did not seek to be in the forefront but at the same time she spoke with pragmatic elegance on the issues that have changed children's literature from stories about the trip to grandma's farm to a narrative loaded with pain and despair. The new attitudes in fiction did not always set well with librarians who believed that children should be protected from harsh realities however vicarious, and book selection lines in the library were on occasion taut with tension.

Leadership does not always require overt action. Her positions on books and services, particularly for the inner city and barrio, brought, as she has said, "A number of people to my corner." It would be incorrect to assume that her career has been narrowly conceived. The entire community of children and young people is her bailiwick, with special emphasis on selection and services. She understands the common denominator of childhood that insists upon directness and honesty without equivocation. For Ms. Wilkin, the story is a primary concern.

She became a Senior Children's Librarian in the Los Angeles Public Library in a federally funded project. Working with nine branches in the central region, she assessed community needs, worked with parents, programmed children's services and assisted children with remedial reading problems. Her "Bookbagger" program distributed free paperbacks to the children. The project "A is for Africa" was a heritage experiment that preceded <u>Roots</u> by a few years. Several thousand children and adults have seen her interpretation of African folktales through narration, music and dance.

The Los Angeles experience was broadened through workshops on inner city services for various Library Association meetings. This led to writing and articles in <u>Library Journal</u>, <u>Interracial Books for Children Bulletin</u> and the anthology, <u>Advances in Librarianship</u>, documented her professional work.

In 1970 she joined the University of Wisconsin Library School for two years, training minority librarians as community specialists. This led to a specific interest in teaching and when she returned to California she taught courses on Children's Literature, Book Selection and Inner City Services at the library school of California State University, Fullerton. In 1976 she became a Lecturer in the Graduate School of Library and Information Science, UCLA, and taught Children's Libraries, Children's Literature and Library Services for Youth.

Among her ideas about books for children she believes that a realistic presentation of human existence will help them develop their own capabilities in problem solving. The books she selects are intended as samples that offer certain sensitivity to some of the individual and societal issues of the day. The choices include a wide swath of basic childrens books extending to the 1970s. Some of the issues are friendship, aloneness, feelings, sexuality, identification and self image. Picture books make up some of the selections. She prefers challenging and provocative issues as background for her perceptive and straightforward comments. The selections indicate a belief that books will help young people achieve a sense of values through an awareness of self and environment.

> JEROME CUSHMAN
> Senior Lecturer, Literature
>   for Children and Adolescents,
> Dept. of English, UCLA

INTRODUCTION

Before the advent of print, audio and visual systems, communication evolved from body language, dance, art and verbal forms. Gradually, an oral tradition developed which probably became the basis for all current literary structures. The story and other narratives, passed down through generations, documented history, modes of survival, and theories of man's existence. Lore was of interest to all and, where it was thought necessary, translations for the young were provided by storytellers, griots, wise men, monks, philosophers and teachers.

These early narratives were collected in the first stages of writing and printing, and records reveal that few of these materials were specifically directed toward children. It is commonly recognized that many fables, myths, and fairy tales, classified today as children's stories, were actually written for the perusal of the entire community. Even Mother Goose rhymes, said to have passed down to common folk from royalty, are linked by literary experts to political satire. Later classics such as Robinson Crusoe and Gulliver's Travels, which were also written for adults, through their popularity with children may have brought the potential of a juvenile market into focus. The surprising response to Alice in Wonderland and Through the Looking Glass possibly encouraged the development of a European market for children's books, which was later duplicated and expanded in America.

The earliest literary works in America were largely transplanted from England and reflected European rigidity and the Puritan tradition. Few attempts were made to make the books appealing to children; young people were treated as miniature adults. Paul Hazard, in Books, Children and Men,[1] suggests that children's dress reflected adult attitudes toward them. If adults didn't give children appropriate dress, he asks, how could they be expected to provide them with good books?

Societal structures may have barred the development of a separate literature for children prior to the seventeenth century. Childhood merged into adulthood at puberty and major responsibilities were assumed by the young. The period of childhood, as currently perceived, did not exist sociologically. But when a new social consciousness developed in Europe and America during the late nineteenth century, concepts of childhood changed. Child labor and child protection laws were passed, and a "leisure class" of children emerged which had previously been found only among royalty and the rich. Thus, cultural norms encouraged changing attitudes toward children, and childhood gradually came to be seen as a period during which one lives outside of adult realities.

More emphasis was placed on the child in the early twentieth century. The beginning of kindergartens brought a new interest in early childhood development and education. This may have accounted for the eventual spread of picture books. In any case, it seems apparent that during this period the focus on childhood as a unique and separate term of life increased.

The growing emphasis on public education encouraged the mass production of printed materials for support of curricula. An enormous expansion of children's publishing produced information books, biographies, histories, etc. directed toward educational and public markets.

Underlying this production were complex questions concerning the child's ability to cope with certain types of materials. Even in books of information, authors struggled to structure their texts in accordance with expert analyses of the child's capabilities at various age levels. The growing market led to fiction factories introducing series such as Tom Swift and The Bobbsey Twins, series which capitalized on formula stories with mass appeal. Some publishers turned out a book a month, with only minor plot changes. Literature documenting cultures, philosophies, and problems of the world was sparse, and what there was was sometimes grossly stereotyped. Societal mores did not allow for complete openness in presenting difficult subject matter to adults and the new attitudes toward childhood allowed for much less in children's materials.

Concern grew among librarians and educators, and they sought methods to raise the level of respect for children's materials. Review media, prizes, and awards were initiated. The critical analysis of books challenged publishers to set better standards.

By the mid-twentieth century, books for children were being published in large numbers. Information books were not only designed to support curricula, but often the format was improved to appeal to a broader audience. In some cases the books presented accurate and detailed information, simplified for the child's uses. Although history and social studies publications were plentiful, they usually did not include in-depth examination of issues. Political structures and forms of government other than democracy were not discussed. Biographies were greatly fictionalized and sometimes only covered the childhood of famous persons. Technically, books were more attractive, with better bindings and paper, excellent illustrations, graphics and color. In regard to content, however, publishers found it hard to keep pace with the world's social and technological changes. Current editions often did not reflect changes in communication, values, and issues. Fast marketing frequently took priority over quality production.

Some early books of fiction focused on pioneer life, poverty, war and various regions of the world, but with few exceptions, what is commonly called "realistic" fiction is a twentieth-century phenomenon. When television opened up, to children of all ages, a world of conflict, passion, and hostility, some authors and publishers of juvenile materials responded with books which touched upon these and other political and social issues. Children could hardly escape the impact of the bomb, war, politics, religion. Physical and social survival became factors important to all.

Books for children had progressed from a few puritanical views of "the hard life" to some attempts to present the "realities" of living. Subjects such as abortion, racial conflict and sexuality have subsequently been presented among the multiplicity of media available for all ages. Possibly because of the massive quantities of materials dispensed and because of the consideration of children's literature as a separate entity in the body of information, realism again became secondary to "childlike appeal." But evidence of new pressures upon the young has promoted a trend toward subjects of survival in fiction as well as non-fiction, and the survival significance of a story becomes again an area for consideration.

4 / Survival Themes

The purpose of this volume is not to argue the validity or otherwise of children's literature designed for simple enjoyment. The level of enjoyment vs. information in children's materials has always been determined by societal perspectives of childhood and of the needs of children. An attempt is made in this volume to focus on some elements of survival as a method of measuring and interpreting fiction for children and young people. "Survival" is broadly interpreted to include introspection, absorption of values, presentation of role models, etc. It is proposed, first, that children are involved in the discovery and exploration of their worlds, in search of leadership in formulating directions for living; second, that communication materials can provide vicarious experiences and observations not accessible to the child in close human relationships; third, that it is essential that children be exposed to some realistic presentations of the human existence as they develop capabilities for problem solving; and fourth, that good fiction is often the vehicle for all of these.

The selected materials here include some which have withstood the test of time, but most are writings produced in the latter half of the twentieth century. Concentration is on those offerings which reflect sensitivity to the individual and to societal issues. Some emphasis is given to bias and omission in various categories. Because of the enormous amount of material available, no attempt has been made to be all-inclusive; I have tried to find a reasonable sampling of materials to exemplify the subject categories. Although the major stress is on fiction, some non-fiction materials have been noted. The story as a medium for transmitting information for survival is of primary concern.

Introductory information in each chapter includes educational, psychological and sociological notes regarding attitudes toward youth and/or the subjects being discussed. Various sources were chosen to give a broad perspective, but in each case articles were chosen to coincide with the selected books which follow. Quotations from taped interviews held with young people in the Los Angeles area are added to give insight to young people's thoughts on the selected subjects.

The following historical outline is presented for those who wish to study further the social elements which have affected the development of children's literature as a genre within the total literary world. Of importance here are the indications of the ways in which the story or novel and the social and political developments of the western world impacted on each other.

HISTORICAL OUTLINE

The following outline is presented as a brief overview of historical developments in England and America which may have affected trends in the production of children's materials. Books listed have been gleaned from standard sources for the study of children's literature. Interwoven with this listing are historical notes presenting some of the educational, social, political and literary ideas evident during periods of production. Notes concerning child labor are added to show possible dichotomies between the reality in children's situations and the adult fantasies about youth. Comments are presented as a challenge to further study, but generally no attempt has been made to draw conclusions. One conclusion is evident, however: children's literature is and always has been an adult process. Materials for children expose the adult's view of self as well as adult perspectives of childhood.*

> In fact, we find that most distinctions between good adult literature and good children's literature dissolve under careful scrutiny; the main difference between the two is not the essential nature but in the age level of the largest number of readers. Hence evaluating and understanding children's literature has a direct kinship to the critical reading of any work of literature. [2]

1400-1625

This was a period of enthusiasm, change and open-minded search for information in most parts of the world. In Europe, however, it was also the period when decadence and materialism were questioned by reformers such as

---

*Starred items represent materials directed at children, or those published for adults which have large child readerships.

6 / Survival Themes

Martin Luther. Rigid traditions of the middle ages were being rejected. Classics were read by the common people. A great curiosity about the world grew into great explorations.

The Renaissance was late reaching England, but when it did, great literature and authors emerged, including Francis Bacon, Marlowe, Shakespeare, Edmund Spenser, Ben Jonson, Robert Greene and Thomas Nash.

Children in these early times commonly labored at a young age. Early pictures show very small children working in the fields or at apprenticeships. Education was the only recourse for improving the plight of poor children, although education almost always led into the church. Apprenticeships with tradesmen were a system of both labor and training.

1430-1440* Book of Courtesye. This title may have been available in manuscript before the invention of printing (about 1456). It was later issued by Caxton, about 1479. The 848-line rhymed poem, in three books, portrayed well-bred English youth. Such books were used in the "great houses" to train children of noble families. Caxton also issued such titles as Morte d'Arthur, The Historye of Reynard the Fox, and Aesop's Fables.

1540* The Primer of Salysbury Use, both Englyshe and in Laten, by John Gough. This Catholic primer was among the first primers for children. It contained alphabets and devotions.

The English Reformation, essentially an effort to de-Catholicize the church, had begun. Various religious movements initiated books of instruction.

1549* A Dialogue of Communicacyon to be had at a table between two chyldren, gathered out of the Holy Scriptures, by John Bale for his two yonge sonnes Johan and Paule. Arguments on points of theology by Bale, a reformist.

1550* The Hornbook. This date probably applies to the devotional hornbook. The existence of hornbooks has been noted as early as 1450.[3] The hornbook was a simple leaf pasted on board and covered with horn. Printed on the leaf were alphabets and

Introduction / 7

prayers. The hornbook seems to be peculiar to English-speaking people, and was extensively used in England and America.

From 1547 to 1553 a strong Protestant movement in England, under Edward VI, was followed by Catholic reaction to reformists, 1553-1558. Some settling in America of English colonists was due to "counter reformist" reactions during this period. Calvinism formed the basis for Puritanism in England and was the basis for social and political thinking in the colonies. Predestination, self denial, and preparation for future life after death were strong elements of this doctrine.

1560   Book of Nurture, by Hugh Rhodes, urged that children should be kept from reading fables, fantasies and stories of love.

1563*   A Booke in English metre of the great marchaunt man called Dyves Pragmaticus, very pretye for chyldren to rede, wherby they may the better and more readye read and write Wares and Implements in this worlde contayned. Aimed at teaching children to read and write.

1625-1750

This period is often called The Age of Reason. The Protestant Reformation had brought a belief in individualism and reason became the order for societal unity. Classics were viewed in a different way; basic truths of former writers were sought. Because leaders and writers of this age did not trust feelings, and emotions such as love, hate and fear were not allowed to surface, literature became cold and artificial. In England, writers like Bacon, Hobbes and Locke tried to show the importance of logical thinking. The foundation was laid for modern science. Poets wrote of universal truths.

Puritan theology saw no innocence in the child; instead, children were viewed as sinners, surrounded by the evils perpetrated by the devil. Books considered appropriate for children often included tales of horror and torture for those who sinned. Lesson books contained religious teachings and warnings against misbehavior.

1625*   Spiritual Milk for Boston Babes, by John Cotton,

presented theology in question and answer form. This may have been the first book for children printed in North America. (About fifty years later, Boston became the center for the book trade, followed by Philadelphia and New York.) A sample of Cotton's text: "How did God make you? I was conceived in sin and born of iniquity."

1678* Pilgrim's Progress, by John Bunyan, told the somber tale of a soul's pilgrimage to everlasting life. The book was not written for children, but later became a children's classic. Newer editions excluded some of the sermonizing text.

1679* The Prodigal Son Sifted or the Lewd Life and Lamentable End of Extravagant Persons Emblematically Set Forth for a Warning to Unexperienced Youth. Emblem books like this one were illustrated with objects from real life; the text was heavy on morality.

1686* A Book for Boys and Girls or Country Rhimes for Children, an emblem book by John Bunyan. In 1724, the title was changed to Divine Emblems: or Temporal Things Spiritualized. Some lightness was found among the stern verses, which used frogs, bees and other animals to teach lessons: "this bee the emblem of sin, whose sweet unto death has been."

From 1688 to 1689, the revolution in England dethroned the Catholic ruler, and Protestants William and Mary came into power.

Reverberations from the English revolution were felt in the American colonies, but religious tolerance was slow to appear. Puritan thought still held firm underneath the growing democratic political thought. An ever-increasing number of immigrants came to America as shifts in power took place in European nations. In 1700, all the thirteen colonies had been established.

1685- The New England Primer, published in Boston by
1690* Benjamin Harris, sold over five million copies. The text emphasized stringent religious principles; e.g., "Heaven to find, the Bible mind; deluge drowned, the earth around; Elijah hid by Ravens fed; the judgement made Felix afraid."[4]

Introduction / 9

In the early eighteenth century, John Locke's theories on education were becoming widely respected. He recommended that easy and pleasant books be written for children, but none that were "useless trumpery." Morality took precedence over religion as Puritan fervor seemed to be subsiding.

During the century, the industrial revolution gathered impetus. Machines replaced hand labor. Children from ages five and six tended machines and worked in coal mines. Ironically, it was during this period that English children's books really got underway. (France's Perrault is sometimes given credit for the beginning of the development of children's materials.) The new parliamentary form of government upgraded the middle class and more people could afford books and education. Books for children still gave instruction on virtue and hard work, although some were more attractively designed.

1702* A Little Book for Little Children (Boston, 1702) contained preachments and tortures from Foxe's Book of Martyrs.

1715* Divine Songs, attempted in easy language for use of children, by Isaac Watts. Watts, a nonconformist preacher, maintained a strong moral and religious emphasis in his rhymes but showed some sympathy toward children. The famous "Cradle Hymn" is one among the songs based on the everyday lives of children, at home, in the streets and fields.

1717* The Holy Bible in Verse, written by Benjamin Harris. Probably published in Boston, this is considered the earliest compilation of the Bible published for children.

1719* Robinson Crusoe, by Daniel Defoe (first edition, 1714), was written for adults but was later adopted by children. Although often appraised as an adventure story, this title in its original editions was an allegory with very deep meanings. Because of its popularity, many imitations were to follow.

1726* Gulliver's Travels, by Jonathan Swift, was also written for adults, as a political satire. However, the giants and little people had enormous appeal for children.

Historians refer to the period from about 1715 to 1774 as The Age of Enlightenment. During this period, emphasis was placed on the natural sciences as well as social conditions, politics and ethics. The first two titles to follow indicate the influence of science.

> The Knowledge of the Heavens and Earth Made Easy as The First Principles of Geography and Astronomy Explained.

1736*   A Description of a Great Variety of Animals and Vegetables ... especially for the entertainment of children, by Thomas Breman.

1740-1743   Gigantick Histories were published by Thomas Boreman. These were tiny books, the size of a snapshot, mainly concerned with the history of London.

1744*   A Little Pretty Pocketbook, by John Newbery. "Intended for the instruction and amusement of Little Master Tommy and Pretty Miss Molly, with an agreeable letter to read from Jack the Giant Killer, or also a ball and a pincushion, the use of which will infallibly make Tommy a good boy and Polly a good girl." Following Locke's recommendation to provide the child with "some easy book suited to his capacity," Newbery printed readings in morality with entertaining formats. Newbery is credited with having printed a version of Mother Goose, but the evidence for this is not clear. Nursery rhymes did appear in many of his volumes.

1749*   The Governess; or Little Female Academy, by Sarah Fielding. A sample of the stories of school life, this one depicts life in the boarding schools, with Mrs. Teachum as head of the institution.

1750-1850

This period, known as the Age of Romanticism, saw a revolt against the Age of Reason and a new interest in the traditional literature of the common folk. Writings gave praise to man's natural feelings as being a guide to wise conduct. Enthusiasm was again respected and artificiality criticized. Nature was portrayed as the "soul of the universe" and simple life in the wilds was romanticized. City people were portrayed as the most artificial, while the "uncivilized" were often seen as noble. There was renewed interest in Greek and Roman classics, which were studied along with the works of the Middle Ages.

While democratic principles grew out of the new attitudes reflected in the writings of Wordsworth, Shelley, Keats and others, children on both continents still worked long hours. In England, children were reported to have worked as many as sixteen hours a day; twelve hours a day was the minimum. In America, children worked on farms, in various household industries, as apprentices, at sea, as indentured servants, and as slaves. Around 1787, textile manufacturing was transplanted to the United States. Children became the bulk of the labor force (later, women took over because there was no large available group of pauper children as there was in England). In 1791, Alexander Hamilton, Washington's Secretary of State, made a statement favoring child labor.

1765*   The Renowned History of Little Goody Two Shoes, thought to be the work of Oliver Goldsmith, was published by John Newbery.

1772*   A Poem, on the rising glory of America, being an exercise at the Public Commencement at Nassau Hall, Sept. 25, 1771 (Philadelphia: Joseph Cruikshank for R. Aitken). This publication indicates that the new nationalism in America was being reflected in the literature.

The strong influence of women was beginning to appear during this period, especially in England where the Sunday School movement to educate the poor was supported by women such as Sarah Trimmer.

1778-1779   Lessons for Children, by Mrs. Anne Letitia Barbauld.

1783   Blue Backed Speller presented simplified and standardized American spelling.

1786   Fabulous Histories, by Mrs. Sarah Trimmer.

1786   Thoughts on the Education of Daughters, by Mary Wollstonecraft. Her ideas were not greeted with general approval. She also wrote Vindication of the Rights of Women.

12 / Survival Themes

1789	<u>The History of Sanford and Merton</u>, by Thomas Day.
1789	<u>Songs of Innocence</u>, by William Blake. Not originally written for children, they presented God and life in a much lighter vein than former poets had.
1789	<u>American Universal Geography</u>, by Jedediah Morse.
1793	<u>Cooper's History of America</u>, abridged for the use of children of all denominations.

Although developments in England in the latter half of the century were very different from those in America, similarities in attitudes toward children can be seen. Education in the colonies had forged ahead, but for many of the poor and those on farms, schools were not available.

In England, rising religious feelings about middle-class obligations to the poor brought about the development of Sunday Schools. These schools were devoted to reading, writing and arithmetic, not religion. (These later became parochial schools.)

1800-1850

In the early nineteenth century, a new humanitarianism emerged and brought some changes in the treatment of children. As the century opened, poor children in English cities still lived in dark holes in cellars with their families. Sometimes a whole family occupied one room. Many children were thrown in debtors' prisons with their families.

In 1802, the first Factory Act included children under the poor laws, and from 1819 to 1878 a series of other factory acts shortened the hours children might work. The age when children could start work was also raised. Parliament set up a commission in 1830 to look into the problems of working children, and children aged <u>eight</u> were found to be working from 6 a.m. to 8 p.m.

Romantics of the eighteenth century had stirred people out of their acquiescence. New writers were concerned with social abuse and political evils. There were strong movements for the reorganization of society. New religious movements appeared. Politically there were the Socialists and the Economists and in religion there were the Evangelicals and the

Nonconformists. The people's movement was reflected in the writings of Tennyson, Macaulay, Browning, Carlyle, Dickens and Ruskin. New interests in science were developed and efforts were made to find answers to moral, social and religious questions. This was the period of the development of the novel as the creative format for the expression of realism. Playwrights often used symbolism to express the cause of the common man.

In America, the Transcendentalist movement of the 1830's greatly liberalized Puritan theology. Elements of this movement were idealism, romanticism, mysticism, individualism and self reliance. Transcendentalism also led to human reforms and new social and political thought. Emerson, Thoreau, and Hawthorne were exponents of this trend. Other American writers emerging in this period were Longfellow, Poe, Whitman, and Melville.

In 1830 Horace Mann led the fight for "common schools" in Massachusetts and in 1832, Massachusetts law required schooling for working children.

Connecticut and Massachusetts limited the working hours for children employed in the textile mills to ten hours a day, in 1842. Later, in 1848, Pennsylvania outlawed the hiring of children under twelve in the mills.

The changes on both continents were reflected in the overt production of tales of the common folks. The breakthrough in children's materials was probably due in part to the growing literacy. Adult fiction was being produced more rapidly and new status and methods existed for publishers.

In the early 1800's children's books were still not plentiful, nor was writing anywhere near the quality found today. Fairy tales were frowned upon, but could be found in chapbooks. Yet the first English translation of Grimm's appeared during this period. Some of today's classics also were produced. Although still heavily moralistic, some materials included poems, rhymes, and fanciful stories with childish experiences.

1800	<u>New England Primer</u> was re-edited with a less pious tone.
1804	<u>Original Poems for Infant Minds</u>, by Anne and Jane Taylor, included the famous "Twinkle, Twinkle, Little Star."

14 / Survival Themes

1809	*The Butterfly's Ball*, by William Roscoe, was published by John Harris.
1812	*Swiss Family Robinson*, by Johann David Wyss. This German classic was introduced in England about 1814. The story, written by Wyss for his sons, was probably patterned after the earlier *Robinson Crusoe*, as were many adventure stories for boys during this period.
1818	*History of the Fairchild Family*, by Mrs. Sherwood. These stories were filled with fear and damnation, but the children were portrayed as real and believable persons.
1822	*A Visit from St. Nicholas*, by Clement Moore.
1823	*Grimm's Fairy Tales* were translated into English by Edgar Taylor.
1823	*The Adventures of Samboe*, by Mrs. Hofland. This and other stories by Mrs. Hofland were among the growing number of stories reflecting concern about slavery. Others were *The Adventures of Congo, Radama, or The Enlightened African*, and *The Babes in the Basket*.
1826	*The Last of the Mohicans*, by James Fenimore Cooper. Written for adults, but popular with children. Cooper was the first American novelist to win international fame.
1834	*Eclectic Readers*, by William H. McGuffey. These were the primary literature for elementary grades in the U.S. and were printed until about 1900. The tone of these readers was one of patriotism, including speeches of Daniel Webster and other American leaders.
1839	*Holiday House*, by Catherine Sinclair. Strong morals, but child characters were more human than in many other titles.
1843	*A Christmas Carol*, from the *Christmas Book* by Charles Dickens.
1846	*Book of Nonsense*, by Edward Lear.

1846   English translations of Hans Christian Andersen's
        Fairy Tales.

1850-1900

1850 is commonly seen as the beginning of the Modern Period. The industrial revolution brought new modes of travel, breaking down barriers between continents. Works of each country became read in various places and styles were copied.

Ferment on both continents peaked in the middle of the century with the Civil War in America and a second Reform Movement in England. Post-Civil War societies were more complex than ever, with the now freed Blacks, a growing women's movement, and the fast expansion westward. Rising merchantilism in the United States brought views of the "good life" to the forefront. In England, the electorate had been broadened as never before. Non-Anglicans were gradually permitted to vote. Even agricultural workers, who still could not vote, had representation.

Developments which may have affected children and the progress of children's literature may be found in educational trends. The child labor movement also continued to have important implications.

The educational system in America was seriously disrupted by the Civil War. In the South, numerous schools were destroyed or used for military purposes and many teachers were killed in battle. After the war Black and White legislators in the South passed laws encouraging free schools. Beginning about 1870, more and more states made laws favoring compulsory education at the elementary level. High schools had been mainly private academies before the Civil War but by the last quarter of the century, public schools became more widespread. Also, new immigration in the 1880's strengthened the Catholic church in America and lent support to the growth of parochial schools.

In England, education for children was not made compulsory until 1880. Between 1870 and 1890 primary attendance was tripled but free education for all came almost a decade later. The Reform bill of 1867 had brought a grave question regarding the need for education of the working class, who now had the right to vote.

Action against child labor and child abuse continued and in 1853 the Children's Aid Society was established in New York City, by Charles Brace. This was a non-sectarian organization serving all races and creeds of orphaned and destitute children. Even so, the 1870 census reported child labor in a separate category, citing about 750,000 children aged fifteen and under in the labor market. After 1870, rapid industrialization came to America, and in the South from 1890 to 1900 child labor increased almost threefold.

In England in 1891, a new factory act was passed which forbade the employment of children under the age of eleven. It is interesting to speculate on the possible connection between Hans Christian Andersen's story of the "Little Match Girl" and an exposé of the atrocious working conditions of London girls in match factories. An article by Mrs. Besant exposed these conditions. She later gave support to the strike of the "match girls" in 1889.

Children's materials during this period, both in England and America, were a mixture of fantasy, social comment, sentimentality and realism. Few experts attempt to explain the arrival of Alice in Wonderland in such a period. Its tremendous success may have been the spark for future fantasies. Reportedly, the popularity of the realistic family story was as much a surprise to literary critics as "Alice" was. The flow of exchange between England and America increased as the American book trade grew.

1851	The King of the Golden River, by John Ruskin.
1852	A Wonder Book for Boys and Girls, by Nathaniel Hawthorne, introduced Greek mythology to children. His Tanglewood Tales appeared a year later.
1856	The Daisy Chain, by Charlotte Yonge, was a popular novel about a middle class Victorian family.
1863	The Water Babies, by Charles Kingsley. Beginning with realism and moving into fantasy, this book is highly moralistic.
1865	Alice's Adventures in Wonderland, by Lewis Carroll, published by Macmillan.
1865	Hans Brinker and the Silver Skates, by Mary Mapes Dodge, was one of the pioneering stories of American origin about people in other lands.

Introduction / 17

1868   Little Women, by Louisa May Alcott.

1869   The Story of a Bad Boy, by Thomas Bailey Aldrich.

1870   Twenty Thousand Leagues Under the Sea, by Jules Verne.

1871   At the Back of the North Wind, by George MacDonald.

1872   Sing Song, by Christina Rossetti.

1873 saw the first public kindergarten, an indication of the new trend toward early childhood education.

Libraries and library publications gained impetus. The Library Journal began in 1876, the same year that the U.S. Bureau of Education published Public Libraries in the U.S., which discussed the necessity for a place in public libraries for the young. In 1895, the Boston Public Library assigned a room as the children's section.

During this period, American influence was seen in the establishment of English public libraries. It should also be noted that historical reports reveal a growing imperialistic urge toward conquest in England, and some feel that the works of such authors as Kipling contributed to these nationalistic dreams of voyage and conquest.

1875   A Young Folk's History of the United States, by Thomas Higginson.

1876   The Adventures of Tom Sawyer, by Mark Twain.

1877   Black Beauty, by Anna Sewell, is a document of social history which has continued to survive.

1878   The House that Jack Built and the Diverting History of John Gilpin, by Randolph Caldecott.

1880   The Peterkin Papers, by Lucretia Hale.

1881   The Prince and the Pauper, by Mark Twain.

1883   Treasure Island, by Robert Louis Stevenson.

1885   A Child's Garden of Verses, by Robert Louis Stevenson.

1885	Little Lord Fauntleroy, by Frances Hodgson Burnett.
1886	Pepper and Salt, by Howard Pyle.
1889	The Blue Fairy Book, by Andrew Lang.
1891	Rhymes of Childhood, by James Whitcomb Riley.
1891	Pinocchio, by Carlo Lorenzini (1st English edition). This was one of the first Italian children's books to win international fame.
1892	English Fairy Tales, by Joseph Jacobs.
1894	The Jungle Books, by Rudyard Kipling.
1898	Wild Animals I Have Known, by Ernest T. Seton--a forerunner of the realistic animal narrative.
1896	Poems of Childhood, by Eugene Field.

20th Century

At the dawn of the twentieth century, the American nation was convulsed by political, social, and economic reform movements. Critics became numerous and vocal. Those who wrote about America's ills were dubbed "muckrakers." John Spargo wrote The Bitter Cry of Children, an exposé of child labor abuse. By 1900, about half the states had placed some restrictions on child labor, but more were needed. In 1904, The National Child Labor Committee was launched by labor unions and social workers, and in 1912 Congress established a children's bureau. In 1916, President Wilson's "Keating and Owen Act," barring from interstate commerce articles produced by child labor, was passed. The act was declared unconstitutional in 1917 but was reenacted in 1918.

Affecting education was John Dewey's Democracy and Education, published in 1916. The Progressive Education Association was formed in 1918, composed of persons dissatisfied with the inflexibilities that had settled in education in the latter part of the nineteenth century. Also in 1918, aims for secondary education were enacted by the National Education Association, including "preparation for health, command of the fundamental processes, home membership, vocation, citizenship, leisure and ethical character."

1902	<u>The Tale of Peter Rabbit</u>, by Beatrix Potter.
1903	<u>Johnny Crow's Garden</u>, by Leslie Brooke.
1903	<u>Rebecca of Sunnybrook Farm</u>, by Kate Douglas Wiggin.
1904	<u>The Bobbsey Twins</u>.
1908	<u>The Wind in the Willows</u>, by Kenneth Grahame.
1910	<u>Tom Swift</u>.
1910	<u>The Secret Garden</u>, by Frances Hodgson Burnett. Moral lessons are very evident in this appealing book.

A postwar recession was experienced from 1920 to 1922, but then came the "golden age" of the twenties. Spiritualism was engulfed by materialism. This was the period of the rise of jazz, Dr. Sigmund Freud's publications, flappers, and gin fizz. Although many authors still wrote on conventional themes, cheap, sexy magazines were on the rise. The 1920's are sometimes called a "backward looking time," when people retreated into fantasy to forget World War I.

Popular novels included Fitzgerald's <u>This Side of Paradise</u> and Dreiser's <u>An American Tragedy</u>. Prohibition spawned an outburst of organized crime.

Schools were making steady progress. More states required that children remain in school through high school. Scientific developments were increasing and an open fight developed between fundamentalists and those who embraced Darwin's theories of evolution.

The scene was set for the forthcoming increase in production of children's materials. Education was expanded and Dewey's theories of progressive education were given support (response to Dewey was not totally positive; negative reactions came from parochial schools and other educational theorists). Dewey basically believed that education was the process by which the child could become increasingly socially conscious.

Children's Book Week had been started and the Newbery Award, established by Frederic Melcher to encourage more and better publishing in the children's field, was first awarded in 1922.

1921   The Story of Mankind, by Hendrik Willem Van Loon.

1926   Winnie the Pooh, by A. A. Milne. Some critics view this title as being extremely important as a trendsetter in writings for children, because it is well written yet free of moralizing.

1928   Millions of Cats, by Wanda Gag.

1928   Abe Lincoln Grows Up, by Carl Sandburg.

1929 marked the year of the stock market crash, followed by the great depression of 1930.

By 1930 publishers had begun to set up separate editing departments for the production of children's materials. Children were more than ever portrayed as individuals in literature rather than as spokesman for morals, religion and politics. The latter tendency did not entirely disappear, however, and after the depression children's materials reflected enormous variations in social, political and religious thought. Generally, in literature, there was a new emphasis on democracy as a group process rather than on the individual finding his place.

To consider the plight of the child, the White House Conference on Child Health and Protection was held in 1930. In 1938, the Fair Labor Standards Act struck at child labor. Employers engaged in interstate commerce could not hire workers under sixteen or in hazardous occupations under eighteen. In certain circumstances, children aged fourteen to sixteen could be employed. Little progress was made in agriculture, for children of all ages still labored long hours on farms and as migratory laborers.

1932   Little House in the Big Woods, by Laura Ingalls Wilder.

1934   Mary Poppins, by Pamela Travers.

1937   The Hobbitt, by J. R. R. Tolkien.

1941   Blue Willow, by Doris Gates.

1941   George Washington's World, by Genevieve Foster.

1943   Johnny Tremain, by Esther Forbes.

1944   Rabbit Hill, by Robert Lawson.

1947   The Twenty One Balloons, by William Pène DuBois.

Developments in English book production in the latter half of the century were quite different from those in America. Some of the most highly proclaimed modern fantasies were produced by English authors during this period.

In America, trends in the 50's, 60's and 70's can almost too easily be linked to educational, social and political and economical concerns. "With the end of World War II in 1948, another period of expansion began and children's book departments achieved major status in trade publishing. Prior to this time they had been pleasant and respected adjuncts, but adult departments were considered more prestigious... International publishing relations could be resumed once more. Books in translation began to appear, including many distinguished picture books. Family stories like those by Eleanor Estes and Elizabeth Enright, biographies like Genevieve Foster's, natural science books like Herbert Zim's all flourished. The world had once again been saved, and ever optimistic; children's book editors saw a bright future ahead for the children of this country and the world."[4]

But changes came in the 50's. The arrest of Rosa Parks on December 1, 1955 for violating Montgomery, Alabama's bus segregation laws marked the beginning of a period of protest. The movement gained impetus in the 1960's, resulting in growing unrest in the nation's cities.

Social and political unrest in America and the world during the sixties and seventies exposed and actively involved many young people in violence in the streets, protest movements, and political advocacy. They witnessed the quest by minorities for respect and equality. They saw the assassination of a president and other political leaders. Many revolted against American involvement in the Vietnam War.

Governmental and other institutional responses included new programs, new designs, even new laws. Almost all levels of society were challenged to respond to the growing activism. Book publishers responded with new materials reflecting dominant concerns. Distress about children's reading problems, federal responses to urban unrest, the youth movements, new openness about sexuality, religious protest, etc. were reflected in children's books.

22 / Survival Themes

Thus materials for children were published on subjects rarely handled in the past. Writers, publishers and critics warn against a new didacticism as the quality and durability of these materials is being assessed.

1950	The Lion, The Witch and the Wardrobe, by C. S. Lewis.
1952-1961	The Borrowers' series, by Mary Norton.
1952	Charlotte's Web, by E. B. White.
1958	Tom's Midnight Garden, by Philippa Pearce.
1958	South Town, by Lorenz Graham.
1959	Mary Jane, by Dorothy Sterling.
1963	Roosevelt Grady, by Peter Burchard.

Having briefly outlined some of the historical and social phenomena affecting the development of writings for children, in the following sections an assessment of some modern stories is made. Selections are examined for their reflection of current social, educational and psychological ideas, as well as their projections toward the future.

NOTES

1. Books, Children and Men, by Paul Hazard. 4th ed. Boston: Horn Book, 1960.

2. A New Look at Children's Literature, by William Anderson and Patrick Groff. Belmont, Calif.: Wadsworth Publishing Co., 1972. (Preface.)

3. History of the Hornbook, by Andrew W. Tuer. New York, London: Benjamin Blom, 1897; reissued, 1968.

4. "The Best Times, The Worst Times, Children's Book Publishing 1917-1974," by Margaret McElderry, Horn Book, October 1974, p. 89.

OTHER SOURCES FOR FURTHER STUDY

American Labor: The Twentieth Century, ed. by Jerold S. Auerbach. New York: Bobbs Merrill, 1969.

Bibliophile in the Nursery, A Bookman's Treasury of Collector's Lore on Old and Rare Children's Books, by William Targ. Metuchen, N.J.: Scarecrow Press, 1969.

The Bitter Cry of Children, by John Spargo. Introduction by William Trottner and an introduction to the 1906 edition by Robert Hunter. New York: Quadrangle Paperbacks, 1968.

The British Empire and Commonwealth, 1500-1961, by W. D. Hussey. New York: Cambridge University Press, 1963.

Chapbooks of the Eighteenth Century, notes and introduction by John Ashton. New York: Benjamin Blom, 1966 (reprint of 1882 ed.).

Child Labor Facts, by Gertrude F. Zimand. New York: National Labor Committee, 1940. (Publication No. 37a.)

Cobwebs to Catch Flies: Illustrated Books for the Nursery and Schoolroom, 1700-1900, by Joyce Irene Whalley. Berkeley: University of California Press, 1975.

Concise Cambridge History of English Literature, by George Sampson. New York: Cambridge University Press, 1970.

A Critical History of Children's Literature, by Cornelia Meigs, Anne Eaton, Elizabeth Nesbitt and Ruth Hill Viguers. Rev. ed. New York: Macmillan, 1969.

Early American Children's Books, by A. S. W. Rosenbach. New York: Dover, 1970 (reprint).

English Literature 1789-1815 by William L. Renwick. New York: Oxford University Press, 1963.

From Primer to Pleasure, by M. F. Thwaite. London: Library Association, 1963.

Guardian of Tradition, American Schoolbooks of the Nineteenth Century, by Ruth Miller Elson. Lincoln: University of Nebraska Press, 1964.

The Growth of American Thought, by Merle Curti. New York: Harper and Row, 1961.

History of Childhood, ed. by Lloyd DeMause. New York: Harper, 1974.

Labor in America, by Foster Rhea Dulles. 3rd ed. New York: Crowell, 1968.

Literature for Children, History and Trends, by Margaret Gillespie. Dubuque, Iowa: Wm. C. Brown, 1970.

The United States to 1865, by Michael Kraus. Rev. ed. Ann Arbor: University of Michigan Press, 1969.

The United States since 1865, by Foster Rhea Dulles. Rev. ed. Ann Arbor: University of Michigan Press, 1969.

White House Conference for Children in a Democracy. U.S. Dept. of Labor, Children's Bureau, 1940.

Written for Children: An Outline of Children's Literature, by John Rowe Townsend. New York: Lothrop, Lee & Shepard, 1967.

PART I

THE INDIVIDUAL

Aloneness and Loneliness

Feelings

Sexuality

Images

INTRODUCTION

Much of human survival lies in the individual's ability to find himself within the complexity of a developing society. When mechanisms and sources for self-evaluation and growth are not otherwise provided, young people will seek their own. Evidence of this was seen in the nineteen sixties and seventies as the world witnessed thousands of young people leaving home to join social, religious and other experiential groupings. It was reported that children as young as eleven and twelve became actively involved in movements for social change. Institutional value systems were questioned and challenged as individuals seeking their place in a world of turmoil joined in various group actions.

Volumes have been written about poor children frustrated in their attempts to find methods for survival in cities, ghettos and barrios. Numerous educators, sociologists and psychologists acknowledge that agency systems have failed to present images, role models, and positive mechanisms for children in crisis. There is general agreement that individuals, lacking sufficient equipment for problem solving, run when faced with pressures and conflicts. Running away takes on many forms--alcoholism, drug abuse, fadism, isolation, retreat, alienation, and even insanity. The Runaway Generation, by Bibi Wein (see Sources and Notes, No. 97), is one title which presents a view of young people searching for their own answers concerning love, family, values, war and peace. She concludes, however, that "we are fortunate that more and more of our adolescents are rising above our fears and falsehoods and mistakes and claiming their right to a voice in their own lives and the world we live in."

Although the junior novel and books for younger children have been seriously criticized for inept handling of the deepest human feelings, some evidence indicates that through the vicarious experience of involvement in vital media, young people can establish and appreciate their own uniqueness. One author considers adolescent materials only a way to lure the reader to good adult materials; others feel that junior materials are important because they provide roles and situations with which the young person can identify. Clues can be provided for children at various steps in their lives, particularly as they face decisions about themselves. Answers need not be pat, but well-written introspective materials may offer young people clues to the decision-making process.

It is probably safe to say that any good novel expresses some level of human feelings, positive and negative. Selected here are only a few titles which seem to have as their focus a view of the individual and the expression of that person's feelings in various situations and relationships.

1. Aloneness and Loneliness

YOUNG PEOPLE SPEAK FOR THEMSELVES

Loneliness is something that everyone have to hack with every now and then. It's a sad feeling when you don't have nobody to talk to or to hold you close.
>   --DOROTHY, 19

All of us go through it once in a while. Sometimes when we go through pressures and everything, everybody feels loneliness. It's not such a good feeling. It's good if we can put off a part of our loneliness because there are so many lonely people in the world.
>   --MARCY, 18

I'm kinda lonely, I'm always alone.
>   --MARGARET, 17

I'm always lonely, mostly by myself. I got friends I can turn to sometimes, but.......
>   --KAREN, 19

When you're very lonely and you need someone to talk to. When you have a problem and you want to talk it over with someone, it's bad when you're lonely. Everybody need somebody to talk to some time. I know I be lonely sometimes. I be sad got nothing to do, I be wanting to talk to someone and tell them my problems. It's sad when a person can't find anybody to lean on sometimes.
>   --LEOLA, 18

I feel aloneness is something that you need once in a while,

but not too often. Sometimes it helps you to think over your problems--helps you be a better person.
                              --JANE, 15

                      *   *   *

Loneliness seems to be a growing problem in our society, affecting both young and old. In April 1975, the <u>Los Angeles Times</u> printed a series of articles about the effects of loneliness on various parts of the population. One of the articles,* concerned with young people, reported several suicide attempts, caused primarily by the individuals' inability to deal with being or feeling alone. It was reported that in 1974, 30 per cent of the calls at the Los Angeles Suicide Prevention Center were from people aged 15 to 29, of both sexes. It was suggested that the situation is so critical that an organization similar to Alcoholics Anonymous, cutting across all ages and sexes, should be formed. Isolation because of physical and social differentness is cited as one problem, while others reportedly feel alone in facing problems and crises. The most critical feeling of loneliness seems to be loneliness within a group.

<u>ALONENESS</u>, by Gwendolyn Brooks. Detroit: Broadside Press, 1972.

An extremely perceptive poetic view of the child alone. Simply and effectively, the text reveals one's need to be alone--in contrast to loneliness. In a society where group processes have sometimes become so overwhelming that aloneness is often feared, children find it increasingly hard to view moments alone in a positive way. Independent play and creativity have become more difficult. Books like this one challenge the individual to deal creatively with aloneness.

> Loneliness means you have not planned to stand somewhere with people gone

---

*Stumbo, Bella. "The Lonely Young ... Sometimes the Way Out Is Suicide," <u>Los Angeles Times</u>, April 28, 1975, Part II, p. 1.

....

    Loneliness does not have a lovely sound
    It has an under buzz
    Or it does not have a sound

....

    But aloneness is delicious
    Sometimes aloneness is delicious
    Once in a while aloneness is delicious

....

    Rest is under your eyes
    and above your eyes
    and your brain stops
    its wrinkles and is
    peaceful as a windless pond.

CALL IT COURAGE, by Armstrong Sperry. Illus. by the author. New York: Macmillan, 1940.

    Call it Courage remains one of the better books dealing with the need to conquer fears through aloneness. Mafatu, son of the Great Chief Hikueru, feared the sea because as a baby in his mother's arms, he was swept out to sea during a hurricane. His mother died and Mafatu is scarred by his memories of the ordeal and the "sound of his mother's despairing cry." The realization of Mafatu's fears brings agony to Chief Hikueru, who feels that Mafatu will never earn his proper place as head of the tribe.
    Driven by shame, Mafatu sails off alone to gain and prove his courage. Led by his pet albatross, he survives a storm at sea and lands on an island used by a neighboring tribe for human sacrificial rituals. In the manner of his people, Mafatu builds a canoe for the trip home, after encounters with a tiger shark and a wild boar. Narrowly escaping the cannibal tribe, he sails home triumphant, with a new sense of courage.

THE DREAM WATCHER, by Barbara Wersba. New York: Atheneum, 1968.

    Various perspectives of human interaction and needs

are presented in this title: relationships between the old and young, parental insecurities, understanding and appreciation of family, and the development of the individual's sense of self. The central concentration, however, is on a lonely person, seeking positive allegiances.

Albert Scully is a loner, because his interests do not fit into the usual mold. He likes Shakespeare and collects recipes; he doesn't want to go to college; and he likes to quote Thoreau. Albert's life is miserably isolated and his relationship with his parents is quarrelsome. He is directionless until he meets Mrs. Orpha Woodfin, a great old lady who lives near him.

The friendship which develops between the two proves to be the beginning of Albert's appreciation of himself. Mrs. Woodfin is different and special. She tells him tales of her days of fame and glory, and he doesn't realize until later that they are imaginary. They recite Shakespeare together and discuss those things which are meaningful to Albert. When Mrs. Woodfin dies and Albert learns from his mother that she has lied to him, the old lady's words of wisdom and her spirit of love remain in his heart and mind.

Albert's alienation from his peers, his rejection of his parents and alliance with Mrs. Woodfin all seem psychologically accurate. The author presents adolescent conflict with self, with believable resolution.

Note: Numerous inferences are made regarding the allegiances formed outside the home in materials surveying the problems of adolescents. Frustrated or isolated adolescents often seek reinforcement from their peers, but many relieve their agony through associations with older people, by acquiring pets, or sometimes through retreat into an imaginary world.

ISLAND OF THE BLUE DOLPHINS, by Scott O'Dell. Boston: Houghton Mifflin, 1960.

To explore human emotions, many authors place the individual alone in extreme circumstances. A book of this kind, based on a true story, is Island of the Blue Dolphins, which describes Karena's eighteen years of lonely survival on an island off the coast of California. Her tribe flees the warring Aleutian seal hunters, mistakenly leaving Karena and her brother behind. Later, her brother is killed by a pack of wild dogs. After she wounds the dog and nurses him back to health, the leader of the wild pack becomes Karena's sole companion.

This story is sometimes viewed as having a female Robinson Crusoe theme, but some exceptions should be noted. The main character is left alone in her natural habitat, so environmental patterns for survival have already been established. Although Karena is forced to step out of the role usually assigned to women, the ways of her people provide support as she seeks weapons, searches for food and repairs her clothing.

Karena's adjustment to being suddenly separated from all human companionship is the issue. Although she faces loneliness with strength, her vulnerability is exposed when the hated seal hunters return to the island. Fearing for her life, Karena succumbs to the enticement of companionship when she is discovered by a young girl with the hunting party. However, the girl does not expose Karena's presence, and when the hunting party leaves, Karena's loneliness is even more acute. The girl's developmental handling of herself in these extreme circumstances is portrayed quite well.

THE LONER, by Ester Wier. Illus. by Christine Price. New York: David McKay Co., 1963.

The theme of the story is exposed in the title. The Loner, an abandoned boy, attaches himself to a group of migrant workers, who give him shelter and food for his work in the fields. After his friend Raidy is killed, the boy starts out alone, heading for California. Later, exhausted and ill, he is found by a Montana Shepherdess called "Boss." The boy becomes a "bum lamb" for Boss, whose only son was killed by a bear.

An acute battle for love and identity begins for the boy, who has no name before being found by Boss. After selecting the name "David" from the Bible, it seems evident that the boy will become a shepherd. David struggles to live up to Boss's expectations; in his mind this means being a model of her dead son. Since David's systems of survival have earlier been developed in isolation, his feelings of responsibility are largely to himself. He is highly introverted; hence, when he encounters this situation which could prove to be a permanent home, he lacks trust. His misinterpretation of the relationship between himself and Boss causes him to place unreasonable demands on himself.

The strongest elements of this novel are the profound insights about basic human survival as reinforced by self-concept. As the situation resolves itself, the human interaction is believable, although deeper development of the characters might help the reader more. It also seems, as Rebecca Lukens notes (see Sources and Notes, No. 40, p. 68), that the element of coincidence here is too much to accept.

Note: In an article titled "Developing the Adolescent's Self-Concept with Literature," Flora Fennimore (see Sources and Notes, No. 74, pp. 138-144) examines this novel and proposes that the chance for adolescents to view themselves in stories can help them get involved in the process of change.

ONE IS ONE, by Barbara Leonie Picard.   New York: Holt, Rinehart and Winston, 1960.

Set in medieval society, this is the tale of a boy's lonely struggle to prove himself. Stephen's life from early childhood to adulthood is covered in three powerful segments:

AMILE: Having been bitten at the early age of fifteen months, Stephen develops a dreadful fear of dogs. This, added to his basic sensitivity, makes the boy a target for ridicule by his peers and adults. Later, an affectionate puppy "Amile" helps destroy his fear of dogs. However, Stephen, still considered a weakling and a coward, is sent to a monastery.

PAGAN: The sensitive thirteen-year-old escapes from the monastery and is later rescued by Sir Pagan. As Pagan trains him for knighthood, Stephen hopes the venture will eventually bring him respect from his family. When his hero and benefactor meets an untimely death, Stephen is again left alone. His newly gained prowess as a fighter brings him recognition and he accepts responsibility for training a young and difficult squire, Thomas.

THOMAS: Stephen gradually wins Thomas's love and respect, only to see him die of smallpox. Stephen then returns to the monastery, choosing to pursue his talent as an artist and to live up to Sir Pagan's instructions:

> Live your life as you want to live it, not as others think you should. Be yourself; and whatever you want to do do it with all your heart and soul above all, always be yourself. Do not be afraid to do what you want to do so long as it hurts no one else. We are each of us as God made us and if God has seen fit to make you in an uncommon mould, be brave enough to be different.

SIMON, by Molly Cone. Illus. by Marion Friedman. Boston: Houghton Mifflin, 1970.

Simon isn't part of the young "set" in his neighborhood. He spends a lot of time in the library, reading a little about a lot of things, and he is often teased by the boys on the block. He finds it difficult to communicate with his parents and angers them with his tendency to daydream and forget things. So, Simon finds an old deserted car (an imaginary cave), to which he withdraws to be alone with his fantasized adventures.

A mentally retarded girl named Julia lives next door to Simon. He often observes and pities her antics, until the day she follows him to the "cave." Sam's anger at finding Julia in his cave is compounded when the neighborhood boys see him taking Julia home. They tease him about his "new friend." In spite of this, one day he finds himself protecting Julia from the rather cruel treatment of her peers.

His action brings him respect from his parents and associates. Most importantly, Simon feels better about himself. This is a humorous, perceptive, but slight story of one summer in the life of an adolescent boy, who retreats from the world in his confusion about growing up.

THE STONE-FACED BOY, by Paula Fox. Illus. by Donald McKay. Scarsdale, N.Y.: Bradbury Press, 1968.

This title presents a poignant example of the damage to self-concept caused by a lack of family understanding and support. Exclusion from loved ones can be more seriously damaging than outside rejection.

This is the story of a shy and withdrawn boy who feels misplaced within his boisterous family. Overwhelmed by the personalities surrounding him, Gus Oliver is unable to express himself. He retreats by never showing emotion in his face. He fails to communicate at school. The "stone face" becomes his protective device.

The problem of loneliness within the group is approached with humor and insight as a visit from Aunt Hattie and the emergency of a trapped dog combine to resolve Gus's problem. Aunt Hattie gives Gus a geode, a symbol of the sparkle within the stone. This, plus Gus's handling of a difficult situation, causes the family to view him differently, which in turn improves Gus's feelings about himself.

Note: Paula Fox has written several other books with real insight into children's feelings in various situations: How Many Miles to Babylon (see page 99); A Likely Place, the story of Lewis, who wants to be his own person, even at nine years old; Maurice's Room, about a boy who collects all kinds of junk and keeps it in his room; and Portrait of Ivan, an engrossing story of a lonely boy whose father has no time for him. The story follows the strange companionships he forms as he resolves his negative feelings toward his father.

TAKE WING, by Jean Little. Illus. by Jerry Lazare. Boston: Little, Brown, 1968.

Jean Little has written some of the most realistic, poignant and believable stories about the special kind of aloneness and loneliness experienced by the handicapped. She is also very successful in her insight to the special problems of families of the handicapped.

This story is about Laurel, whose brother is retarded. Laurel is the first to become aware of her brother's special problems. At seven years old, James wets the bed and needs help with his clothing. Laura hides her fears about her brother until she has to assume care of the child while her mother is absent. She is unable to make friends because of her own insecurities, which are complicated by the time she must spend with her brother. She finally approaches her father and suggests a medical examination, which exposes the boy's retardation.

In the end, James will receive training and Laura finds a new friend. The only contrived portion of the book is the discovery that Laurel's new friend also has a retarded sister. The rest of the book is well worth reading.

THERE IS A TIDE, by Elspeth Bragdon. Illus. by Lillian Obligado. New York: Viking Press, 1964.

This story examines the trauma of a lonely boy whose exhibitions of antagonism cause him to be sent from school to school and to be expelled from all of them. At the suggestion of his last schoolmaster, Nat and his father travel together to "Outcrop," a huge summer home at the edge of an island off the coast of Maine.

Experiences on the island bring Nat to terms with himself. He also realizes that his father, almost a stranger to him, is a very lonely man. Gradually Nat gains friends among his peers on the island.

Although the average person will not have access to an island retreat, this story shows how moving away from

36 / Survival Themes

the routines of a situation can open up communication, and how some of the barriers which reinforce loneliness can be recognized and removed. The issues and possible solutions are set within a well-written story.

ZEB, by Lonzo Anderson. Illus. by Peter Burchard. New York: Alfred A. Knopf, 1966.

Father, Abel and Zeb set out from the Connecticut Territory to find land west of the Delaware River. The three of them form an advance party to clear the land and build shelter for the rest of the family, who will join them in the spring. But Zeb's father and brother are killed in their misjudged attempt to cross the rising river in a storm. Only Zeb and his dog are saved.

Although gripped by sorrow and loneliness, Zeb determines to survive. "The dreadful loneliness, the horror at what happened so suddenly to his father and brother, the awful feeling of being cut off from his family, kept welling up in Zeb and threatening to paralyze his will to go on. But the deadly peril of his situation and the need to do something about it pulled him up and held him there and made him think."

Bits and pieces of information learned from his grandfather and from his life on the Connecticut farm aid Zeb in finding shelter and food to survive the winter. Other methods for sustenance are discovered by chance and ingenuity. As the fascinating, menial processes of subsistence are detailed, Zeb's fight to maintain a sense of meaning and hope is successfully portrayed.

According to Piaget, the very young child can reason about things but not about verbal propositions. Therefore, books which present pictures along with simple language can provide an accurate or close-to-accurate view of feelings for the child in an early developmental stage. Following are some titles for young children which portray aspects of loneliness or aloneness.

ANDY, by Eleanor Schick. New York: Macmillan, 1971.

This title is more a mood piece than a story. Andy plays on littered inner city streets, imagining himself in various roles. A realistic portrayal of a child creatively using his moments of aloneness.

CROW BOY, by Taro Yashima. New York: Viking Press, 1955.

Crow Boy is a picture story set in Japan. The theme of aloneness is characterized through Chibi, a mountain boy attending a village school. He is fearful of everyone and everything, and he can't make friends. Daydreaming, imaginative play, and watching insects provide him with amusement.

This simple story, beautifully illustrated, has depth in its discernment of children's reactions to people who are different. When Chibi reaches sixth grade, the new teacher gives him affirmation and encourages him to do his imitations of "crow voices" for the class. This leads to the discovery that "Crow Boy" has trekked miles each day from a distant mountain to put in perfect attendance at school.

J.D., by Mari Evans. Illus. by Jerry Pinkney. New York: Doubleday, 1973.

Eight-year-old J.D., who lives with his mother in a housing project, is lonely and sometimes frightened. Four short scenarios from the life of this boy, wise beyond his years, are presented. He plays imaginatively, is very brave in a fight with a bully, and sees the tragedy of heroin use by a neighborhood sports participant.

JUST ME, by Marie Hall Ets. New York: Viking, 1965.

A young boy alone expresses how wonderful it is to be "just me." He can't fly like a bird, but he can walk like a cat, and take a nap and a bath like a pig. He can hop like a rabbit and wriggle like a snake, but when dad calls and they go together to the pond at the end of the cornfield, he is content to be his real self.

MARY JO'S GRANDMOTHER, by Janice Udry, with pictures by Eleanor Mill. Chicago: Albert Whitman Co., 1970.

Mary Jo is the only one at home when grandmother

falls and hurts her leg. When Mary Jo realizes her grandmother is unable to move, she sets out in a snowstorm to get help. A lesson in decision-making for the young child facing an emergency.

PLAY WITH ME, by Marie Hall Ets. New York: Viking, 1955.

A little girl longs for some animal playmates. She learns the difference between holding animals captive and communing with them. Her frustration in aloneness at the beginning dissolves into joy in companionship with the animals in the end.

TIM ALL ALONE, by Edward Ardizzone. New York: Henry Z. Walck, 1957.

Tim returns home from a trip and finds his whole family gone. He sets out alone to search for them. His lonely trek takes him to sea and into the city, where he is almost taken to a home for orphans. But he escapes, and gradually finds clues to the whereabouts of the family, who have presumed him dead.

Other Ardizzone books place very young children in lonely situations where they must use their own mental resources to survive.

TONY'S HARD WORK DAY, by Alan Arkin, with pictures by James Stevenson. New York: Harper and Row, 1972.

Tony is not allowed to help with anything around the house, because he is too young. When he wants to help with something, he is constantly told to "go and play." Feeling left out and alone, Tony builds a house of his own.

2. <u>Feelings</u> (Expressions of Love, Hate, Power, Violence, Anger)

YOUNG PEOPLE SPEAK FOR THEMSELVES

Love and anger are two of the most important feelings, because if you don't love somebody else you won't love yourself. You also need anger, you need to express it; if you don't and you keep it all in, you will explode one day.
--JANE, 15

* * *

Feelings or emotions are mostly intangible, and the printed word is often inadequate in expressing them. However, this intangibility does not remove responsibility for concern about feelings in personal associations. Recognition and respect for human feelings can lead toward meaningful interaction and order for living.

Although words may not duplicate feelings, they can show some of the effects of feelings and bring one closer to an awareness of them within oneself. The story or novel can also expose the manipulative power of human feelings.

Traditionally, materials for children have presented feelings of love, hate, violence, etc., particularly in fantasy and folklore, but often the feelings do not emerge as realistic because they are so interwoven with fantasy and magical responses.

Modern realistic materials explore characters with which children can relate. It can be assumed that the children also identify with the feelings associated with these characterizations, particularly since some psychologists believe children even identify on a feeling level with animals and other characters of fantasy. (One common example is the reported reaction to <u>Charlotte's Web</u>. Children often cry when the spider heroine of the tale dies in the end.)

Love

In <u>Power and Innocence</u>, Rollo May (<u>see</u> Sources and Notes, No. 88) presents an interesting thesis about human feelings as related to the quest for power in our lives. For example, he states, "the boundaries of power and love overlap each other" and "love makes the person who loves want to be influenced and want to do what the loved one wishes." The balance of love and power, he believes, keeps the individual from being swallowed up by another, and allows for respect and concern for the dignity of the other person.

According to May, love and power are not interrelated, but interdependent. He projects that the person having no sense of self has nothing to give, and thus cannot love. Further on this theme, he proposes that it is our understanding of the Christian ethic of love, colored by other fantasies, which forces us to view love as only emotion, while we view power as compulsion.

Good literature dealing with love as a theme should probably present evidence of this interdependence. This bars dishonesty in writing for children, who often visualize love as only what May calls "nutrient," rather than manipulative. (See RUBY, reviewed in this section, as an example of manipulative love.)

Violence

Some psychologists and philosophers attribute violence to conditions of the society, thus allowing for prevention through social training and exposure. Some feel that the recognition of good and evil allows for the victory of good over evil, or the achievement of positives in the face of negatives.

Numerous articles have challenged the media for being a stimulus to violence and for creating an acceptance of violence as a way of life. Proponents for media presentations of life in its most real form argue that it is only by recognizing and viewing violence that it will be conquered. May suggests that one essential in overcoming violence is development of the individual's sense of self. To achieve this, power must be shared so that every person feels that he counts for something in the world.

Few books successfully depict the human needs which are sometimes the background for violence, but most novels explore emotions in some way. Chosen here are a few which seem to have various types of feelings as central themes. Titles addressed to young children often single out one emotion for explanation.

ANTONIO, by Bronson Potter. Illus. by Ann Grifalconi. New York: Atheneum, 1968.

This story could be used as a companion to Call It Courage (see page 30) because of the setting in a fishing village.
A twelve-year-old Portuguese boy, son of a fisherman, longs to participate in the work and adventure at sea. Instead he serves as the oxen boy, because of a stiff hand he sustained from a childhood injury.
Later in the story, Antonio devises a plan to save the fishing boats which are caught in a storm at sea. He becomes a hero, and his job as oxen boy is viewed with a new respect. Although it doesn't happen in the story, one gets the impression that his dreams of going to sea will one day be fulfilled. The dramatic rescue adds excitement and suspense.
Although only briefly, a view of Antonio's feelings and longings is offered. Many young people will identify with his longing to be in a different situation in life.

BLESS ME, ULTIMA, by Rudolfo A. Anaya. Berkeley, Calif.: Quinto Sol, 1972.

A beautiful story of a boy growing up with his family in New Mexico. It is a legend of the people, showing the contrast between life on the llano and in the towns. It is a tale of men, women, and children struggling with the mysteries of life, the conflicts between good and evil, and the meaning of their Gods.
Ultima, a curandera, comes to live with the Marez

family. She is known to have the power and skill of healing, although some believe that she is a witch. Ultima becomes the strongest force in the life of Antonio, the main character.

While growing up, Antonio spends much time with her, gathering roots and herbs for various ailments. They talk about his future, and Ultima quietly but forcibly helps him gain direction. Through Antonio's dreams we are aware of his fears and conflicts. He is troubled about himself and his family. But Ultima proclaims that he will be a man of intellect, so this becomes his aim.

His brothers return from the army and can't seem to find their place within the local society. Two of them leave, causing the mother and father grief, but their hopes are still strong for Antonio and the one brother who remains with the family.

Eventually the cruel forces of life cause greater conflict. Ultima heals Uncle Lucas and in the process Tenario's daughters are cursed. Tenario vows revenge and eventually kills the owl to which Ultima's soul is linked. Ultima has no fear of death, for she believes that her spirit will be released in another form and will always be there to come to Antonio's aid.

A moving and beautiful story portraying complex conflicts based in cultural beliefs and in the struggle for life.

DORP DEAD, by Julia Cunningham. Illus. by James Spanfeller. New York: Pantheon, 1965.

This story of Gilly Ground is an unusual junior novel, exploring the depths of human feelings. When his grandmother dies, Gilly is thrown into an orphanage where he is subjected to very restrictive treatment. Not allowing his spirits to be crushed, Gilly escapes periodically to a nearby tower where he meets "Hunter," who carries a rifle for protection.

When Gilly's overnight escapes to the tower are discovered, he is sent to live with Kobalt. The foster-father is a weird old townsman who beats his dog unmercifully and who builds a cage just right for Gilly. Suspecting the worst, Gilly flees toward the tower, pursued by Kobalt. Mash, the dog, comes to his rescue and Gilly goes off to join Hunter, leaving a sign on Kobalt's door--"Dorp Dead" (Gilly deliberately spells words wrong.)

The author grants the reader a view of emotions such as hate, violence, fear, and suspicion. The first person telling of the story allows the author to express her interpretation of Gilly's innermost thoughts.

Note: A detailed discussion of this title as a "dramatic novel" is found in A New Look at Children's Books by Anderson and Groff (see Sources and Notes, No. 85, pp. 105-112). The subtle meanings of the story are interpreted and devices used by the author are noted.

ELLEN GRAE, by Vera and Bill Cleaver. Illus. by Ellen Raskin. Philadelphia: J. B. Lippincott, 1967.

Ellen Grae is an unusual personality, an individual resisting the influences of society in her early years. She tells imaginative and disturbing tales to adults and her peers, but the story she eventually tells about her friend Ira is true. Ira has told her that he killed his mother and father and buried them in the swamp. Ellen is caught between the horror of knowing an awful truth and what will happen to Ira if she tells.

Ellen loses weight and retreats from everyone, causing her parents great concern. Finally she decides to relieve her conscience and tell the truth, but no one believes her story. In a way, Ellen's fantasies have saved her--her conscience is clear, but Ira remains free.

Note: Other titles by the Cleaver writing team are included in various parts of this volume. For an interesting commentary on the books written by these authors see the article, "Vera and Bill Cleaver Know Their Whys and Wherefores," by Patricia J. Cianciolo in Top of the News, June 1976 (see Sources and Notes, No. 113).

GRETTIR THE STRONG, retold by Robert Newman. Illus. by John Gretzer. New York: Crowell, 1968.

Ancient sagas often deal in more depth with feelings than many modern tales, as is true in this tale of Grettir, who kills in self-defense at the age of 15. This is a saga which explores humans who possess mythological strength and the violence which results from their use of it.

After several violent chapters describing Grettir's conquering feats, he encounters and kills "Glan's Ghost." Before dying, the ghost curses Grettir, declaring that he will acquire no greater strength, that all luck will leave him and that he will be "hunted like a wolf."

Grettir continues his exploits, searching for safety and haunted by the ghost's curse, until he meets a death as violent as the life he has lived.

THE HOUSE OF WINGS, by Betsy Byars. Illus. by Daniel
    Schwartz. New York: Viking, 1972.

   Sammy and his parents have started out on a trip to
Detroit, where they plan to relocate. They stop for the night
at the old dilapidated farmhouse of his grandfather.
   Sammy awakes the next morning to find that his mother
and father have left him behind to live with his grandfather
until they have settled in Detroit. At first Sammy doesn't
believe it. They had started out together and there was no
mention of his staying with his grandfather. It just couldn't
be true! Later, realizing the truth, he feels angry and deserted. He turns his anger on his grandfather, shouting at
him and then running away from the old man.
   The confusion ends suddenly when Sammy and his
grandfather spot a crippled sand crane. Temporarily forget-
ting his own problems, Sammy becomes engrossed in the capture and care of the crane. Gradually he becomes entranced
with the life his grandfather lives, caring for birds at "The
House of Wings."
   The boy's anger and frustration ring true, as does his
quizzical enrapture with the stories his grandfather tells about
the birds.

RUBY, by Rosa Guy. New York: Viking Press, 1976.

   Another view of the family presented to us in The
Friends (see page 99). In this book the focus is upon Ruby,
who, like Phyllisia in The Friends, finds herself alienated
from her classmates. The girls are now teenagers, living
alone with their father since their mother's death. The
strict and insensitive father allows them no male associations
and hardly any female companionship.
   Because of her needs and thwarted male relationships,
Ruby gravitates toward Daphne. Daphne exudes confidence
and beauty, often expounding her strong view on Blackness,
and seems to have some hold over the teacher. The relationship grows from companionship and dependency on Ruby's
part to intense and passionate love--a love built on selfishness and insecurity.
   Many aspects of humanity and human relationships are
presented in this delicately handled novel: a rigid, overpro-
tective father who finds it hard to show the love he feels for
his girls; Phyllisia, who finds escape in reading and compels
her father to respond through humor and chiding; the teacher,
ruthless and harsh, lacking interest in her student's needs;

Daphne, arrogant and self sufficient, hiding her own weaknesses in attacks on others; and Ruby, self-centered and weak, having lost her major support when her mother died.

The pain and poignancy of the love affair between the two girls are no less than those in many heterosexual affairs. In the end the girls part, Daphne strong and determined to start a new life, and Ruby, lost in love and dependency, threatening suicide.

A SLIPPING-DOWN LIFE, by Anne Tyler. New York: Alfred A. Knopf, 1970.

An intriguing story about young love unfolds as Evie Decker, the second fattest girl in her school, pursues a relationship with Drumstring Casey, a local rock singer.

After a rather bizarre incident in which Evie carves the singer's name in her forehead, she becomes protagonist and publicist for Casey. This begins the "slipping-down" relationship between the two, which eventually ends in marriage.

Their confusion and lack of responsibility, and the selfishness in their relationship are all important parts of the resulting story, told humorously and well.

The manipulative interplay of loving and needs are evident as Evie plays the part desired to give Drumstring publicity. Pregnancy and the death of her father are elements which cause Evie to question her relationship with Casey. She then makes a thoughtful decision to end the "slipping-down life" by getting a divorce.

WILD IN THE WORLD, by John Donovan. New York: Harper and Row, 1971.

A rather fast series of tragedies brings death to all of the Gridley family of homesteaders except John. For a time, John lives in the New Hampshire hills with only the companionship of a "wolf dog." The last part of the story details John's slow death from pneumonia.

Some have argued that this book presents circumstances which are improbable, but situations where whole families are eliminated in a few days are conceivable. The novel was probably designed for impact, and it is this element that makes it an important book. Within a few pages the author portrays a sense of family, the stark factor of loneliness and the natural acceptance of death. These elements characterize the lives of many who are poor and of others who have found means for adapting to the "hard life." This brief story immediately involves the reader in intense feelings which are relieved for only brief moments here and there before the tragic ending.

Many books for the very young still present only surface treatment of the reality of human feelings. Simple questions about love, hate and hostility, and expressions of emotions, however, are fairly presented in a number of picture books.

Elkund, in his interpretative essays on Piaget (see Sources and Notes, No. 25), states that in providing answers for the young child about his world, we must be aware of that child's unique view of the world. The following titles attempt to deal with feelings on the level of the young child.

BENJIE ON HIS OWN, by Joan Lexau. Illus. by Don Bolognese. New York: Dial Press, 1970.

When granny doesn't come to pick him up from school, Benjie has to find his way home alone for the first time. After several frightening encounters on the way, Benjie arrives home, only to find that granny is ill.

Benjie doesn't have a dime and he is too short to reach the telephone, but people in the neighborhood respond to his need for help.

Benjie's fears of inadequacy seem real, and the response of the neighbors offers a message of hope.

GREEN AND SOMETHING ELSE, by Gunilla B. Norris. Illus. by Charles Robinson. New York: Simon and Schuster, 1971.

Feelings of insecurity and fear are adequately explored in this story of a young boy who faces up to the challenge of saving a pet mouse. Green acquired his name because his sister once painted his hair that color. Even when the color wore off he retained the name because he turned a sickly green when frightened.

Green's friends taunt him because of his fear, but he surprises them and himself when he enters an abandoned house to retrieve his pet mouse.

THE HATING BOOK, by Charlotte Zolotow, with pictures by
    Ben Shecter. New York: Harper and Row, 1969.

    Surface treatment of hate feelings as a little girl faces the rejection of her best friend. Later it is discovered that their alienation from each other is based on a mistake.

HE'S MY BROTHER. Story and illustrations by Joe Lasker.
    Chicago: Albert Whitman, 1974.

    A picture story about the special child who is slow to learn and is sometimes overactive. Jamie's family shows him love and support. Even his older brother makes up stories to tell Jamie, to show him that he loves him.

HOW DO I FEEL? by Norma Simon. Pictures by Joe Lasker.
    Chicago: Albert Whitman, 1970.

    A picture book designed to make the very young child respond to feelings such as lazy, hungry, poky, cozy, mad and sad, smart, stupid, strong, brave, big, tired, worried, etc.

I KNOW WHAT I LIKE, by Norma Simon. Chicago: Albert
    Whitman, 1971.

    Exploring likes and dislikes with humorous pictures and text.

IF I HAD MY WAY, by Norma Klein. Illus. by May Cruz.
    New York: Pantheon Books, 1974.

    This is an imaginative picture story of how things would be if Ellie could have her way at home. The child's frustrations about the new baby and about her parents are touched upon.

I'LL PROTECT YOU FROM THE JUNGLE BEASTS, by Martha Alexander. New York: Dial Press, 1973.

    As in a dream, a child's fears are explored when he and his teddy bear walk through the woods and hear noises like jungle beasts. The boy is first brave, then his fears creep up on him....

JOSHUA'S DAY, by Sandra Lucas Surowiecki. Illus. by Patricia Riley Lentholl, lettering by Naomi P. Slifkin. Chapel Hill, N.C.: Lollipop Power, 1972.

When a truck hits his tower of blocks, at the day care center, Joshua screams and shakes with anger. The children and the adults allow him to express his anger, and later all is resolved. Lollipop Power published titles which are aimed at reducing stereotypes for children and also presenting the realities of life. Another of their publications dealing with feelings is Grownups Cry Too, by Nancy Hazen (1972), in which it is acknowledged that everybody cries sometime.

LOVE IS A SPECIAL WAY OF FEELING, by Joan Walsh Anglund. New York: Harcourt, 1960.

In this tiny book, the sentimental positives of loving are expressed poetically.

> It is the good way we feel when we talk to someone and they want to listen and don't tell us to go away and be quiet.
>
> Love comes quietly, but you know it is there because suddenly you are not alone anymore and there is no sadness inside you.

MONSTER'S NOSE WAS COLD, by Joan Hanson. Minneapolis: Carolrhoda, 1971.

Bedtime loneliness and fear are chased away by a blanket, the child's imaginary playmate. The substitute playmate is no longer necessary when brother becomes old enough to play.

NO FIGHTING, NO BITING, by Else Holmelund Minarik. Pictures by Maurice Sendak. New York: Harper and Row, 1958.

From a story about two alligators, two children learn

a lesson about fighting and biting. When the two alligators stop to fuss and fight, they are almost eaten by a big alligator.

PLINK, PLINK, PLINK, by Byrd Baylor. Boston: Houghton Mifflin, 1971.

    Children are reassured about night noises through pleasant rhymes and pictures.

THE SHY LITTLE GIRL, by Phyllis Krasilovsky. Illus. by Trina Schart Hyman. Boston: Houghton Mifflin, 1970.

    Anna is shy, thinks she's ugly, and doesn't communicate well with anyone. Then Claudia comes to school. She is also a loner. The two respond to each other and gradually are able to share with the rest of the class.

THE SOMETHING. Story and pictures by Natalie Babbitt. New York: Farrar, Straus & Giroux, 1970.

    In this picture book exploring fears, Mylo (resembling prehistoric man or monster) is afraid of the dark. He fears a "something" might come in through his window. His mother buys him some modeling clay and Mylo tries to design the "something." He finally forms a figure which is just right, and that night he meets the "something" in his dreams--a real little girl who is afraid of _him_.

STEVIE. Story and illustrations by John Steptoe. New York: Harper and Row, 1969.

    Feelings of jealousy and later, realization of caring are beautifully treated in Stevie. Young Robert's mother assumes care of a younger boy, Stevie. Robert resents everything about his mother's ward. He dislikes having Stevie play with his toys and interfere with his games. When Stevie leaves, Robert realizes that he misses having the little boy around.

TEMPER TANTRUM BOOK, by Edna Mitchell Preston. New York: Viking, 1971.

Having a fit of temper is shown as being normal for every person at some time in their lives.

<u>WHAT IS FEAR? AN INTRODUCTION TO FEELINGS</u>, by
Jean Rosenbaum, and Lutie McAuliffe. Illus. by Tomie de Paola. Englewood Cliffs, N.J.: Prentice-Hall, 1973.

The author differentiates between fear which provides protection and fear of things that won't harm. Also discussed are fear of the dark, fear of strangers, fear of authority and punishment, fear of school, fear of failure, fear of being different, and what you can do about fear.

Although the feelings discussed here are very real, the ways of handling them may be too simplistic, as in the section on fear of strangers. In their attempt to explain which strangers to avoid, the authors suggest that there is no need to distrust strangers who simply ask a question or genuinely offer help, but it isn't at all clear how one differentiates between these and those who might do harm. The book is probably best used as the basis for discussion on the subject.

3. <u>Sexuality</u>

YOUNG PEOPLE SPEAK FOR THEMSELVES

A lot of people should wait until they get married, but the reality is that people are doing it before, instead of marrying. It's all right if you've got the right person and you care for that person.
> --KAREN, 19

I like it, with somebody you care something about. I don't believe in getting down with anybody. These days all men want to do is get down. A young lady these days better get all the education they can get, because all these men want to do is get over. First thing they want you to do is smoke a joint and then the next thing is to let your drawers down. Men aren't men any more, they're sex maniacs.
> --LEOLA, 18

Sex is cool, as long as you handle it right. I don't like homosexuality, I think it's a sickness. A lot of them are crazy freaks.
> --JILL, 19

I feel that some people are getting out of hand, but in general, the way people express their sexuality is their business, as long as they don't harm anyone. Whatever they do is all right for them and what I want to do is all right for me as long as I don't harm anybody.
> --JANE, 15

I don't believe in sex before marriage. I believe you should give all to your husband.
> --MARCY, 18

* * *

Although the question of sex is critical to the young person's understanding of self, life's beginnings have traditionally been translated through myths and fairy tales. Adults and children alike have understood little about the physical processes of their being.

In this open age of communication and scientific discoveries, documenting human sexuality is still problematic for writers. There is an obvious lag between the development of scientific knowledge and changes in social and cultural mores. With apparent weakening of cultural sex taboos, materials for children approaching the subject of sexuality have appeared. Currently the media on this subject include everything from near myths to clinical, graphic and explicit documents. Few books, however, even in the non-fiction category, present details about sexual intercourse.

Research in sexuality is extremely complex. Some agreement seems to have been reached regarding sexual "norms" in our society, but problematic areas such as homosexuality still provoke heated arguments among experts. The morality of sex also prompts a variety of opinions. Fiction materials can focus in any or all of these directions. Essential to the child is the presentation of enough materials to arrive at some reasonable conclusions.

Taking a look at one viewpoint on adolescent sexuality, Reuven Kohen Raz, in his book reporting developmental research regarding preadolescence as a separate period of development rather than a continuation of childhood, presents an interesting thesis regarding the "development of psychosexual and psychosocial identity" (see Sources and Notes, No. 24). He believes that there are definite patterns which isolate this period as a critical stage in the child's development. Following are some of the points made which might be considered while reviewing materials designed for youth.

a) The preadolescent male demonstrates his struggle to free himself from mother attachments by overtly rejecting everything feminine: softness, sensitivity, docility, neatness, etc. He acts out his masculinity by using obscene language and by humiliating females. These actions are reinforced by the social norms of his peers and the adult community.

b) Although the monosexual activities of boys at this stage allow for mutual sex experimentation, touching, masturbating, exhibitionism, etc., this should not be defined as homosexuality. They are a phenomenon of a transitional character in the average male. Combined with these patterns is an inquisitiveness about heterosexual activity, sometimes acted out in exhibiting oneself to the opposite sex or in actual touching or sometimes, intercourse.

c) At puberty, there is a tendency for preadolescent aggressions to turn inward, as the young man deals with the emotions and tensions of his physical development. Solitary daydreaming and masturbation accompanied by guilt feelings are evident at this stage. If both these stages are completed without serious conflicts, the male passes into later adolescence developing wider contacts and strengthening his identity. Problems occur with the late development of either of these stages or with pressures applied by peers and adults, causing the formation of guilt feelings and self-rejection.

d) The dynamics of development in the preadolescent girl are primarily the same as in boys, except that the evidence of a girls' emotions and rebellion against mother are shown in different kinds of behavior. Girls dream they are already grown up and try to act out maturity that is not real. Acting out is important to girls at this stage, so they become obsessed with clothing, hair dress, makeup, etc., portraying their assumptions about the seductive role of the adult female. Other females act out their aggressions by attempting to duplicate everything males do. They dress like boys, join male activities and thus receive male approval on another level. These girls, loosely defined as "tomboys," are, according to Kohen Raz, experimenting with their typically feminine erotic role, the same as the girls who display femininity in socially acceptable forms. However, a fixation to masculine behavior after adolescence could show evidence of problematic rejection of the feminine role.

e) The conflicts between the preadolescent girl and her mother are more complex than is the case with boys. Her sexual curiosity is more pronounced and more real. Girls do not congregate and act out sex roles in groups as boys do, but they form more temporary small group alliances.

f) "With the approach of the menarche, the early adolescent girl enters a phase of tense anticipation." However due to new approaches to sex education, few girls experience the "traumatic surprise" common in years past with the beginning of menstruation.

g) Preadolescent antagonisms between males and females are often misunderstood. Boys' seeming rejection of girls may be aggressive expressions of erotic excitement, until in later stages their sexual identity is strengthened. Girls accept their ability to get boys riled up as an accomplishment, meaning they have succeeded in seductively disturbing the male.

h) The wayward adolescent boy is often unsure of his sexual image, and does not know whether he is a boy, a girl, or a child. Without a clear-cut image of his masculinity, this child may be reduced to passive homosexuality, allowing adolescents or adults to exploit his confused sexual image. This sexual deviation (homosexuality) is usually formed at preadolescence or puberty. This type of child is also susceptible to other types of misbehavior if the person advocating the action shows strength and determination.

i) The preadolescent girl who lacks close maternal exposure and identity is often unable to develop and internalize the erotic aspects of her femininity. These girls are more susceptible to primary experiences with sex. Educational intervention can alter fallacies formed at this stage.

j) Evidence shows that in the past ten years the behavior of American preadolescents is similar to that of adolescents. This may be because discrepancies between the habits of adults and the habits of children have narrowed since World War II. This means that patterns of social behavior naturally advance by imitation. Also there is evidence that the current generation is experiencing the onset of puberty at an earlier age.

These are but a few of the theories presented by Kohen Raz, chosen because of their relation to areas overlooked or mishandled in children's books. Young people may be not only physically but experientially ready for more information at an earlier age than they were in the past. Teen novels may be presenting psychosocial behavior related to sex which is in variance with the research.

Although the concentration here is on fiction materials, it is probably worthwhile to extend some cautionary suggestions regarding non-fiction:

Some books deal in too many pat generalities and declarations about what is "normal"--for instance, in one book a man's penis is described as "normally" the length of a finger although somewhat thicker. The author doesn't take into account the well-known problem of male "hang ups" about penis size.

Many authors escape into moralizing, making assumptions of love and marriage before sex in the text. One book, for instance, even discussed the possible kind of wedding one might have. Added to this is the general conclusion that marriage will result in having children.

In many titles the sex act between animals is described, but not human intercourse. In one book, after a description of intercourse among animals, human sexuality is simply declared "special."

Most of the books are inadequate in their dealings with preadolescent homosexual play and masturbation.

Sexist typecasting statements are also a problem. For instance, in one title the following statement is made: "being a lady you would expect her to be smaller." And in another title the man's role in marriage is described as "to provide her with security," while the wife is described as "giving pleasure." The wife is shown making the meals.

Books about how babies are made often completely leave out the role of the father. From many of these books, a child could assume virgin births.

As with other subjects, one could assume from the illustrations that sex is a lily-white affair. Few visuals include Blacks or other minorities.

Wickes's challenge regarding problems of sex (<u>see</u> Sources and Notes, No. 66) provides a good perspective for evaluating sex materials for the young: "Let us try to look behind existing sex manifestations to the underlying conditions of relationships and to the inner attitude toward life, and not attempt to consider sexual difficulties as things in themselves, apart from the whole psychological attitude."

Fiction books for children and young adults have for the most part excluded mention of bodily functions. Little guidance is given regarding the decision-making process. Issues and options are often not presented fairly, if at all.

These novels do, however, generally consider in some way the psychological attitudes about the physical relationship. The peripheral circumstances around a sexual encounter are detailed. This approach, however, pictures the sex act as only "the ugly incident." The possibility of overpopulation and the cultural affirmation of sex outside of "sin," it is to be hoped, will move society toward a point where sex can be dealt with as a subject natural and basic to human survival.

Several of the titles included, designed for young adults, deal with questionable or pathological sexual relationships rather than with accepted norms. As is true with other difficult subject matter, the first attempts to deal with a subject often are focused on extremes.

FLY AWAY PAUL, by Peter Davies. New York: Crown, 1974.

Paul is the child of estranged parents who lives at the "Home" in Montreal. The Home and its staff are like backdrops lifted from a Dickens novel--the facilities are filthy and depressing and the staff, with a few exceptions, are depraved and ugly. Paul, like most of the boys at the Home, is not a criminal but he and the rest are treated like offenders locked into a community which creates and germinates physical, mental and sociological illness.

Life among the residents in this boys' home represents all the hope and pathology of other social ghettos. The boys struggle to survive within the outer structure by devising their own individual and group subsystems. Thus we view Paul as he maintains his sanity by talking to his dead brother David and searches for positive relationships which constantly elude him. Wolf, a younger boy from Germany, becomes his blood brother. Paul protects Wolf from the victimization of the gangs and perverted minds of some of the inmates. But after their loving relationship has been established, Wolf returns to Germany to live with his uncle, leaving Paul a note which says simply "I LOVE YOU." Paul's best friend, Campbell, an orphan who considers this place his only home, dies. When Paul strikes up a relationship with a lovely Portuguese girl, that association is severed by a strict and suspicious father.

Paul wants to believe that either his mother or father

will eventually take him from the school, but his father dies and his mother marries a man who refuses to allow Paul in his home. Paul's only hope is to "fly away," although each of his four earlier attempts to run away were thwarted and followed by severe beatings.

Although the setting and the lives of the boys seem altogether depressing, their are some humorous incidents and the reader is compelled by Paul's obvious determination to cope and to eventually escape.

Views of adolescent sexual awakening are included, with scenes of overt masturbation and homosexual rape, balanced by a view of the innocent naïveté of a young fourteen-year-old kissing a girl for the first time. Paul is also shown in an embarrassing moment, purchasing his first "safes."

In the end, Paul escapes on a train to Toronto, hoping to find a job and start a new life. This is indeed a powerful novel of social realism, a view of humanity, young and old, caught in the turmoil of survival. Sexual awakening, fantasies and practices are presented as a part of living in this forced community.

Note: Barbara Wersba reviewed this novel in Psychology Today (January 1975), suggesting that "novels of social justice can change the attitude of society. More often they wind up on the scrap heap of good intentions. For the novel, despite its beginnings as a social genre, is really more interesting when it deals with individuals rather than issues. Fly Away Paul is such a conundrum, for not only is it polemic against child abuse, but it has been published for children."

THE GIRLS OF HUNTINGTON HOUSE, by Blossom Elfman. Boston: Houghton Mifflin, 1972.

A teacher in a home for pregnant girls recalls her experiences teaching and learning. As the teacher gradually learns that these girls are real people with a variety of feelings, she is frustrated and surprised. She is frustrated by their dramatics and romanticism, and surprised at their naïveté.

The day-by-day experiences at the home are presented with reality and humor, a human drama unfolding the levels of sexual knowledge and experience of the girls who find themselves pregnant. The teacher also learns something about herself as she deals with her own attitudes about love and sex.

GOOD TIMES, BAD TIMES, by James Kirkwood. New York: Simon & Schuster, 1968.

The "times" report the struggles of young Peter Kilburn, eighteen years old, at a prep school of disputed reputation. Peter finds himself entangled in the school's struggle to reestablish its reputation, the funny/sad intergroup activities and exploits, and the latent homosexual frustrations of Mr. Hoyt, the headmaster.

From prison, Peter tells his story in writing, reporting scenes in the school which gradually reveal the complicated human emotionality and horror of his experience.

"Good times" are mainly those with Jordan, a sensitive and loving friend of Peter's. Others include exploits with girls, humor and games in the dormitory, and moments of pure unrepressed giggling. The "bad times" are the accusations of a homosexual affair between Jordan and Peter, and the eventual death of Jordan, partially due to the abusiveness of the headmaster. Added to this is the pain Peter feels for his father, a faded old actor, and finally the death of Mr. Hoyt, killed by Peter in self-defense.

This is an honest and skillfully written novel which points up the pathology which can result from repressed homosexuality, as is the case here with the headmaster.

HIS OWN WHERE, by June Jordan. New York: Thomas Y. Crowell, 1971.

Poetically written, this is a sensitive love story for young people. Placed in the city, it is the story of Buddy and Angela, friends and lovers. Angela is faced with constant accusations and abuse from her father. Her mother is hopelessly weak, and allows the hostilities to ferment. The girl's only real source of support is Buddy, who lives alone with his father in a more positive relationship until his father is hit by a car. Buddy survives alone while his father lies critically injured in the hospital.

Incidents in Angela's home are both painful and explosive. Eventually she is sent to a home for girls but is later rescued by Buddy. At the end, the two of them hide in their meeting place in the graveyard and make love.

The active fact of the love relationship is important, but the author adeptly shows physical needs as being intertwined with emotional needs. Although many see this as a problem novel, the issue of sexuality is not presented as a problem. The two young people move naturally toward closeness. Their hope lies in their feelings for each other and the hope for a baby expressed by Angela in the end.

This book presents love and sex in a natural way. It is also important because the love story is told through Black characters and with a rhythm of blackness in the language.

THE MAN WITHOUT A FACE, by Isabelle Holland. Philadelphia: Lippincott, 1972.

Fourteen-year-old Charles Norstadt has problems with his family and with school. At a summer island home, he meets Justin McLeod, badly scarred on one side of his face from an accident. Charles asks Justin to tutor him, so that he can pass tests for entering boarding school in the fall.

The relationship between the two develops from near hostility to one of closeness, culminating in a homosexual incident. Again, this author presents sexuality as interwoven with social and psychological needs. The subject is handled well. There is no preaching and emotions are described sensitively. At the end Justin encourages Charles to consider the affair from the point of view of mutual need and not as a physical handicap.

MY DARLING, MY HAMBURGER, by Paul Zindel. New York: Harper and Row, 1969.

Maggie and Dennis, Liz and Sean are the pairs formed in this novel about high school romance. Central in this study in social and sexual pressures is the fact that Liz gets pregnant. Marriage is considered but she decides to get an abortion.

The conversations, interaction, and reactions to the eventual pregnancy present no in-depth insights about possible choices, but the author's intent may have been to present the naïveté with which many young people face the seriousness of personal relationships, especially when they are uninformed. At least the emotional pressures of decision-making, when faced with pregnancy out of wedlock, are conveyed.

Young people will probably read this book as a popular romance written with some humor and perception. The issues of sex and love are not presented in any depth, but many conclusions can be drawn from the incidental relationships presented.

60 / Survival Themes

PHOEBE, by Patricia Dizenzo. Adapted from the film Phoebe produced by the National Film Board of Canada. New York: McGraw-Hill, 1970.

    The somewhat outdated film is made current through text which chronicles a perennial problem--a girl growing up. Phoebe is sixteen and pregnant. She faces the problem alone as those around her are shown in their relationship to Phoebe. Her mother is concerned but lacks rapport with her daughter. Her father is remotely interested in her welfare. Paul is the father of the child, but so much a child himself that he doesn't sense the seriousness of Phoebe's moodiness and the frustrations arising from her knowledge of her pregnancy.

    Phoebe daydreams about broaching the subject with her parents and her boyfriend, but she knows how much her life will be changed by the fact of her eventual motherhood. She finally has to tell someone, a friend who is shocked but offers to try to help her. Phoebe tries to seek help from her doctor, considers an abortion and visits a girl from school who had a baby a few years earlier. None of these approaches works out, and we follow the day-by-day agonies Phoebe suffers as she wonders where to turn next. In the end, with acute frustration she simply blurts out the truth to Paul on the phone, and thus the story ends and begins.

TOO BAD ABOUT THE HAINES GIRL, by Zoa Sherburne. New York: Morrow, 1967.

    Melinda is pregnant and doesn't know where to turn. She doesn't want to be a disappointment to her parents, who trust her. She's afraid of putting a stigma on her younger sisters.

    After Melinda and her boyfriend discuss the matter and consider some options, she decides to get an abortion. When she arrives at the doctor's office and observes the filthy surroundings, fear overcomes her and she flees. The only thing left to do is to tell her parents--which she does.

    No pat solutions are given at the end. The truth is out in the open. The parents of the two arrange to meet and talk over the matter. It can be assumed that because Melinda's family situation is a good one, she will receive support in this traumatic situation. Melinda's frustrations throughout seem real.

TRYING HARD TO HEAR YOU, by Sandra Scoppettone. New York: Harper and Row, 1974.

A complex story of youth, growing up, and sexual relationships is told through Camilla, who discovers that Phil, the young man she likes, is involved in a homosexual relationship with her friend Jeff.

The story is told in the group setting of a summer theater for youth. Camilla and the rest of the group, when they discover the relationship between Phil and Jeff, react with questions, taunting behavior, and even violence.

In the end, Phil's tragic death in a car accident leads Camilla to new considerations of humans in all their variations and differences.

Some scenes in the story are much too didactic and message-oriented, but possibly not so much so as to discourage the reader. Solutions to incidents and problems often lack credibility, as in the scene in which one boy tries to discourage a mob from tarring and feathering Jeff and Phil. At best this is an open and forthright attempt to present a very complex question in novel form. Fly Away Paul and Good Times, Bad Times are more realistic and less stereotyped introductions to the subject of homosexuality, as also are Ruby and Man Without a Face, which explore the very human aspects of the phenomenon.

Because sex is such a problematic area, it might be expected that very few titles for the very young child, other than non-fiction, give any indication of sexuality. Even non-fiction titles seldom portray the human body in full view. Following are a few titles which pioneer in this area:

BODIES, by Barbara Brenner. With photographs by George Ancona. New York: Dutton, 1973.

A photographic essay for the young which makes a simple statement about the body and body functions. It is not a scientific explanation, but a helpful approach to seeing the body without fear or bashfulness. Pictures include a pregnant woman, nude children at play or in the bath, a child sitting on the toilet, etc.

IN THE NIGHT KITCHEN, by Maurice Sendak. New York: Harper, 1970.

A nude boys falls out of a dream into the "night

62 / Survival Themes

kitchen," into the wetness of the milk and the softness of the dough. Pictures are nostalgic, joyful and sensuous.

LEELA AND THE WATERMELON, by Marilyn Hirsh and
   Maya Narayan. Illus. by Marilyn Hirsh. New York:
   Crown, 1971.

This is a beautifully illustrated story of a young girl who discovers that having a baby has nothing to do with swallowing a watermelon seed. Leela's fears are dispelled, but nobody tells her where babies really come from. This is one of the few stories for children to show a mother breastfeeding her baby.

LOVING CHOICES*

ALA YASD Media Selection
and Promotion Committee

As individuals, we may approve or disapprove of present-day sex practices and attitudes, especially among the young. Hardly anyone would deny that the scene is exciting and worthy of attention. For most of us, the subject is

---

*This article is a joint effort of members Elaine P. Adams, Bob Barron, Barbara Duree, Helen Kreigh, Helen Lloyd, Marie O'Day, Don Reynolds, Ruth Smith, Susan Uebelacker, and Rosemary Young of the ALA YASD Media Selection and Promotion Committee, and the following interested persons: Doris Bass, Rita Broughton, Gwendolyn Clark, Becky Collins, Richard Douglass, Claudine Kelleher, Doris Losey, Jane McFarlane, Cherie Maylis, Sheryl Meerman, Jeanann L. Montney, D. F. Poertner, Jerri Quinn, Carol Sayle, and Carol Starr. Ms. Kreigh served as chairperson of the committee and prepared this article for publication. The article is reprinted here from Top of the News, January 1974, pp. 191-204, by permission of the American Library Association.

fraught with opposing views and still edged with Victorian bias and blindness. In assembling this report, the YASD Media Selection and Promotion Committee has accepted this condition as the challenge and, in spite of sure knowledge that however brave the lip-service we pay to intellectual freedom, many an actual local librarian says of such materials, "I can't use them in my community."--and doesn't--we're assuming insight and understanding at the national level that may help move us along in our local library communities.

Librarians serving young adults--people of junior high school through young-married and young-college age--in contributing items for this piece, responded to the questions highlighted and discussed throughout. They were asked to cover as wide a range of media as possible and to recommend only materials with which they had had direct experience. Consensus favored "a few good, sure-fire, objective entries rather than a whole list of duds."

> Are some young people sophisticated in many ways, yet naive about their sexual selves? How can the library help balance 'street' or 'behind the back fence' information?

The question is directed toward needs of young adult library users, but several contributors suggested, first, general works which speak to the possibility of naïveté on the part of librarians working with young people. Let us begin, then, by citing for professional enlightenment: The Sorensen Report: Adolescent Sexuality in Contemporary America, New Edition (World, 1972, $20.00) by Robert C. Sorensen, a comprehensive work to be skimmed at the very least, and Untapped Generation (Zondervan, 1971, $4.95), a discussion of problems confronting youth by David and Don Wilkerson who co-direct Teen Challenge, a religiously oriented rescue operation for teens in trouble. Although some librarians may prefer not to use a religious approach in reaching out to youth, much of the information about the authors' counseling experiences will be useful to anyone trying to serve young adults. It should be noted that the Wilkersons write of "curing" the homosexual, promote "sex within the boundaries of marriage," consider abortion and forced marriage to be poor solutions for the unwed, pregnant woman, counsel offering the child for adoption as the best remedy, and advise on "making clean" the prostitute. Other titles listed as helpful to both parents and educators: Oh, Sex Education by Mary Breasted (Praeger, 1970, $7.95; pa., New American Library, 1971,

$1.50), a sincere, provocative appraisal of opposing attitudes toward sex instruction in American schools and Sex in the Adolescent Years: New Directions in Guiding and Teaching Youth by Isador Rubin and Lester Kirkendall (Association Press, 1968, $4.95).

As for books directed primarily towards helping young people develop sexual self-understanding, perhaps we should consider to what extent home-based commercial television has built "sexploitation" into life. On the one hand, the very young have grown knowledgeable and sophisticated enough to resist and resent sermonizing and condescension; on the other, they have developed a champagne appetite for excitement. How can the nonfiction writer achieve objectivity, avoid hypocrisy, and yet find and hold an audience? And what of the librarian who seeks to choose nonfiction materials that will fill the needs of young people and promote their use without drawing a deluge of community flack? Our contributors thought these titles might fill that difficult bill. Abigail Wood's The Seventeen Book of Answers to What Your Parents Won't Talk About and Your Best Friends Can't Tell You (McKay, 1972, $7.95) and Elizabeth C. Winship's Ask Beth: You Can't Ask Your Mother (Houghton, 1972, $5.95) are written in popular, readable style. The Hard Life of the Teenager (Four Winds, 1972, $4.95), by James L. Collier, contains several chapters which emphasize feelings as well as physiological aspects, including "Right and Wrong" which discusses differing views of morality. (However, at least one young adult dubbed this author sexist in his discussion of "Sex and Social Problems.") Alan Guttmacher's Understand Sex: A Young Person's Guide (New American Library, 1970, pa., $.95) deals with sexual and reproductive functions without false morality. He is the doctor who heads the Planned Parenthood Federation. Helen Burn's Better Than the Birds, Smarter Than the Bees (Abingdon, 1969, $2.50) contains nononsense answers to honest questions about sex and growing up. In Interracial Marriage: Expectations and Realities (Grossman, 1972, $12.50), Irving R. Stuart and Lawrence E. Abt present another facet of modern life that confronts young adults with complexities their grandfathers did not face. Still in galley proof at this writing, but promising for general information, is a new book by Dr. E. James Lieberman and Ellen Peck, Sex and Birth Control: A Guide for the Young (Crowell, scheduled for publication in June 1973, $5.95). The authors consider, temperately and without cant, issues of a changing sexual morality and their implications. A mature young married adult, after undergoing a painful tubular pregnancy, thanked the librarian for recommending On Being a Woman, The Modern Woman's Guide to Gynecology, Revised Edition (Macmillan, 1971, $6.95) by W. Gifford-Jones. She said, "Most women know little about such matters, and it's scarey." Whereas, Eric W. Johnson, in Sex: Telling It Straight (Lippincott, 1970, $3.95; pa., Bantam, 1971, $.75), uses simple, straightforward language to offer a frank introduction for the junior-high-age person with the aim of helping him establish a healthy and positive approach to sex and family living. Another title by Johnson, Love and Sex in Plain Language (Lippincott, $3.50; pa., Bantam, $.75), although last revised in 1967, is still hard to keep in stock, librarians report.

So-called educational films, on the other hand, seem to have been liberated by the technological brilliance of television and the sexual openness spinning off from crasser uses of sex on film. A Child Is Born (Holt Reinhart, 16mm, 22 min., color, 1971), Swedish film about childbirth, refutes the often-heard objection that sex education is clinical and amoral. Human values are clearly evident in the careful handling of the infant, the father's participation, the attendants' sympathy, and that triumphant parental twin-smile as the child is borne out of the hospital for home. The film includes a breast examination and the live human birth, untidied and all the more splendid for that. The Rose (Films Inc., 16mm, 25 min., color, 1971) adds soft-focus, symbolic photography to the same happening.

A set of six 8mm film loops, averaging 3-1/2 to 4 minutes in length, which were clipped from A Child Is Born, are distributed by Ealing under the title Human Reproduction and Birth: #81-6611, Menstrual Cycle; #81-6629, Sexual Intercourse; #81-6637, Fertilization and Early Development; #81-6645, Embryo and Fetus; #81-6652, Human Birth; and #81-6660, The Newborn Baby. This set of loops, in addition to its obvious value for independent, "private" viewing where that is needed in school and public libraries, can also be loaned to expectant mothers' classes; city health departments, "free" school groups, and so forth. (Has any librarian thought of offering it to taxi drivers?)

Another film which eloquently emphasizes the joy and wonder of pregnancy and delivery, heightened by the husband's participation, is Story of Eric (David Seltzer, Centre Films, 16mm, 35 min., color, 1971) which details preparation for and delivery by the LaMaze Method.

Urban teenagers, led by Angel Martinez, discuss a variety of sexual topics, including body development, masturbation, homosexuality, pregnancy, and birth control in <u>About Sex</u> (Texture Films, 16mm, 23 min., color, 1972). Lighthearted in style but serious in content, the coed group displays emotions ranging from shyness to super-bravado during the conversation. Martinez excels as a warm and understanding counselor-leader. In the final portion of the film, he presents some straight facts assisted by interesting photography. This segment includes brief scenes of nudity and lovemaking.

In <u>A Three Letter Word for Love</u> (Texture Films, 16mm, 27 min., color, 1970), Puerto Rican teens living in New York display honesty and humor as they rap about sex. Topics covered include childhood sexual awareness, masturbation, courtship, birth control, and sexual myths and taboos. Interspersed throughout the dialogue are scenes depicting episodes in the romantic relationship of a young couple portrayed by an actor and actress from the Soul and Latin Theatre. To clarify some of the mistaken beliefs expressed by the teens in the films and possibly shared by members of the viewing audience, a sex-guidance counselor should be available as a resource person.

A group of sound-filmstrips, produced by Guidance Associates, Pleasantville, New York, covers the gamut of all questions discussed in this report. They have been outstandingly successful with young people of junior high age who, singly and in groups, often view them repeatedly at one sitting. Typical of the firm's offerings and especially recommended are:

<u>The Future of the Family</u> (two parts, 8F-101 566, 1972, $37.50): An excellent treatment of challenges to the nuclear family structure--overpopulation, women's roles, decaying cities, sterile suburbs, inability to guide children. Proposals for solutions are included. <u>Love and Marriage</u> (two parts, 8F-102, 705, 1970, $40.00): Three couples with different personal arrangements are seen from the standpoint of a marriage counselor as they cope with their problems. <u>What Is Marriage</u> (two parts, 8F-106, 1971, $37.50): Explores the traditional concept of marriage, its advantages and disadvantages, and looks at alternatives. <u>Young, Single and Pregnant</u> (two parts, 8F-102 226, 1971, $37.50): Choices which must be made by young people who are sexually active are discussed objectively without moralizing--avoidance of

pregnancy, alternatives to consider if it happens, the father's responsibility, the girl's education, whether to keep the baby, how to support it.

Another sound-filmstrip set in six parts, Human Birth, Growth and Development (Warren Schloat, 1970) includes The Times They Are a-Changing; Above Love: Beginnings; Should You or Shouldn't You--and When; Sex: Problems and Possibilities; DNA and You; and The Miracle of Birth. The information, visuals, and tapes are all of high quality; discussion is of changing sex roles, morality, premarital sex, contraception, homosexuality, heredity, and venereal disease.

Love and the Facts of Life (Sound-Filmstrip, Cathedral Films, 1967) is a summary of Evelyn Duvall's book of the same title (Monona, 1963, $4.95; pa., Association Press, $.95).

> Do some young people choose to live together without marrying? If so, what kind of library materials may they need?

A member of the committee commented: "I have made numerous inquiries among the staff, my acquaintances, and teenagers and have yet to come up with one couple of high school age that is living together. In my opinion, this is a post-teen problem."

The point is well taken, for the question does hopscotch all the young people who face the more common problem of deciding whether, at what point, or how to limit sexual experience before marriage. A majority of the materials being produced still tend towards sexual prudence, however, as, no doubt, does the practice of many librarians. For example, it was suggested that the film AMBLIN (UPA, 16mm, 24 min., color, 1970) is shown back to back with A Child Is Born, discussed above, to contrast a "casual sexual encounter" with a "committed" one. Whereas, it should be noted that AMBLIN, though it deals with a less long-lived sexual alliance is nevertheless a respectful consideration of that relationship. The sexual intimacy, including a semi-nude love scene, is one important but not exclusive factor in the developing self-recognition of the two young people involved. They have met as hitchhikers, joined forces rather reluctantly, sparred a little, grown intimate, and parted. The film's mood, greatly enhanced by exquisite scenic photography, is romantic but real. Both young and older people who viewed the film at the committee's open-for-participation meeting at Oxon Hill Branch of the Prince George's County (Maryland) Memorial Library during the 1973 American Library Association's Midwinter Meeting, commented that it should be "enjoyed but not analyzed." A serious effort, though, as contrasted with filmed fluff, can stand a searching eye. It will be an injustice to view AMBLIN as only fun and games, especially because there is danger that the "only entertainment" assessment could be an excuse for ducking the film's refusal to make a moral judgment about a relationship that is at odds with the assumed conventional code.

As books are chosen to meet the needs of young people ranging from omnivorous, precocious readers all the way to functional illiterates, so viewers "read" a film with all degrees of sophistication or lack of it. Thus, during the Oxon Hill meeting, a prep school student from an urban milieu pronounced AMBLIN "already dated." On the other hand, in the midwest, a young black girl, resident of a small city ghetto, having watched The Party (CCM Films, Inc., 16mm, 27-1/2 min., color, 1971), a technically less polished, self-conscious but affecting indictment of peer pressure that leads to premature sexual experience, wrote on her evaluation form: "The film meant a lot to me. Too bad I couldn't have seen it before now. It's also a film which I hope a lot of young girls could see. To let them know more about life and sex which can mean a lot to some people. I myself think the film will make a lot of young girls think more about sex before they jump into it and have it with anyone. Thanks for showing it."

And the parents of young adults react to films as well as books! After viewing Phoebe--Story of Premarital Pregnancy (McGraw, 16mm, 29 min., b/w, 1965), in which a pregnant, teenage girl fantasizes while trying to pluck up courage to "break the news," one mother said on a long-drawn breath, "Well, they would never have made a movie like that when I was eighteen." A father replied, "But you must admit that's Sunday School stuff compared with M*A*S*H." And the group of parents came to the conclusion that nothing about Phoebe recommends premarital sexual experience. Most importantly, when their sons and daughters saw the film a few days later, it was evident from the discussion that some trans-generational communication had been achieved after all.

The Game (McGraw, 16mm, 28 min., b/w, 1967),

also open-ended, has been used by young adult librarians as a companion film with Phoebe. It deals with peer pressure on a young man to "score" with his girl and is the other side of the coin examined in The Party. As a matter of fact, these three films could be used effectively in series for young adults.

Although they have received a rather rough go in the library press and among professional reviewers, most practicing librarians who serve young adults will freely admit that the sex-problem oriented novels for young adults--cop-outs or not--really circulate. Phoebe, by Patricia Dizenzo (McGraw, 1970, $4.95; pa., Bantam, $.75), based on the film mentioned above, does so. You Would if You Loved Me, by Nora Stirling (Evans, 1969, $3.95; pa., Avon, $.75) may be "teachy-preachy," coming down heavily on the side of conventional sex mores, but it gets checked in and out, ripped off, replaced, and ripped off again. For junior high school students in protected communities, where sexual explicitness and liberated language are still anathema, such works are better than nothing which may, in the most real sense, be the alternative. Other titles in this much-read genre are Paul Zindel's My Darling, My Hamburger (Harper-Row, 1969, $3.95; pa., Bantam, $.75); Ann Head's Mister and Mrs. Bo Jo Jones (Putnam, 1967, $5.95; pa., New American Library, $.75); June Jordan's His Own Where (Crowell, 1971, $3.95; pa., Dell, price not set)--in beautiful black language; John Townsend's Good Night, Prof. Dear (Lippincott, 1971, $4.50); Barbara Wersba's Run Softly, Go Fast (Atheneum, 1970, $5.75; pa., Bantam, $.95); Herman Raucher's Summer of '42 (Putnam, 1971, $5.95; pa., Dell, $1.25); and Lee Kingman's The Peter Pan Bag (Houghton, 1970, $3.95; pa., Dell, $.75).

One notch up the sophistication ladder for young adults come titles like Raucher's A Glimpse of Tiger (Putnam, 1971, $5.95) and Zindel's not too well received I Never Loved Your Mind (Harper-Row, 1970, $3.95; pa., Bantam, 1972, $.75). As usual, labels get us into difficulties: a high school sophomore, writing an extended review of A Glimpse of Tiger, so well done that it was published without editing in the local newspaper's book section, never even mentioned the bizarre life style it describes.

The Cheerleader (Putnam, 1973, $6.95), by Ruth Doan MacDougall, may be one of those novels young adult librarians hope their clients will find without specific direction. It is as sexually explicit as most of the classic intellectual freedom causes célèbres. The strong sexual line is used not only to hold keen interest throughout a long novel, but, more importantly, as a probing weapon to examine a value system-- purportedly that of the '50s, but at least as applicable today. The ending of this novel, where the cop-out usually comes, is a stunning self-confrontation for both the heroine and the reader. Its impact is heightened by the fact that the author has refused to "tone down" the preceding sexual explicitness and hard language to buy readership from timid librarians and protected young adults.

Relatively speaking, it is quite true that not many young people have begun to practice communal marriage, but turnover on the shelf suggests that someone is interested. To satisfy lively curiosity, librarians may consider stocking The Alternative (Macmillan, 1970, $7.95; pa., $3.95), by William Hedgepeth and Denis Stock, a pictorial presentation of communal life; Becoming Partners: Marriage and Its Alternatives (Delacorte, 1972, $7.95) by Carl R. Rogers; What the Trees Said (Delacorte, 1971, $5.95; pa., Dell, $2.45) by Stephen Diamond; Open Marriage: A New Life Style for Couples (Evans, 1972, $6.95) by Nena and George O'Neill; and, academic but interesting, Harry L. and Joan Constantine's Group Marriage (Macmillan, 1973, $8.95).

> Do some young women consider abortion as a solution to unwelcome pregnancy? Has the library any responsibility in this case?

Increased premarital sexual exploration, whether fleeting or long-lived, particularly where the practice outstrips community attitudes, inevitably confronts young people with the need to choose among the alternatives to bearing unwanted children. Information is needed about human reproduction, birth control methods, the prevention and cure of veneral disease.

At the top of our contributors' list, in response to this question, was emphasis on the library's responsibility to supply specific information--names, addresses, costs, confidentiality or lack of it, etc.--about community agencies, hot lines, and other sources of help. Here are typical ways in which such information is being made accessible:

American Friends Service Committee--Vocations for

Social Change: <u>The People's Yellow Pages</u> (353 Broadway, Cambridge, MA 02139, 1973, $1.25). An indispensable where to, how to book with specific information and addresses.

State of New York--Department of Health (Albany) Hospital Memorandum, Series 72-16. (Request most recent revision.) Subject: <u>Abortion Facility Inventory</u>. Lists certified health facilities in the state which will perform abortional acts.

<u>Help for Girls,</u> Everyday and Special Assistance Available in Boone County. Brochure prepared by Service to Girls Committee, Quota Club of Columbia, in Cooperation with School of Social Work, University of Missouri, Columbia, 1972. (Sample available from Coordinator, Young Adult Services, Daniel Boone Regional Library, Columbia, MO 65201, upon receipt of stamped, addressed envelope.)

<u>Momma,</u> a newspaper produced for the purpose of assisting single parents (926 Marco Place, Venice, CA 90291).

<u>I'm 17, I'm Pregnant, and I Don't Know What to Do</u> (Children's Home Society of California, 3100 W. Adams Blvd., Los Angeles, CA 90018, 16mm, 28-1/2 min., color) includes abortion among a range of choices open to several young women who are pregnant and alone. All are members of a process group whose facilitator is a social service worker. Cases described are actual, although the young women are actresses portraying roles. One girl decides to keep her baby and later realizes her decision was a mistake. The film has won several awards.

In the many states where, as one librarian put it, "it is still touchy to give out abortion information in spite of the recent Supreme Court decision," books like Ruth Pierce's <u>Single and Pregnant</u> (Beacon, 1971, $5.95; pa., $1.95) and other media which present the subject as one of several alternative solutions not only make the full range of possibilities accessible, but also keep alternatives in perspective.

The who, why, and when of legal abortion is set forth effectively on p. 67-70 of the September 27, 1971, issue of <u>Time</u> magazine. Concise presentations like this lend themselves well to photocopying. On an audio cassette, <u>How to Get an Abortion</u> (2) (#21629, 26 min., $13.95, University Microfilm, 300 N. Leeb Rd., Ann Arbor, MI 48106, CCS Catalog 701B) executives in law and social services answer questions about abortion. Again, these media allow for the "privacy" many patrons require and, perhaps, cut down on the high loss of more expensive items. For medical perspective, Robert E. Hall offers Doctor's Guide to Having an Abortion (New American Library, n.d., $1.00).

For those who decide against abortion as an alternative to unwelcome pregnancy, in addition to general works already discussed, there are films and books that provide not only information but, through humor and a nonjudgmental approach, may offer reassurance and comfort as well. House of Tomorrow (Harper, 1967, $4.95; New American Library, 1968, $.75) by Jean Thompson and Blossom Elfman's The Girls of Huntington House (Houghton, 1972, $5.95) are believable, appealing stories set in a home for unwed mothers, and the film, A Statistic Named Ann (WJZ-TV, 16mm, 27 min., b/w, 1966), if a little dated technically, is superior in terms of content and approach. Though daughter confessing to mother that she had decided to have an abortion may no longer be outré, even in novels for young people, an openness that allows mother to admit she once did the same is unusual. Such is the case in Norma Klein's It's Not What You Expect (Pantheon, 1973, $4.95).

> Are more young people than ever before contracting and communicating venereal disease? If so, how can the library assist in their need for cure and prevention?

Even allowing for journalistic overstatement and manipulation of statistics by alarmists, it seems obvious that venereal disease is increasing in the direction of epidemic proportions in the United States. By making printed materials and film showings readily accessible to the total public, free of charge, the library can be a viable factor in moderating this trend. In this connection, especially, our contributors emphasized the need for the librarian to become acquainted, first-hand, with local referral services. Do they give help without judging; are confidences respected; medical credentials valid? Because the subject lends itself so readily to scare tactics and grisly details, the young people remind us: "Just give us the facts. Shut the barn door on moralizing; it's too late for that when someone has contracted and may be spreading a venereal disease." Holders of this view should approve a recent release by See-Saw Films, called When Love Needs Care (16mm, 13 min., color, 1972), a semidocumentary in which a young man and a young woman visit their respective doctors; venereal disease is diagnosed; and they are treated for it. The doctors are models--objective, reassuring, informative, relaxed.

Although rather long, young adults seem to find the recent television presentation VD Blues, narrated by Dick Cavett, the right blend of information and entertainment. It will be available shortly on 16mm film from Indiana University Audio-Visual Center, Bloomington, Indiana. Mr. Stephen Johnson at that address can be contacted for further information and to arrange a preview. A paperback book based on the program is also available (VD Blues, Avon, $.95); it should be especially useful, one contributor noted, for libraries in areas that cannot receive educational telecasts.

A Half Million Teenagers (Churchill Films with the cooperation of the Los Angeles School System, 16mm, 16 min., color, 1968) clearly and objectively presents information about VD recognition and treatment of gonorrhea and syphilis with emphasis on curability through proper medical care. Microscopic views of spirochetes and gonococci are shown, and the routes these organisms travel within the male and female body as the disease progresses are diagrammed.

The problem from a girl's point of view is set forth in the 16mm film, Kathy (AIMS Instructional Media Services, 10 min., color, 1969). Kathy's suburban bubble bursts when she learns that she has gonorrhea. After a nightmare sequence when she envisions various home remedies and their results, she decides to seek clinical advice. The remainder of the film focuses on the patients seated in the VD clinic and their difficulties in coping with gonorrhea. Myths are clarified, statistics presented, and medical procedures explained. Sometimes the film comes off a little too sugary, but it's a fairly good presentation for suburban "innocents."

VD--Prevent It! (Perennial Education, 16mm, 11 min., color, 1972) focuses on typical questions asked by high schoolers on how and where people get venereal disease with an authoritative voice offscreen providing the answers. It treats teens with dignity and spares the viewer phony acting out of calamitous situations. VD Attack Plan (Disney, 16mm, 16 min., color) covers the subject using the technique of animation.

The Lunatic (CEN, 16mm, 23 min., color, 1972) is

an engrossing dramatic film about the human implications and individual responsibilities in dealing with venereal disease -- not a clinical study but, rather, a highly personal film to be used in conjunction with clinical materials on the subject. A girl learns that she has contracted a venereal disease, and the film explores a whole range of interpersonal relationships involving trust, responsibility, love.

Recommended books and pamphlets that avoid condescension and sensationalizing are: VD: Facts You Should Know (Lothrop, 1970, $4.25) by M. D. Blanzaco; VD: The A B C's (Prentice, 1971, $4.95) by John W. Grover and Dick Grace; and, one of the best pieces of straightforward information on the subject to fit the most limited budget, VD Handbook (Handbook Collective, P.O. Box 1000, Station G, Montreal, Quebec 130, Canada; $.25 first copy, $.10 thereafter) by Donna Cherniak and Allan Ferngold.

Available and useful sound-filmstrips on the subject are: VD Myth and Reality (Projects for Peace, 1972) which emphasizes prevention and control through understanding and Venereal Disease: A Present Danger (Guidance Associates, 2 parts, 8F-105 906, $40.00) which stresses the confidential patient/MD relationship.

Are some young people unsure of their sexual role? Can the library offer insight and reassurance?

Martin Duberman, discussing "Homosexual Literature" in the December 10, 1972, issue of the New York Times Book Review, bids for careful scrutiny of materials on the subject because the literature of homosexuality is also just emerging from the closet and may be clouded for a time by undue commercialism and controversy.

Bibliographies like Homosexuality: A Selective Bibliography of Over 3,000 Titles by William Parker (Scarecrow, 1971, $9.00); A Selected Bibliography on Homosexuality, 5th ed., 1972, available from the Homosexual Information Center, 3473 1/2 Cahuenga Blvd., Los Angeles, CA 90068; and A Gay Bibliography, 2d rev. ed., 1972, produced by the Task Force on Gay Liberation of the ALA Social Responsibilities Round Table, available from Barbara Gittings, P.O. Box 2383, Philadelphia, PA 19103.

Overviews of the homosexual experience are explored

in The Gay World by Martin Hoffman (Basic Books, 1968, $5.95; pa., Bantam, $1.95); What About Homosexuality? by Clinton R. Jones (pa. Nelson, 1972, $1.95); and Society and the Healthy Homosexual by Dr. George Weinberg (St. Martin's, 1972, $5.95). The Invisible Minority: The Homosexuals in Our Society (Unitarian Universalist Association, 25 Beacon St., Boston, MA 02108, $60.00) is a sound filmstrip program by Deryck Calderwood and Wasyl Szkodzinsky who deal with "The Changing View of Homosexuality," "Understanding the Homosexual," and Questions and Answers Concerning the Homosexual Way of Life."

Personal life experiences are shared in Sappho Was a Right-on Woman by Sidney Abbot and Barbara Love (Stein and Day, 1972, $7.95; pa., $1.95); Lesbian/Woman by Del Martin and Phyllis Lyon (Glide, 1972, $7.95; pa. Bantam, $1.50); The Gay Mystique by Peter Fisher (Stein and Day, 1972, $7.95; pa., $1.95); and On Being Different by Merle Miller (Random, 1971, $4.50; pa. Popular Library, $.95). The Gay Crusaders by Kay Tobin and Randy Wicker (Paperback Library, 1972, $1.25) presents in-depth interviews with fifteen gay people who are committed to improving life conditions for homosexuals. The authors give personal histories as well as an excellent overview of the gay liberation movement.

A new film, Lavender (Perennial Education, 16mm, 13 min., color, 1972), is a sensitive portrayal of two young girls that shows glimpses revealing their lesbian life at home and with friends in contrast to their other straight life at work, at church, and with their families.

Six homosexuals define their roles in a heterosexual society on an audio cassette, Homosexuals and Society, available from University of Michigan Microfilm (address above), CCS Catalog 701B #23636, 53 min., $14.95).

Are some young people unsure of their social role?

In a similar way, the Women's Liberation Movement, confronted with apathy and passiveness in women and ridicule and resistance from men, complicates the selection process. The January 1, 1973, issue of the American Library Association Booklist carried a selected multimedia list of materials on women's liberation.

76 / Survival Themes

Our Bodies, Ourselves: A Course by and for Women by the Boston Women's Health Collective (c/o New England Free Press, 791 Tremont St., Boston, MA 02118, $8.95; pa., $2.95), written by twelve women in their twenties and thirties, is a collection of facts from medical and popular literature on the physiology and psychology of women treating such subjects as the anatomy and physiology of reproduction, special problems of female nutrition and exercise, birth control, abortion, and childbearing with plenty of diagrams: "An admirably clear and truly humane 'course' on the functioning of women."

In Born Female: The High Cost of Keeping Women Down, rev. ed. (McKay, 1970, $5.95; pa., Pocket Books, $1.25), Caroline Bird maintains that having babies and being committed to a specific role because they happen to be born female is costly to women from the social, moral, and personal standpoints because it destroys talent, wastes talent, and hides talent. Dr. Joyce Brothers offers a formula for achieving equality with husbands in The Brothers System for Liberated Love and Marriage (Wyden, 1972, $5.95). As contemporary thought focuses on the relationship between the sexes, Margaret Mead's classic Male and Female: A Study of the Sexes in a Changing World (Morrow, 1949, $10.00; pa., Dell, $.95) remains significant because of its examination of male and female roles in seven primitive societies and how those attitudes operated in America in 1949 as compared with today. Kate Millett's Sexual Politics (Doubleday, 1970, $7.95; pa., Avon, $2.95), which discussed patriarchy as a political institution and as an attitude reflected in literature is not for the reluctant reader, but its point of view is unusual and interesting for the serious and mature student of the movement.

Free to Be ... You and Me, starring Marlo Thomas and various guest stars (Bell, 1110, $5.98), records in charming and hilarious story, song, and humor, a thoroughly entertaining attack on all the stereotypes sexist theories of our lives; good for fifth or sixth grade up through senior citizens.

Two cassette tape discussions give women an opportunity to be heard on the subject: Selma Greenberg interviews Elizabeth Janeway about Women's Role in Society (Classroom Materials, n.d.) as four women--a college president, a gynecologist, a psychologist, and a dean of women--talk about how they see themselves in relation to the current identity crisis; and Gloria Steinem narrates an introduction to the Women's Liberation Movement in a sound-filmstrip discussion of The Forgotten Majority (Denoyer-Geppert Audio-Visuals, 1971).

Confusion about sex and social roles in general is graphically and hilariously treated from the woman's point of view in a 16mm film, Anything You Want to Be (Brandon, 8 min., color, 1971) which depicts a teenage girl growing up with the notion that she can be anything she wants to be, but finding that her intention is on a collision course with reality; deservedly a Blue Ribbon Winner at the American Film Festival.

Books that suggest guidelines for both sexes are William Braden's The Family Game: Identities for Young and Old (Quadrangle, 1972, pa., $2.95) and Ralph Blum's Old Glory and the Realtime Freaks (Delacorte, 1972, $5.95; pa., Dell, $1.25), in which a teenage boy almost makes a cult of interpersonal communication: his most meaningful relationship is with his dying grandfather ... a person who listens, shares his thoughts, but does not preach; the labels of young and old are forgotten in the warmth of this rapport.

There has been, too, a recent rash of stories for young people which one librarian facetiously calls "The Groping Group." Usually humorous or ironic, as the tag implies, these deal in contemporary terms with the age-old awkward, tentative reaching for adulthood on the part of the untried and painfully unready segment of the younger generation. The sheltered quality of both the writing and the people involved virtually requires that these novels concern the society's majority rather than otherwise. Some recent examples are: Dinky Hocker Shoots Smack (Harper-Row, 1972, $4.95) by M. E. Kerr and I Will Go Barefoot All Summer for You (Lippincott, 1973, $4.95) by Katie Letcher. One young adult reader summed up the latter by reporting, "It filled a desire which people of my age group look for in books." In Hope Campbell's No More Trains to Tottenville (Saturday Review Press, 1971, $5.95; pa., Dell, $.75), it is middle-aging parents who seek to redefine their roles, while their daughter, reacting to their confusion, has an idyllic sexual encounter which is unrealistic but not unreal. Recent novels in which homosexual experiences have been sensitively and normally set forth are Lynn Hall's Sticks and Stones (Follett, 1972, $4.95; pa., Dell, price not set) and Isabelle Holland's The Man Without a Face (Lippincott, 1972, $4.95; pa., $1.95).

In Norma Klein's <u>Mom, the Wolf Man and Me</u> (Pantheon, 1972, $4.50), an engaging girl has a different problem from that usually confronting an illegitimate child: basking in an exceptionally warm relationship with her mother--possible because both are strongly independent spirits who respect one another--she speculates about changes that may occur if her mother marries.

<u>Penny Wars</u>, by Elliott Baker (Pocket Books, pa., $.95) deals movingly, frankly, and humorously with teens and sex hang-ups, and a perennial favorite of this genre, <u>The Bride Wore Braids,</u> is now available in an attractive paperback edition under the title <u>Ask Me If I Love You Now</u> (Scholastic, $.75).

4. Images

CHILDREN SPEAK FOR THEMSELVES

An anxious mother decided to test with her six-year-old child a picture book using symbolically distorted pictures of Blacks. As an artist, she hoped that the child would understand the pictures without adult interpretation. She gave him the book, without comment, and waited for his response.

At first, it seemed the child's reaction would be okay, although he commented more about the colors, the bugs, etc., not mentioning the people. But later, when he closed the book and seemed again to be at play, he yelled out a question, "Hey ma, how come the people in that book are so ugly?"

The question indicated his need for an interpreter of the symbolism, which would probably have been obvious to an older child or to an adult. Left alone with no discussion, the child's view of the images presented was exactly as he saw them--ugly. One should note however, that after discussion, the child seemed to understand that the pictures were not a photographic view of real people but an artist's portrayal symbolizing the horrors of slavery.

>   --Interview held with mother and Raymond, aged six.
>   Altadena, California,
>   February, 1974

Psychologists present evidence that a child reaches the lowest level of self-acceptance at puberty. This is the period when family relationships and social alliances often break down. Part of the conflict is based on the child's desire to be like someone else or to fit a certain image. Often conflicting with this is the young person's perception of the view held of him by others. Healthy attitudes, therefore, require positive reinforcements, so that the adolescent sees some reality in selected goals or realizes that all criticism is not actual rejection.

It is not clear what effects written images have upon a child's developmental processes. However, psychologists and sociologists alike agree that young people at all levels imitate live role models. It seems reasonable to assume that the child who depends partly upon literature for resources might absorb and imitate written images. Children at play have often been observed imitating roles from literature as well as life.

Racial Images

One of the most complex areas of image formation is that involving race. Some experts believe that racial prejudice is based on cultural exposure, not personal experience. Generally, it is theorized that the child makes negative and positive associations about race at an early age, and that these associations become stronger as the child grows older. Gradually, links include attitudes about clothing, work, living quarters, personality and abilities. Logically, it can be assumed that limited exposure allows for limited associations. Images in our society must be presented fairly and include varieties in social class in order to allow the child to develop healthy perspectives.

In literature for children, early portrayals of Blacks were scant and extremely stereotyped. With the civil rights movement of the late nineteen fifties came various publications portraying Blacks attempting to integrate schools, neighborhoods, etc. Few of the authors of these books were themselves Black. Today, more children's materials are being written by Blacks. These books present Blacks in social situations as well as in a world aggravated by racial biases.

Positive images of other minorities are equally hard to find, particularly those placing Indians, Chicanos, Asians, Puerto Ricans and others in modern settings. Historical perspectives are often patronizing and stereotyped. As with Blacks, the development of materials has followed social and political protest movements. Some attempts are being made to reevaluate old materials and to fill the void of positive media in these categories.

Sex Roles

In the past, women's movements have had little effect

on the images of women as portrayed in literature. Books featuring females still placed women primarily in the roles of mother and housekeeper. Currently, the open communication of the space age has brought wider attention and impetus to the women's movement and some attempts have been made in children's fiction to present women in a new light, although the overwhelming majority of books still present women as subservient to men, not capable of leadership, as nagging mothers lacking understanding of their children and their husbands, and assuming work roles only in the home. Most of the new enlightened materials are biographical and historical rather than fictional.

It can be expected that changes in views of women will also alter the approach to males in literature. As the social situation changes, males will be presented in a different relationship to the family and will be allowed to show feelings which in the past have been considered not masculine.

Self-Esteem

Positive image materials may be considered as those which help the child to build self-esteem. (The presentation of alternative value systems allows children to find elements contributing to belief in their own worth.) Romanticized values and a favorable emphasis on beauty permeate children's stories. Children who cannot aspire to such standards can feel seriously insecure. This problem of self-esteem is important at all levels of the child's development, but it can become all-consuming during adolescence.

The problems involved in selecting a list of image-forming materials are complex. It certainly means more than merely identifying an item as having a character from a given ethnic group or of a given sex. The question is whether the story or novel is written so that the child identifies with a given character, and what negative or positive reinforcement is offered for the child? Is the child's self-esteem being bolstered by negative reinforcement through the portrayal of one group or one sex as inferior to another. Stories which present both positives and negatives of all human behavior help children to understand that everyone has strengths and failings.

Because of the difficulty in finding this kind of balance, only a few books have been selected for this section. Minority materials were found to deal primarily with a given social issue rather than focusing on people. Stories which are historically accurate are often socially false, and vice versa. Some titles offering a view of minorities or of women are included in other sections because they focus on one of the other selected themes. For other opinions and examinations of literature presenting minority images and sex roles several sources are included in the Sources and Notes.

ANGELITA. Story by Wendy Kesselman. Photographs by Norma Holt. New York: Hill & Wang, 1970.

    Photographs and story portray the positives of Angelita's life in Puerto Rico in contrast to her life after the family moves to New York City. In Puerto Rico there are the outdoors, the birds, the chickens, a horse and the joy of love and family. In New York there is no coquille bird, it's hard to make friends and some boys steal her favorite doll. In the end the doll is returned but Angelita still dreams of Puerto Rico.

CLAUDIA, by Barbara Wallace. Illus. by Charles Liese. Chicago: Follett, 1969.

    Only Claudia's brother sympathizes with the fact that she plays boy's games with her friend Duffy and is not ladylike. Pressures placed on her cause her to react with anger. She spoils a party because she knows her invitation was the result of parental pressure. Claudia is then accused of stealing a teacher's watch, which is later found.

    As is true of many books of this type which present strong young women whose behavior is "boyish," solutions for Claudia's problems lie in signs of more "girlish" endeavors. She becomes friends with a girl and takes a job babysitting, which the author presents as signs of her beginning to "bloom."

DRAGONWINGS, by Laurence Yep. New York: Harper and Row, 1975.

    Moon Shadow tells the story of coming to San Francisco when he was eight to join his father. Reinforced by the warm and close community of which he is a part, Moon Shadow is able to survive the hostile ways of the "white demons." Moon Shadow and his father do acquire two white friends, Miss Whitlaw and her niece Robin. All of them join together doing rescue work after the great earthquake.

Windrider, the father, has always had a dream of building an airplane and flying it. That dream is realized. (The story is based on a true story of a Chinese flier who flew a biplane for 20 minutes over Oakland in 1909.)

ESTANBANICO, by Helen Parish. New York: Viking, 1974.

The first-person account of the adventures of the Black man who accompanied and sometimes led the Spanish to the east coast of the Gulf of Mexico, in 1528.

A warm, positive and historically accurate account presenting a strong and positive Black image. The hero Estanbanico projects strong feelings about the positives of his heritage, his blackness, his abilities and his physical beauty, sometimes in contrast to the accompanying whites. It is one of the few books that documents the revering of blackness by many Indians. Black masks which symbolize luck and happiness can still be found in many areas of Mexico.

It is also important that the hero, in spite of his strength and positiveness, remains human and vulnerable in the end.

Although some of the negative language used seems unnecessary, and Estanbanico's views of his slave counterparts are tinged with ridicule, for the most part this book presents positive image material.

FROM THE MIXED UP FILES OF MRS. BASIL E. FRANKWEILER, by E. L. Konigsburg. Illus. by the author. New York: Atheneum, 1967.

This author presents fanciful tales with unusual but believable images of children. In this story Claudia carefully plans to run away from her surburban home. She takes along brother Jamie because he has money. Their place of refuge is certainly unusual--the Metropolitan Art Museum in New York City. After six days, Claudia has established a new identity which prepares her for life at home.

This writer's Jennifer, Hecate, Macbeth, William McKinley and Me, Elizabeth also gives an unusual modern view of children. In another book, George, the reader is presented with a brilliant boy with an alter ego, George. Approaching schizophrenia, he sees a psychiatrist and begins to recover from what could have been a most serious mental collapse.

GUESTS IN THE PROMISED LAND, by Kristin Hunter. New York: Scribner, 1973.

Stories in this collection portray various aspects of Black living. The characters are real in their relationships to their world. Each story presents a view of blackness in a special situation.

HALF BREED, by Evelyn Sibley Lampman. Illus. by Ann Grifalconi. New York: Doubleday, 1967.

Pale Eyes decides to leave his Crow Indian home and search for his father when his mother decides to remarry. He moves into Oregon Territory, facing the prejudices and strangeness of this new environment. When he finally finds his father, his hopes for a new and secure life are almost shattered, except for the fact that his Aunt Rhody appears on the scene. She is a woman of strength and character, who first tries to change all the boy's Indian ways while strongly acknowledging their kinship. The two develop a positive and believable relationship which enables Pale Eyes to face the new environment in which he meets different ways and frequent rejection. (See Sources and Notes, No. 87)

HE BEAR, SHE BEAR, by Stan and Jan Berenstain. New York: Random House, 1975.

A beginning-to-read book which establishes through the female bear that gender should be no barrier to jobs formerly seen as for males only. Male bear meantime successfully knits socks and paints pictures.

IN-BETWEEN MIYA, by Yoshiko Uchida. Illus. by Susan Bennett. Scribner, 1967.

Twelve-year-old Miya is the daughter of a Buddhist priest, whom she feels lacks ambition. She also resents being the middle child, questions her life style, etc. Her resentments are typical of those found in adolescents in various cultures in the modern world. A visit with relatives in Tokyo, where city friends appreciate her simple life style in the country, helps Miya to see things differently.
A view of culture and a young girl's development are seen as Miya tries to change her life. Also pictured is a very understanding family.

LONG JOURNEY HOME: STORIES FROM BLACK HISTORY, by Julius Lester. New York: Dial Press, 1972.

Based on historical facts, Julius Lester presents six stories of the Black perspective, during and after slavery. The stories portray the conflicts, emotions, withdrawal and resistance of Blacks caught in the vise of a system of slavery, which persisted even after "freedom." Symbolized is the frustration experienced by slaves after emancipation, seeking means for survival in a system based on land and ownership. Without either, many retreated and others rebelled.

The story of Ben, told from the point of view of a white lawyer, dispels the myth of the contentment of slaves, even those who were well treated.

These stories present both the negative image of Blacks, filled with self-rejection and subjecting themselves to cruel self-hate mechanisms, and the positive image of those who maintained a sense of pride and strength in their humanism.

Other books by this author dealing with the Black perspective which should be considered are: To Be a Slave, Search for the New Land, The Seventh Son: The Life and Writings of W. E. B. Dubois, among others.

OUR CUP IS BROKEN, by Florence Means. Boston: Houghton Mifflin, 1969.

Sarah, a Hopi Indian girl, spends eight years of her life with white people, after the death of her parents. When a romance between her and a twenty-year-old white boy is broken up by his parents, she returns to the reservation. Sarah faces many difficulties adjusting to life with her own people because she has absorbed the values and customs of whites. She leaves the reservation after being raped and bearing first a blind child and then a stillborn baby. Sarah finally finds happiness away from the reservation with her Indian husband. (See Sources and Notes, No. 87)

PLANET OF JUNIOR BROWN, by Virginia Hamilton. New York: Macmillan, 1971.

This author of numerous books portraying Blacks presents images noteworthy for their perception, creativity and variety. One of her most memorable titles is the story of

Junior Brown, who lives in the city, likes the piano, and has a mother who suffers from asthma. His constant companion is Buddy, a street kid who daily skips classes with Junior to meet with the janitor in the basement of the school. There, the three of them build models of the solar system.

Junior Brown's life gradually becomes overwhelming. His visits to a harmless deranged music teacher, his mother's illness, his lack of opportunity to release his creative energies, and other pressures drive him to the point of insanity. But Buddy emerges as a true hero as he determines to save Junior from a life of confinement. He and the janitor rescue Junior and take him to one of the survival satellites Buddy has established for himself and other homeless children in vacant buildings.

This story is complex, with an element of surrealism, but the character images emerge with great reality. Although some characters may seem lost and hopeless, hope for humanity is strong in Buddy, who finds the resources for survival within himself and who reserves strength to help others. Buddy becomes the positive image of a young Black hero.

Other titles by this author include: House of Dies Drear, in which the mystery of a house where Dies Drear maintained an underground railroad station in Ohio is unfolded; The Time-Ago Tales of Jahdu, tales told to Lee Edward by Mama Luke while Lee waits for his mother after school each day. The setting is Harlem; M. C. Higgins the Great, the award-winning story of M. C. Higgins growing up in a strip-mining area on Sarah's Mountain near the Ohio River. His dreams of the family moving to the city while his mother pursues a singing career are thwarted and M. C. rises to the occasion with plans for bettering their situation; and Arilla Sun Down, presenting the complexities faced by an interracial family, Black and Indian, in the Midwest.

THE RAVEN'S CRY, by Christie Harris. Illus. by Bill Reid, a descendant of the last Haida chief. New York: Atheneum, 1966.

When the white men came, in 1775, to hunt the sea otter, the Haida people suffered many problems. The white hunters cheated the people, destroyed their way of life and pillaged the land until only a few of the tribe remained. This is an important title for its historical and cultural accuracy.

Note: This title was recommended among others by Rey

Mickinock in a Library Journal article titled "The Plight of the Native American" (see Sources and Notes, No. 87).

THE STORY CATCHER, by Mari Sandoz. Illus. by Elsie J. McCorkell. Philadelphia: Westminster Press, 1963.

    Lance, son of Good Axe, catches the story of his people in pictures drawn in the sand, or with sticks on skins. But according to the ways of his people he must earn the right to be the "story catcher," recorder of the history of his people. The story takes Lance through the processes of growing into manhood: on the hunt, in wars, and in his love for the beautiful maiden, Dawn.

    The traditions of the Plains Indians are beautifully depicted as the story develops. Ceremonials, family life, and many of the old ways are captured positively and realistically.

UPTOWN, by John Steptoe. With pictures by the author. New York: Harper and Row, 1970.

    In Uptown, two Black boys consider their world and what they are going to be when they grow up. Role models from the city and neighborhood are examined through their eyes as they consider several possibilities: junkies, a Brother, a karate expert, a hippie, and a cop. With keen perception the author presents the child's perception of adult role models.

WHEN THE LEGENDS DIE, by Hal Borland. Philadelphia: Lippincott, 1963.

    Thomas Black Bull's father escapes to the wilds with his wife and child, after killing a scheming crook who has stolen from him. Later, father is killed in a landslide and mamma dies from grief. Thomas Black Bull is left to survive alone. The boy has learned the old ways of survival well. He lives in communion with nature, becoming brother to a bear. The bear becomes part of his Indian soul.

    Later, Thomas is discovered and taken to an Indian school where he is taunted and ridiculed by his peers and some of the adult teachers. Several times he attempts to escape but succumbs to his entrapment when his brother bear's life is threatened. The bear is allowed to go free.

    Gradually, the boy subverts his strong cultural feelings,

although longings for the old ways haunt him. He learns to
eat the new food, responds to the classes, but finds himself
unable to enjoy most of the work until he is taught to break
horses. He breaks horses with all his pent-up hostility,
showing almost a desire to kill.

Subsequently, Thomas becomes involved with Red, a
drunken cowboy who uses Tom to make money at rodeos.
He enters Tom in small rodeos, as a beginning rider. Faking a loss, no one suspects Tom's skill. In later challenges,
he wins and they take all the money and leave. These experiences are demoralizing for Thomas, but he has lost his desire to fight. When Red dies, Thomas becomes a rodeo star
until he is critically injured. He fights his way back to
health and becomes a shepherd.

While working as a shepherd, Thomas encounters
brother bear. Their meeting one lonely night arouses all his
suppressed cultural feelings. The soul of the past returns
as he sings the bear chant and responds to the spirit of the
mountains challenging him to return to the old ways.

This book is powerful in its imagery, symbolism and
poetic quality, portraying both violence and love. Thomas
Black Bull conquers his conflicts and finally understands the
strengths of his beliefs and culture.

WOLF RUN: A CARIBOU ESKIMO TALE, written and illus-
    strated by James Houston. New York: Harcourt, 1971.

Punik, defying tradition, seeks food for his starving
village. He hopes to find food to replace the caribou which
didn't come as usual that year. Unsuccessful and near death,
Punik is saved by two wolves, which kill a caribou and unbelievably walk away and leave it for him. This is a stark,
intense fifty-page mood piece which gives an excellent picture
of Eskimo life.

Note: James Houston has written a number of titles about
northern peoples, including Tikta'liktak, which won the 1966
Canadian Library Association Award for the best book published in the English language in Canada.

A WOMAN NAMED SOLITUDE, by André Schwarz-Bart.
    Translated from the French by Ralph Manheim. New
    York: Atheneum, 1973. (Excerpt printed in MS magazine, February, 1973.)

This compelling and tragic tale of slavery traces Solitude from life as a baby on a slave ship through transfers from one plantation to another. Solitude remembers her mother as being strong and black; in contrast, she is mulatto and has strange eyes of two colors.

As her life progresses, Solitude develops a protective mask of unresponsiveness which moves her to an almost zombie-like state. She becomes a legend of strength and strangeness as she moves from one experience of servitude to another. Throughout the horror and sorrow, Solitude remains a striking and independent character supported by her "soul" base in Blackness.

ZEELY, by Virginia Hamilton. Illus. by Symeon Shimin. New York: Macmillan, 1967.

A young girl's imaginative dreams of a heroine are explored in this book. Geeder observes Zeely, tall and regal and the exact duplicate of an African queen the girl saw in an old magazine. Until Zeely reveals the truth, Geeder is convinced that Zeely is somehow related to the pictured queen.

The story presents positives of heritage and images of Black beauty. It also challenges the child to deal with reality as Geeder separates her fantasy about Zeely from the real story. The illustrations are quite striking.

Several bibliographies and other sources are included in the "Sources and Notes" which suggest titles in this subject area: See nos. 1, 5, 12, 15, 18, 29, 47, 49, 55, 65, 67, 72, 82, 84, 87, 94, 96, 100, 106, 109, 114.

PART II
PAIRINGS AND GROUPINGS

Friendship; Peer Pressures

Families

INTRODUCTION

Psychologist Elizabeth Hurlock (see Sources and Notes, No. 21) indicates that young children want to be friendly. Generally her analysis of the formation of peer associations is as follows:

a) In cases where children have not learned proper ways to make friendly advances toward adults and toward other children, aggressive behavior may be displayed. Mistaken attempts to show friendship in early associations often lead to a quarrel, but young children soon reestablish friendship. Older children are more prone to break off a friendship and establish new ones.

b) Later, when the schooling process begins, the child enters the complex developmental process called "socialization." The establishment of friendships fluctuates in a very complex manner depending on the individual's intelligence, personal ego systems, looks, sex, interests, etc. Although the establishment of companionships and friendships is important to every child, some inevitably are rejected by their peers. Those who are rejected may become completely alienated and hostile to their peers or may seek substitute relationships--friendship with adults, association with imaginary characters, and attachment to pets. Children who establish several good relationships usually advance more rapidly socially because of the value of the variance of peer reaction and challenge.

c) Friendships are important to the child, although adults should be aware that some allegiances are formed for the wrong reasons and can be disastrous. Friends, on the other hand, can broaden or sharpen the child's interests and can provide sounding boards for ideas and problems which can't be shared with an adult. They may also provide healthy comparisons. Whether good or bad, friends may exert the most impact on a child's socialization processes.

d) Children will experience various levels of social acceptance and if their perception of that acceptance is accurate, they will probably be able to handle it. This means that the child must be able to determine that acceptance is not always good. It is apparent then, that adult reinforcement, parent intervention in ego formation, and amplification of a child's positives are important prerequisites to the child's ability to form positive pairings and groupings.

e) As the child develops, he begins to come to grips with the realities of the world around him and the community beyond his family. He gains confidence in himself and reaches out to establish emotional ties beyond the family, lessening his dependence on mother and father. This is the beginning of important peer relationships and influences. As friendships are established, the child learns from this outer relationship and reinforces or forms new mental associations.

Pre-Adolescence

Some psychologists believe that healthy peer relationships are most important in the pre-adolescent years. If preadolescents are not emotionally ready or able to establish contact with their peers, they may not pass through a "normal" adolescent period. The adolescent personality and performance-formation then take on problematic symptoms mentioned in other chapters--such as loneliness, sexual deviations, aggressions, violence, etc.

The pre-adolescent begins the integration of fantasy with the realities of the adult world, forming new and vital conceptualizations. Although there are gross variations, the pattern on the average seems to be: pairings, from five to nine; large group relationships from nine to twelve; and then the splitting off into small groups again at adolescence. In all of these cases--pairings, large group relationships and small intimate groups--the attitudes of the associate have a great influence on the individual. Even in the case of the child who becomes a peer group leader, the reactions of the group are of great importance (perhaps more so in this situation than in others).

Although the development of peer associations may be slightly different in girls than in boys, particularly at the pre-adolescent stage, the synthesis of fantasy with reality begins similarly. Some girls attach themselves to male groups and imitate their attitudes and actions. But it is more common for girls to form small-group peer associations or pairings at the pre-adolescent stage. Their fantasy-reality integregation is evident in their playing with dolls at the same time that they are learning to baby-sit and play at being real mothers. Keeping secrets and diaries which reflect fantasy and views of the adult world is also a common phenomenon. Emotional and social development can often be seen in diary writings.

The structure of the society (or possibly natural drives) draws boys into large active groups where they carry out the rituals of forming laws and social rules. Commonly, activities include mechanical operations such as fixing cars, making electronic devices, and building models.

In a discussion of pre-adolescent peer group relationships, Dr. Kohen Raz (see Sources and Notes, No. 24) analyzes the patterns of such formations briefly as follows:

1) The content of the peer group changes from that of the play groups established in early childhood. Play groups are accidental formations for the sake of games, while clubs and gangs formed later are more firmly organized.

2) The stability of the play group is low. These groups are formed for immediate purposes and then dissolved. Pre-adolescent peer groups, by their design, formulate rules reflecting the members' level of moral development. They usually guarantee unity and mutual support. This kind of organized structure allows the pre-adolescent to further separate himself from adults and adult rules and norms. Each member of the group assumes a place and depends on the group rules even if they are different from the community rules.

3) Leadership in a play group fluctuates, allowing any child a chance to play leader, while gangs and clubs choose a leader who remains dominant for some time. Characteristics of the pre-adolescent group leader are: intelligence; an advanced sense of achievement and socialization; good looks, etc. The bully or person who rules by sheer force is not usually a group leader (this type of leader is more common in poor communities where respect for physical prowess and sexual attractiveness indicates variances in development according to community value systems).

4) Although peer group formations show some

differences according to socioeconomic background, generally there are: a) normal peer groups of the middle class; b) normal peer groups of the poor; and c) the delinquent gang in both communities.

Kohen Raz concludes that normally formed peer groups can represent the highest form of psychosocial development, although there is the chance that any group may deteriorate into mob behavior. The delinquent gang is more prone to extreme and negative behavior because the actual formation often evolves out of emotional and social instability. They generally operate with looser laws and sometimes with neurotic views of themselves and adults.

The role of the adult is not clear, except that there is a clear differential between adult-led institutional groups and naturally formed peer groups. Some psychologists believe that adult attempts to lead the naturally formed groups can lead to extreme behavior. This doesn't bar the possibility of adult intervention after the natural group is formed.

Included in this section are materials written for children and young adults which present seemingly accurate representations of friendship and peer group formations in story form. Relationships in these books often conform to the analyses of the forementioned authors.

1. <u>Friendship; Peer Pressures</u>

YOUNG PEOPLE SPEAK FOR THEMSELVES

Friendship is nothing but a word. A better word is associates.
 --DOROTHY, 19

You don't find much friendship; a lot of people won't accept it. It's hard to find a true friend. Like me, I find pleasure in people, talking to people and helping people, but most people think this is a dud.
 --MARCY, 18

It's nice to have some friends but not too many; too many may take advantage of you. I stick with a couple.
 --KAREN, 19

A lot of people say you can't trust friends, that they will get behind your back and steal your man. But you need a friend, and if you really care for them and they do something to hurt you, you forgive them. I don't care who you are, you need somebody. It's stupid to be by yourself all the time. Everybody needs somebody by their side.
 --LEOLA, 18

I had that problem when I was younger. My friends would always pressure me into doing things. If I didn't want to do something they would pick on me and talk about me. It's changed since I got older; I have friends but they don't force me to do anything. But if it came up, and my friends tried to push me now, I wouldn't hang around them anymore because I can make other friends.
 --JANE, 15

I feel friendship is one thing you have to have because you can tell a friend everything if he's close enough. If you don't tell anybody your secrets and problems, then you won't know what to do with yourself. When you have someone to talk to it helps. Your friend also is your companion, you can go places together and enjoy yourself. That's what I feel is good about friendship: having someone to talk with and be with.

--JANE, 15

BAD FALL, by Charles P. Crawford. New York: Harper and Row, 1972.

Sean Richardson's need for friendship is strongly portrayed as he survives on the fringes of his high school group. He is accepted, but is not important. Later he meets Wade Sabbat, his first "real friend." Beneath a mild exterior, Wade hides a cruel and cunning personality and he manipulates Sean. Sean finds himself doing things he would not otherwise do.

The friendship between the two boys is shown realistically, although the strong portrayal of Wade's character places Sean in the shadows. Some incidents, such as one on Halloween night, are lost in symbolism.

In spite of its limitations, this book may be important for what it implies about the manipulatory power of friendship. Sean graphically represents the adolescent who seeks acceptance and who is trapped in fears of rejection.

THE CHOCOLATE WAR, by Robert Cormier. New York: Pantheon, 1974.

An intriguing and probably controversial story of a fund-raising scheme in a Catholic school. Through the candy sales, gang psychology is exposed along with a compelling view of the depraved Catholic Brother who uses the gang to further his scheme.

Archie Costello is leader of the Vigils, but leadership is a tenuous affair. One has to constantly prove one's capacity to lead. Jerry Renault is the victim--victim of the system. Brother Leon, aware of the power of the Vigils, enlists their aid in compelling the other boys to participate in the candy sales.

Jerry receives an order that he is to refuse to sell candy until he is told to capitulate. Time and time again when the candy sale role is called, Jerry is the only one who refuses. He becomes frustrated by the whole process of having someone else control him, so that when the command is rescinded he still refuses to sell candy, an act of rebellion against the gang and against the corrupt leadership of Brother Leon. Lest he lose control and leadership, Archie must squash this rebellion. He organizes the eventual cruel showdown in which Jerry is unmercifully beaten, while Brother Leon looks on and does nothing. A disturbing view of gang psychology and of the individual trying to beat the system.

DINKY HOCKER SHOOTS SMACK, by M. E. Kerr. New York: Harper and Row, 1972.

Susan (Dinky) Hocker is hooked, not on dope but on food. She eats all the time and is grossly overweight. Her mother works with reformed addicts in a center, but doesn't recognize that Dinky's weight problem is emotionally linked.

Tucker, Dinky's friend, arranges a blind date between her and P. John, who also is overweight. The two of them relate beautifully, to the astonishment of Tucker, who is so shy that he can't communicate with his date. A supportive and positive relationship develops between Dinky and P. John. Dinky goes on a diet and no longer feels her former compulsion to tell horror tales. But her parents dislike P. John's conservative view of life.

As the characters are developed, Tucker's feelings about himself and his first real relationship with a girl are revealed. He and Natalie, Dinky's cousin, have such difficulty communicating with each other that they resort to word games, which Dinky's mother mistakenly interprets as the secret code of a developing love affair. With P. John's support, Dinky continues to lose weight until P. John, after an encounter with Dinky's parents, is asked to leave the house. Eventually, P. John leaves town and Dinky returns, even more voraciously, to her old eating habits.

After living with his aunt for a while, and losing quite a bit of weight, P. John returns to town and pays Dinky a surprise visit. Humiliated at seeing P. John so slim and at being so much fatter herself, Dinky revolts by painting a huge sign on the street "Dinky Hocker Shoots Smack." This incident reveals some realities to her parents.

The need for friendship and support and the difficulties

in establishing compatible relationships are defined but the characters show little depth. The book will probably be popular with teenagers who empathize with the surface problems, but without discussion it is doubtful whether they will gain much perspective from the book.

DON'T SLAM THE DOOR WHEN YOU GO, by Barbara Corcoran. New York: Atheneum, 1972.

Judith, Lily and Flower, all just out of high school, have considered leaving home for months. Finally when Lily's father (the only parent aware of their plan) gets them a car, they leave. They have chosen to settle in Plunketville, a ghost town in Montana.

Backgrounded by their family relationships, the major portion of the story covers the girls' trip and their struggle to survive in a new setting.

On the way they encounter a motorcycle group which intimidates them, but when they arrive in Plunketville they do very well setting up a life style for themselves in some abandoned shacks. Then strange things begin to happen, which they blame at first on the wild animals. They soon begin to realize that the strange incidents have been caused by local people who are hostile to youth cults. Things are further complicated when a hippie group moves into the settlement with them.

By the time their problems are eventually solved, one female member of the hippie commune has died of an overdose; Judith has become very attached to the young son of the dead girl; Flower strikes out on her own following the commune leader with whom she has fallen in love; Eric, son of the dead drug abuser, finds a foster home; Lily finds a job on a horse ranch, and Judith goes to live with her older sister, a nun.

Judith realizes as she leaves that decisions about her future will not be easy. In following Judith's development, some of the links with other main characters are lost, but most of the story is believable. The importance of temporary adolescent associations is apparent, as is the need for adult intervention.

THE FOG COMES ON LITTLE PIG FEET, by Rosemary Wells. Illus. by the author. New York: Dial Press, 1972.

Thirteen-year-old Rachel hates being placed in a boarding school, where she has no rights or privacy. When she gets involved with "the Daggett girl," a troublemaker and eventual runaway, Kathy's problems are compounded. She finds herself caught in a web of lies as she tries to win the approval of her peers and to protect the confidence of the runaway.

The girls and the adult leaders are realistically portrayed. Kathy's dilemma will be familiar to many girls.

THE FRIENDS, by Rosa Guy. New York: Holt, Rinehart and Winston, 1973.

This is not just a book about friendship, as may be indicated by the title; it is a story about a girl's interrelationships with the elements of her world, resulting finally in her reassessment of herself and those around her.

Phyllisia is confronted with the hostilities of her peers because she is West Indian and smart in her classes. She suffers great insecurities because (by superficial standards) her mother and sister are pretty and she is plain.

Her father's false sense of superiority rubs off on her, so she is ashamed of her only real friend, Edith. Edith is poor and wears tattered clothes and socks with holes in them. As the story develops, Phyllisia's mother dies and she begins to view her father more realistically. These and other factors bring Phyllisia to a realization of her mistaken understanding of love and friendship.

The lives of the friends are basically very different, although similar in some ways. Edith, having no mother, has to assume the role of an adult. She resorts to stealing as a method of survival. Edith suffers an aloneness and need for companionship similar to Phyllisia's but the reasons for their rejection from the group are different. Eventually, when her father leaves home, Edith drops out of school to care for her younger brothers and sisters. She rejects outside assistance because she wants to keep the family together. Phyllisia, on the other hand, lives in what would appear to be a stable family situation, but she suffers because of her growing inner turmoil.

HOW MANY MILES TO BABYLON? by Paula Fox. Illus. by Paul Giovanopoulos. New York: David White Co., 1967.

James Douglas lives in a crowded building in Brooklyn

with his three old aunts. They have cared for him since his mother left. Life with his aunts has its pleasures and problems. James likes to hear Aunt Paul tell stories about the old times, but he hates the secondhand clothes and shoes Aunt Althea brings for him to wear. Most of all he hates school. He would much rather play in the deserted house where he fantasizes about being a prince and about traveling to Africa with his mother.

The majority of the story takes place the day James walks out of school and goes to the deserted house where he is discovered by a gang of "dognappers." They force him to join their game of stealing dogs which they return later for a reward.

James succumbs to the wishes of the gang, but looks for every opportunity to escape. After several attempts, James manages to escape, returns a stolen dog and finally arrives home. His anxious aunts are waiting with a surprise --his mother!

This interesting story presents a believable portrayal of a young person pressured into negative behavior. The characters and setting ring true. James's slips into fantasy and reminiscences interrupt the flow of the story, but the excitement of his capture and escape sustain the plot.

This story could also be considered for its presentation of family. The support of the aunts is obviously strong, which adds to the credibility of James's ability to gather his resources and outwit the gang members. This book has appeal for younger and older children.

IT'S LIKE THIS, CAT, by Emily Neville. Illus. by Emily
    Weiss. New York: Harper and Row, 1963.

This story humorously portrays an adolescent's attachment to an animal in lieu of human friendships. Fourteen-year-old Dave Mitchell is alienated from his father. When he acquires Cat from an old and eccentric neighbor, he talks to Cat about his problems and frustrations. Later he finds a new girlfriend, Mary, who helps him see his father differently. His father also comes to some new realizations and finally resolves that Dave is entitled to make some decisions about his life.

Light, perceptive and entertaining, this book explores maturing adolescence and a boy's relationships to his family and peers.

MEANING WELL, by Sheila R. Cole. Illus. by Paul Raynor. New York: Watts, 1974.

Lisa feels sorry for poor Peggy, who is rejected by her peers because her father is "weird." Peggy invites all the class to her birthday party, but no one shows up except Lisa. Subsequently Lisa is also ostracized by the group, including her former best friend, Susan. Lisa's sympathies for Peggy are lost as she tries to regain her former status with the group.

The need for peer relationships is established, as well as the cruelty that can result from young people's gross insecurities about such relationships. There is no happy ending to this story and it provokes much thought from the reader. Familiar to many will be the embarrassment suffered by children when their parents appear at school and make a scene in front of the other children. Others will recognize Susan, social leader among the group, who manipulates the others according to her wishes. Many will also identify with Peggy, who lets down her defenses when she thinks she has found a friend. And last, there is Lisa, torn between her need to be a part of the group and her new relationship with Peggy.

THE OUTSIDERS, by Susan E. Hinton. New York: Viking, 1967.

Personal and group interrelationships are handled with discernment in this book about gang life. The story is told by Ponyboy, a member of the "Greasers," a gang from a low-income neighborhood. The "Greasers" have a long-standing feud with the "SoCs," who are more affluent. Hostilities between the two groups are demonstrated through street fights and competition for girls.

Since his mother and father died, Ponyboy has lived alone with his older brothers. Love and conflict in the three brothers' relationship are revealed as the story progresses. Ponyboy runs away from home with his pal, Joey, who commits homicide in a gang encounter. While hiding out, the two boys risk their lives to save some young children caught in a fire. This brings attention to their whereabouts. Joey dies of injuries from the fire and Ponyboy returns home, where he begins to reassess his gang membership and his feelings for his brothers.

Characterizations of the young people are well handled, showing each individual's unique personality and needs. Their individual needs for involvement with the group are thus better understood.

THE PIGMAN, by Paul Zindel. New York: Harper and Row, 1968.

    This novel is a study in adolescent peer associations and influences as they affect their relationships with, and feelings about, adults.
    John Conlon and Lorraine Jensen meet Mr. Pignati, while collecting money for a fictitious charity. Mr. Pignati is a lonely old man, living with the memory of his dead wife. His main relationship is with a baboon he has befriended at the zoo. A tenuous connection between the young people and Mr. Pignati develops. There are less than noble intentions in the young people's association with the old man, although they later develop true affection for him.
    As the story develops, John and Lorraine use Mr. Pignati to their advantage, realizing, only through the resulting tragedy, the danger in tampering with people's feelings. Group interests and peer pressures have taken precedence over their underlying feelings of guilt. Interwoven with all this is a slight view of the parents and their relationships with the teenagers.

SIDEWALK STORY, by Sharon Bell Mathis. Illus. by Leo Carty. New York: Viking, 1971.

    Friendship in this story truly means helping as best you can in a crisis. Lilly's friend Tanya and her family are being evicted from their apartment. Desperately, Lilly tries to seek help. She calls the newspaper and the police, but to no avail. Real commitment is seen when Lilly tries to protect the family's possessions which have been moved outside to the sidewalk. When it rains she tries to cover their things with anything she can find, including her own body.
    Some will question the success of this nine-year-old's fight against the bureaucracy, but none can question the impact of the portrayal of sincere friendship.

THAT WAS THEN, THIS IS NOW, by Susan E. Hinton. New York: Viking Press, 1971.

    In The Outsiders, there were gang fights between the

"SoCs" and the "Greasers," rival gangs representing the rich and the poor. Then a boy is killed and the gang activities decrease. In this story, young people still are found in pairs and groups and they engage in activities unknown to their parents.

Bryon and Mark are like brothers, although Mark is adopted. The two boys are a constant team, Bryon having all the answers and Mark charming people to get his way. Mark also steals and hot-wires cars but both manage to stay out of serious trouble until...

M&M, a good and trusting friend of the brothers, is attacked by a gang of boys. This results in retaliation, which costs the life of Charlie, poolroom owner and friend of the boys.

Bryon becomes involved with Cathy, M&M's sister, and he gradually grows apart from Mark. Charlie's death and Bryon's relationship with Cathy effect changes in his thinking about the life he leads. He is also disturbed by M&M's growing alienation from his large and loving family, and when M&M joins a hippie commune and starts taking drugs, the impending crisis begins.

In the end, after turning Mark in to the police for selling dope, Bryon faces the beginning of a new life. He has lost Mark, his relationship with Cathy is shattered, and M&M, after taking a bad trip on LSD, is completely changed. Solutions are not readily available for the young man; he is now faced with forming his own individual perspectives apart from the group.

Note: Ms. Hinton is also author of <u>Rumble Fish</u> (Delacorte, 1975), a story about brothers caught in the web of gang violence. This story emphasizes how hard it is for young people living in a gang environment to escape involvement.

<u>VERONICA GANZ</u>, by Marilyn Sachs. Illus. by Louis Glanzman. New York: Doubleday, 1968.

Veronica is a big kid, bigger than anyone in the class. But no one understands that her bullying behavior is the result of her discomfort. More than anything, Veronica wants to get even with Peter Wedemeyer, who taunts, teases and tricks her, but Peter never lets her get close enough for a real fight. At first, everyone sides with Peter, but one day he and some friends attack Veronica. Veronica is rescued by a passerby, who chastises the boys for their behavior. The incident leaves Peter with such an obvious sense of guilt that Veronica realizes he cares.

Veronica's feud with Peter is balanced by a glimpse of her family: mother, stepfather, younger sister Mary Rose, and a five-year-old half-brother. Family problems and sibling relationships are part of Veronica's conflict, but the story is nicely balanced by humor.

The adventures of Veronica are continued in <u>Peter and Veronica</u> (Doubleday).

Added Entries

<u>THE BIRTHDAY WISH</u>, by Chihiro Iwasaki. Illus. by the author. New York: McGraw-Hill, 1974.

A solution for a bad moment between friends. Allison's birthday is the day after her friend June's. Attending June's party, Allison forgets it is not her birthday and blows out the birthday candles. Her humiliation is conquered when she allows June to blow out her candles at the party the next day.

<u>THE CAT ACROSS THE WAY</u>, by Anne Huston. Illus. by Velma Ilsley. New York: Seabury Press, 1968.

A familiar theme of a family moving from the country to the city and the trauma experienced by the child in such a situation. Lacey strikes up a tenuous, quarrelsome friendship with Rosette. In the end the friends' quarrels are resolved and the family establishes better relationships.

<u>GLADYS TOLD ME TO MEET HER HERE</u>, by Marjorie W. Sharmat. Illus. by Edward Frascino. New York: Harper, 1970.

Boy-girl story of friendship. Irving wouldn't dare let Gladys know how much he worried when she was late meeting him. His thoughts about Gladys's friendship and his fears for her safety are exposed.

<u>I WONDER IF HERBIE'S HOME YET</u>, by Mildred Kantrowitz. Illus. by Tony De Luna. New York: Parent's Magazine Press, 1971.

Young children are often selfish about their friendships, as is Smokey, who plans to get even with his friend Herbie for going off to play with someone else--until he realizes that Herbie is at the dentist's office. Then, he can't wait until Herbie gets home.

MEMBER OF THE GANG, by Barbara Rinkoff. Illus. by Harold James. New York: Crown, 1968.

The search, the trauma, and the pressures of gang membership are exposed in this title. Woodie wants to be a member of Leroy's gang, so he pays no heed to his father's warnings not to associate with the boy. Woody becomes involved in a store robbery and is arrested. With the help of a Black probation officer, Woodie gradually begins to see the futility of his gang involvement.

The resolution is less credible than the view of the adolescent needs which sometimes result in this kind of situation. Although Woodie seems to be saved, most of the gang members plan for their return to the streets, which is the common pattern.

NO TRESPASSING, by Ray Prather. Illus. by the author. New York: Macmillan, 1974.

When he wants to play ball with them, Little Charlie is taken advantage of by the bigger boys, but he emerges the hero.

THE ONCE-A-YEAR DAY, by Eve Bunting. Illus. by W. T. Mars. Chicago: Children's Press, 1974.

The development of friendship between two Eskimo girls in Alaska. Emma, an orphan, has been taken in by Annie's family. Annie has looked forward to having the girl, her cousin, as a companion. But Emma rejects her friendship until one day the barge arrives and Annie shares treasures bought from the barge with Emma.

THE SEVENTEENTH-STREET GANG, by Emily Cheney Neville. Illus. by Emily McCully. New York: Harper, 1966.

Peer relationships and pressures are vividly apparent in this story set in New York. Minnow encourages hostility toward Hollis, the new boy in the neighborhood. Although Minnow rebels, the pressures are reversed because the others in the group really like Hollis.

STEFFIE AND ME, by Phyllis Hoffman. Illus. by Emily McCully. New York: Harper, 1970.

Amusing story of friendship, with interracial pictures. Two girls are in the same class and ride the bus together to school. Their view of the classroom is all too familiar and very funny.

WILL I HAVE A FRIEND? by Miriam Cohen. Illus. by Lillian Hoban. New York; Macmillan, 1967.

Fears of the very young child on the first day at school is a familiar theme.

WILL YOU BE MY FRIEND? by Chihiro Iwasaki. Illus. by the author. New York: McGraw-Hill, 1974.

A growing friendship between Allison and the boy who has just moved in down the street. One of the nicer picture stories about very young children seeking friendships.

2. Families

YOUNG PEOPLE SPEAK FOR THEMSELVES

My family, I'm close to them in some ways. I'm not close to my mother, but I'm close to my brother and sister. We're pretty good together, we always have good times together.
                              --JANE, 15

My mother's family raised me. I love them and appreciate them. Someday, when I'm responsible enough, I'd like to have a family of my own.
                              --MARCY, 18

My family is a wonderful family, we all get along pretty good but I don't want a family until I'm 54.

I miss them, they would like for me to come home. I remember when I was little I went to church every Sunday, but now I'm kinda glad. You know, when you get older you appreciate things more. But, I don't want to go home. I want to be on my own. My family can't back me up all the time, I have to learn how to do for myself. I don't want to be dependent on my family. I don't want to have to say mamma did this and mamma did that.

When I have kids, I want to have something, I want to teach them everything--how life is. I'm not gonna hide anything. Kids are okay, but it's best to have a man and have something to show your kid. Of course accidents can happen and a girl can get pregnant, but she's got a problem if she doesn't want an abortion.
                              --LEOLA, 18

* * *

Prominent educators view the child, not as an individual, but as a member of a family. Many agree that most formative development takes place outside the school, nurtured by the family unit, or by the community when the family unit is weak. For example, the construct for Montessori (see Sources and Notes, No. 99) education placed strong emphasis on the parent. Montessori believed that the school was partner to parents, particularly to mothers, who are largely responsible for the child's education. In the original Montessori school the concept of parent involvement included releasing the child from school if the cooperation of the parents was not received. This procedure indicated this educator's strong belief that educational exposure can easily be undermined by attitudes and reactions in the home.

Montessori believed in parent involvement, but she did not view the family as an isolated unit. She felt that such isolation did not allow for the development of attitudes of sharing and brotherhood. She felt that it was often within families that the strongest class barriers and subsequent national barriers were formed. She conceived the school, the parent and the community as a cooperative for the child's benefit.

Kohen Raz (see Sources and Notes, No. 24), in a discussion of the American preindustrial society, explains that during those times an extended family concept was prevalent. Younger people were expected to assume the roles vacated by parents and close relatives. In most cases, it was unnecessary to move far from the original family in order to form a life and work pattern acceptable to the society. Hence there was no need for the preparatory processes of pre-adolescence in which the child could begin to experiment with stepping out into the wider world.

Regarding current trends affecting the American family, Hurlock (see Sources and Notes, No. 21) concludes that with the turn of the century came major changes in family relationships, especially those between children and parents and children and grandparents, which has resulted in a deterioration of the family in general.

She lists parental attitudes which affect the negative developments in the child's family relationships. These include over-protectiveness, permissiveness, rejection, domination, submission to the child and over-ambition for the child. She further indicates that the size of the family affects these attitudes and relationships. Small families are listed as negative in the tendency toward overprotectiveness, while large families lack close parent-child relationships. In small families the application of pressure for achievement is more prevalent than in large families, according to this theorist.

Most importantly, Ms. Hurlock states emphatically that the mass media as well as personal experience strongly influence a person's concepts of proper family roles.

In conclusion, it appears that the American family has reached a critical point in its development. More mothers are heads of households. There are more one-parent families with either the mother or father as a single role model. Extended family involvement is decreasing. And status of children in decision-making is changing.

Therefore, those with peripheral influence on the child's developmental processes may have to assume greater responsibility than ever before. Educators and community leaders will probably be required to present a variety of positive family models to young people. Early instruction will need to include family concepts and problems.

Many materials still present the nuclear family as the ideal, while other common family forms are often omitted or are portrayed as negative. Some recent materials for children present problematic family situations such as divorce, remarriage, sibling rivalry, etc. The presentation of more varied perspectives of the family could help children make choices and develop attitudes which will be helpful to them in the future.

Note: <u>Children's Literature, an Issues Approach</u>, by Marsha Kabakow Rudman (see Sources and Notes, No. 31), includes a chapter dealing with sibling relationships within the family. Some of the titles discussed are included here, but Rudman's book has additional resources for expanding the approach to families in literature. The section following "Siblings," titled "Divorce," also includes a helpful list of titles offering views of families facing divorce.

ALL-OF-A-KIND FAMILY, by Sydney Taylor. Illus. by
   Helen John. Chicago: Follett, 1951.

   It's 1912, on the predominantly Jewish East Side of New York. Ella is twelve, Henrietta is ten, Sarah is eight, Charlotte is six and Gertie is four. These are the five girls in the "All-of-a-Kind Family."
   This story chronicles the humor, adventures, and family experiences of the five girls and their relatives. People are poor and crises must be faced, but strengths and joys of being together in an affirming family are apparent. The religious celebrations are handled naturally as part of the story, as is the anticipation of the new baby whom father wants to be a boy.
   Sequels to this story are More All-of-a-Kind Family and All-of-a-Kind Family Uptown.

THE BEAR'S HOUSE, by Marilyn Sachs. Illus. by Louis
   Glanzman. New York: Doubleday, 1971.

   Ten-year-old Fran Ellen Smith sucks her thumb. She knows that when school is out, someone will be given the bear's house which Miss Thompson keeps in the classroom. Fran wants that house more than anything, even enough to stop sucking her thumb.
   When her daddy left home Fran Ellen's mother retreated into herself, becoming progressively more ill. Fran decides that the truth must be kept from everyone or the social worker will come and take the entire family away. So she and the other children live a pretend life, hiding mother away in the bedroom whenever anyone appears, and taking care of themselves and the baby the best they can. Until-- Miss Thompson comes to deliver the doll house and discovers the truth.
   A poignant, sometimes funny story of young people designing their own pattern for survival. It is the story of a family torn by adult trauma, but of children who determine to stay together.

DANNY ROWLEY, by Reginald Maddock. Boston: Little,
   Brown, 1970.

   Set in England, this story presents a common crisis which often engenders problems for parents and teens. Danny's mother announces that she plans to remarry, triggering such resentment in the boy that he goes out and smashes several street lamps. Later, Danny finds himself hiding out with two Black boys, dubbed "the niggers" by his mother and the police. This encounter and subsequent happenings establish a bond between Danny and the two Black kids.

Laura Higgins, daughter of the groom to be, is no happier about the situation than Danny. But in spite of their protests, the marriage takes place and Danny goes to live at the Higgins' home.

Life is not easy for the new family. Laura intends to be so hostile that the marriage will be forced to break up. Partially because he resents Laura's treatment of his mother, Danny slowly has a change of heart. He learns to respect his stepfather's strength and knowledge. He silently appreciates his stepfather's positive attitude toward Blacks.

Added intrigue revolves around activities of a gang who burglarize and steal. One of the Blacks, Robbo, is accused of a crime committed by the gang leader, Mugsby Jones. Danny, his stepfather and friends devise a plan to trap the real culprits, saving Robbo from being falsely charged.

Ingredients of family and gangs are handled credibly in this story, but the portrayal of the two Black characters is forced, probably because the Blacks remain ineffectively one-dimensional against the whites and their attitudes of prejudice.

THE DOLLAR MAN, by Harry Mazer. New York: Delacorte, 1974.

Positives and negatives of a one-parent family are convincingly explored in this novel about fourteen-year-old Marcus Rosenbloom.

Until his fourteenth year, Marcus has felt reasonably secure in his relationship with his mother, although he has experienced uncomfortable moments with his peers when the subject of fathers has come up. He knows nothing about his father. His mother, Sally, has only explained that she didn't want to marry him.

Over the years Marcus's close relationship with Sally and his positive relationship with her boyfriend has been enough. However, during his fourteenth year, Marcus experiences insecurities about being overweight. He envies his peers and dreams about his father.

Marcus then becomes involved with a new group at school and is suspended on a "bum rap" of marihuana possession. As the result of a confrontation with his mother, he learns his father's name for the first time. Marcus traces the clues he finds and finally locates his father, only to discover that he is not the kind man of his dreams. He is a shallow man with negative values, a man he doesn't know or want to know.

This is an important book because of its realistic exploration of the pressures on a child by his peers and society when he has only one parent. The positives of the mother-son relationship are explicit enough not to be obliterated by Marcus's obsession over finding his father.

THE EDGE OF NEXT YEAR, by Mary Stolz. New York: Harper, 1974.

Family problems are dealt with in this story of Orin Woodard, aged fourteen. His mother is killed in an accident and his father turns to alcohol because of his grief. Orin thus becomes the head of the family but he, too, finds it hard to accept his mother's death. Later, in a harrowing experience, in a cave, Orin accepts the reality of life and wanting to live.

This is an unusual family story. Each person is a unique individual. The father loves to read poetry and was a political reporter for a liberal newspaper. Mother was a bird watcher and brother Victor knows everything about animals.

Orin finds it hard to understand the individual reactions to his mother's death. His father is lost in despair and Victor, obsessed with collecting specimens, doesn't seem to miss her very much. Orin's own return to reality at the end implies his understanding of the others' reactions to his mother's death.

THE FAMILY UNDER THE BRIDGE, by Natalie Savage Carlson. Pictures by Garth Williams. New York: Harper, 1958.

A mother and her three children, evicted from their home, take refuge under a bridge in Paris. Armand, an old hobo who declares he hates children, discovers them there. But it is evident that Armand has a heart, because he shares his food with the family. He also learns that the children can serve to his advantage in his solicitations on the streets of Paris. Armand poses as the grandfather of these poor motherless waifs and it is even more appealing to sympathetic givers when the children sing, for it is the Christmas season.

Armand takes the children to visit Father Christmas and their greatest wish is to have a home where all the family can be together. Later, the children are discovered by two women who decide to seek help for them. To escape social workers they must leave, so Armand takes them to live with his friends in a gypsy camp. All is well for a while, but trouble develops and the gypsies have to leave. There seems to be no place to go, until Armand, now the children's adopted grandfather, decides to take a job. With the job he is able to provide living quarters for the family.

Throughout this story, one is impressed with the strong feeling of families who wish to stay together. We also are introduced, in a warm and positive way, to the life style of a hobo and to gypsies.

A GIRL LIKE ME, by Jeannette Eyerly. Philadelphia: Lippincott, 1966.

Beginning with a double date (in separate cars), Robin finds herself involved in more than she is prepared to handle. She subsequently develops a questionable relationship with Randy Griffin and later discovers that her friend Cass is pregnant.

The story follows the theme of the trials of pregnancy out of wedlock and the unreadiness of teens to face the problems of love and marriage. More importantly, this narrative reveals family relationships. Cass's father and mother had great expectations of her. When she becomes pregnant, her father is so angry that he places her in a home for unwed mothers.

Through her involvement with Cass, and her trauma over what might happen to Cass's baby, Robin, who is an adopted child, has a sudden need to know who her parents are. She starts a search on her own, secretly taking information from her adoption papers. After finding out her mother's name, she locates an old lady who tells her about her mother's death. Robin then realizes the blessings of being loved by a new father and mother.

The search and discovery may seem a little too easy, but the story shows believable insight to the adoptive child's sometimes overwhelming need to know who his or her real parents are.

THE GLASS ROOM, by Mary Towne. Drawings by Richard Cuffari. New York: Farrar, Straus and Giroux, 1971.

Two boys in very different family situations exchange feelings about their pain and frustrations. Robin's family are all musical. He is frustrated by the constant noise and clutter. Simon's mother and father are separated. Simon and his architect father live in a house with a glass room, his father's studio.

Each of the boys finds himself feeling jealous of the other's way of life. Robin thinks the glass room and the quiet and solitude of Simon's home is perfect. On the other hand, Simon finds the humor, noise, and activeness of Robin's family delightful.

An accident, in which Simon breaks his ankle, brings a lot of things into focus. When Robin goes to Simon's father for help, and he refuses to listen, Robin realizes that there is a difference between quietness and really listening and caring.

In the end, the two families get together, including Simon's mother, who has come for a visit. Each boy settles into his own way of life, with a few changes in perception brought about by their summer's relationship.

GUY LENNY, by Harry Mazer. New York: Delacorte, 1971.

This story deals with the problem of families broken by divorce. Guy has lived with his father since his mother left home to marry another man. When the story begins, he is faced with the realization that his father has established a relationship with another woman, which weakens the strong father-son bond. Guy resents the courtship, but doesn't feel the full impact of its meaning until his mother returns to town. His mother, after talking with his father, has come to take Guy to live with her and his stepfather. Guy feels his father has lied to him by implying that they would always be together. He runs away to be alone for a while, and then returns. Nothing is resolved, except that Guy realizes that no matter with whom he lives, now he is somehow apart from both his mother and father and must make decisions for himself.

The presentation of the parents is not as negative as in some novels of this type. One understands that Guy has made it difficult for his father by refusing to relate to the girlfriend, and his mother tries, however unsuccessfully, to explain her earlier decision to leave him.

Families / 115

THE HAPPY ORPHELINES, by Natalie Savage Carlson. Pictures by Garth Williams. New York: Harper and Row, 1957.

 This is the story of Brigitte and the other girls who live in a Paris orphanage. A special kind of family with love and sharing is portrayed through the little girl who wants more than anything <u>not</u> to be adopted.
 This book demonstrates that love can be found in situations other than the nuclear family. It also demonstrates how the child views herself, in contrast to how the world views her. Happy times among the family of orphans contrast with outsiders' view of them as pitiful orphans.

HENRY 3, by Joseph Krumgold. Drawings by Alvin Smith. New York: Atheneum, 1967.

 Through Henry Lovering, who has an IQ of one hundred and fifty-four, the frustrations of the "special" child are revealed. Henry is tired of being ostracized by his peers because of his smartness. When his family settles in suburban Crestview, he hopes to keep his IQ a secret, but Fletcher Larkin discovers his genius and threatens to expose him.
 Added to Henry's struggle to relate positively to his peers is the theme of life in an affluent community. False value systems and pressures are credibly exposed as other members of the family seek position and security in the new community.
 A sudden hurricane takes a couple of lives, shocks residents into new values, brings Henry and father closer together, and adds a new member to the Lovering family.

HOME FROM THE HILL, by Margaret Baker. New York: Farrar, Straus and Giroux, 1969.

 In this pleasant, fast reading book, four children set out to reunite their family by finding a suitable home during a housing shortage in England.
 The family's cottage home is destroyed in a flood and they are forced to move to a crowded flat in town. Mamma has twins and papa is out of a job and the health inspectors remove them from their flat. The family is separated--the two girls sent to a home for girls, the boys to another site, mom and the twins taken care of in a hospital, while father searches for work.

The family still communicates but most of all they want to be together. Although the arrangements are temporary, the children become impatient and hatch a scheme to escape and search for a suitable home for the whole family. Aided by a beautiful African girl, Liberty, the girls escape on bikes to join their brothers in flight from the authorities and in search of a house. They find refuge in the cottage Liberty has suggested as a hideout, but soon they must move on, for the authorities are close in pursuit. They escape to another house, where they encounter a young runaway who aids them in their second escape. When they are later captured, all is well because their friends have helped to arrange for the family to be together again.

An enjoyable and lightly suspenseful story emphasizing strong feelings of family togetherness.

I KNOW YOU, AL, by Constance Greene. Illus. by Bryon Barton. New York: Viking, 1975.

Sequel to A Girl Called Al, which follows Al through the development of family problems when her mom meets a new boyfriend and Al worries about whether she will marry him. Humorous perspectives of adolescent growing pains are seen.

Al was introduced in A Girl Called Al as being different, independent, wearing pigtails, a bit overweight, with a high IQ and wanting to take shop. The concentration is on Al as an individual and her relationship to her friend Kate. The family situation is exposed in this earlier title, however, as we are introduced to Al's divorced parents and her feelings about them. There is also an element of the need for surrogate parentage as Al and Kate spend time with the building superintendent, a friendly and unconventional man.

LIFE OF KESHAV: A FAMILY STORY FROM INDIA, by Rama Mehta. Illus. by Negri. New York: McGraw-Hill, 1969.

Life within a poverty-stricken family in India is exposed through this story of Keshav, who faces many problems when he receives help which enables him to attend a city school. The setting, emotions and conflicts are sometimes better portrayed than the characters. The atmosphere in the home is not conducive to studying. Keshav is caught between the values and rituals of his village life and his desire to get an education. The conflict forms the vehicle by which a view of the family is presented.

THE LONG JOURNEY, by Barbara Corcoran. Illus. by
    Charles Robinson. New York: Atheneum, 1970.

   Thirteen-year-old Laurie takes a long journey to get help for her grandfather, who is going blind. Laurie has lived alone with her grandfather since her parents were killed. They live near an old abandoned mining town, where their life is simple and devoid of modern conveniences. Steering clear of the authorities, who might take her away, Laurie doesn't go to school. Instead she takes a correspondence course and reads anything available. When it is certain that her grandfather is losing his sight, he sends her on horseback to Butte, Montana to solicit help from her uncle.
   On the trip she encounters a weird stranger dressed in black robes. When he threatens her and almost takes her captive, she is convinced that her grandfather is right about the viciousness of the world outside their remote home. She escapes and is later rescued from a storm by a lonely retired school teacher. At the teacher's house Laurie experiences use of many modern conveniences for the first time -- a bathtub, a television, a gas stove, etc. The only person whom she meets and really trusts is an Indian boy who helps her get her bearings when she is lost.
   Finally she arrives in Butte and her uncle arranges an operation to save her grandfather's sight. When her uncle requests that she stay, Laurie is faced with the decision whether to stay and discover more about the "outside world" or to return to her former way of life with her grandfather. She decides to return.
   Variations in life styles provide one of the central themes of this story. Her grandfather distrusts modern ways of living, but he needs modern medicine to save his eyesight. Laurie has learned to enjoy bathtubs, fancy meals, symphonies, libraries, etc. She now faces life with fewer negative attitudes, and accepts the invitation to spend summers in the city with her aunt and uncle.

MOM, THE WOLF MAN AND ME, by Norma Klein. New
    York: Pantheon, 1972.

   Scratcher lives in a liberated world where adults discuss serious matters with children--like love, sex, marriage and divorce. Scratcher's mother is a single parent. She never married and doesn't apologize for it. Her child is not sensitive about not having a father, except that it presents a minor problem when they have father's day at school.

At a political march, mother meets the "wolf man" (he owns a wolf hound). Scratcher likes the wolf man, but she hopes that he and her mom will not get married. Contrary to the liberated view of the mother presented in the beginning, mom does marry the wolf man.

This story is important for its view of contemporary thinking and its presentation of options for life styles. Some roles are a little overplayed, but humor provides a balance.

NAOMI IN THE MIDDLE, by Norma Klein. Illus. by Leigh Grant. New York: Dial, 1974.

Naomi is a seven-year-old second child. She and her older brother face the arrival of a new baby. This rather slight story portrays sibling rivalry and attempts to explore questions of birth and sex. The answers regarding pregnancy and sex are rather inadequate but some may find them appropriate for an early age group.

A QUIET PLACE, by Rose Blue. Pictures by Tom Feelings. New York: Franklin Watts, 1969.

A somewhat slight book about a boy who searches for a quiet place to read, away from the family noises and interruptions, and away from friends who would rather play. More importantly, this is the story of a family of loving parents and foster-children.

In the beginning, Matthew, who is nine, has some bad experiences in foster-homes devoid of love. Then he is placed with a mama and daddy who love him and want him. He also acquires a new sister and a baby brother.

Tom Feelings' illustrations add to the text, making this a warm portrayal of a Black family.

THE ROCK AND WILLOW, by Mildred Lee. New York: Lothrop, 1963.

This story is placed in the 1930's on an Alabama farm where Enie Singleton lives with her family in poverty. During her high school years Enie copes with her mother's death and the death of her sister. When her father remarries she feels resentment and eventually leaves home to pursue her dream of being a writer or a teacher.

There are many ingredients which give power and depth to this narrative. The lifestyle, foods and community surrounding this family are adequately presented. Enie's projection into early adulthood and her assumption of adult chores and roles are credible. The alienation of her sixteen-year-old brother from his father is sharply epitomized by the demands placed upon him to work, which leave no time for recreation. Family selectiveness is shown as Enie's father shows tender feelings only toward the younger sister. Brother Leroy, who is Enie's favorite companion, lives in a world of unreality which is perhaps an escape mechanism. Enie has a brief love affair with a wanderer. When she makes up her mind to leave, she symbolically throws away the strap her father has used for whippings. In conversation with her Aunt, her Aunt says, "you got to ask or take or get left out."

SISTER, by Eloise Greenfield; with drawings by Moneta Barnett. New York: Crowell, 1974.

A Black family's chronicle of joys and sorrows as told by Doretha, aged thirteen. Doretha's older sister Albertha has quit school and spends most of her time hanging around with a gang. Doretha is afraid she will be influenced by Albertha, but determines not to be.

The joys portrayed include happy scenes of the father interacting with his wife and daughters; a trip to hear a favorite singing group; a holiday picnic in the park with family and friends; and attending Sister Shani's School of Black Freedom. Episodes of sorrow include the father's death from a sudden heart attack; mama's retreat from the girls to handle her own sorrow; mama's encounter with a man whom she later discovers is married; and Albertha's involvement in a fist fight, which lands her in the hospital.

Doretha gains strength from the support offered by her family and community, but Albertha's struggle with herself is not won. This is a quietly moving and believable story.

TEACUP FULL OF ROSES, by Sharon Bell Mathis. New York: Viking, 1972.

Elements of survival within an urban Black family are explored in this book. Three brothers, Joe, Paul and Davey, are shown in all their individuality within the family group. Joe has a dream of going to the same college as his girlfriend Ellie. Paul, in spite of his extraordinary talents as an artist, is strung out on dope. Davey is very smart and shows great potential as a basketball player.

Mama becomes so involved in trying to save Paul that she can't provide the reinforcement necessary to encourage Davey and Joe in their endeavors. Pop, who has a heart condition, stays quietly in the background until he can't take it anymore. He gives what encouragement and support he can to the two sons who want to make something of their lives.

The story clearly exposes a family with needs and conflicts. The ordeal of such a family trying to maintain a sense of unity and balance is evident. Also, the positive interaction necessary to reach out to the future is described.

Mama tries to escape the reality that Paul is lost, by maintaining a false sense of hope. She provides meaningless support for him. Joe tells stories, in which he expresses his hope. He finds promise in his relationship with Ellie and in his fierce love for his brother Davey. Davey survives on his ability and inner-strength, supported by Joe's reinforcement.

In the end, tragically, Davey is killed. Paul betrays them all because of his compelling need for dope. Joe is left to reshape his world. Somehow one feels he will do it positively.

A unique view of family and community support systems is offered in the author's <u>Listen for the Fig Tree</u> (Viking, 1974). This is the story of Muffin, who is blind and lives alone with her alcoholic mother. Her notable title, <u>The Hundred Penny Box</u> (Viking, 1975) beautifully portrays the positives of relationships between the very young and the very old.

<u>TUNED OUT</u>, by Maia Wojciechowska. New York: Harper and Row, 1968.

Although this book presents a study of the drug culture, family relationships are basic to the theme. Young Jim worships his older brother, Kevin, and suffers acute disappointment and confusion when he discovers that Kevin is hooked on drugs.

When Kevin is later hospitalized, his basic problem is

revealed. He has found it impossible to handle his family's dependency upon him. Since hearing his parents state when he was younger that they would remain together only because of him, Kevin has assumed that the family's togetherness depended upon him.

The story of Kevin's drug involvement and response to them is not as credible as in some other books, for example, Go Ask Alice. More realistically presented are the themes of hero worship and of pressures in family relationships.

Added Entries

ABBY, by Jeannette Caines. Illus. by Stephen Kellogg. New York: Harper, 1973.

A warm and simple story of an adopted child. Abby is happy, lively and fascinated by the fact that she is adopted. She loves to look at her baby book and hear the story of how she was found by her family. Realizing her need for this affirmation, Kevin, her older brother, takes her to school and brags about having a new sister to keep forever.

ADAM'S WORLD: SAN FRANCISCO, by Kathleen Fraser and Miriam Levy. Chicago: Whitman, 1971.

Part of this loving Black family's strength lies in their cultural identity. Adam and his family live in San Francisco at the top of a tall building overlooking the bay. Father, a seaman, returns home from a trip to Africa, bringing beautiful cloth which mother sews into clothing for the family. All of them feel proud and beautiful when they wear the new outfits to a street party.

BE NICE TO JOSEPHINE, by Betty Horvath. Illus. by Pat Grant Porter. New York: Franklin Watts, 1970.

Families are important, even if it means giving up a day playing ball with the boys to "be nice to Josephine," who is probably pretty and who probably plays with dolls and tea sets.

What a pleasant surprise to discover that Josephine likes to fish and even digs her own fishing worms. But she is also human enough to cry when teased.

122 / Survival Themes

This simple picture book touches upon male and female conflicts arising from learned stereotypes. It also emphasizes the importance of making decisions in support of those close to you.

BOSS CAT, by Kristin Hunter. Illus. by Harold Franklin. New York: Scribner, 1971.

A slight but warm story of an incident in the life of a Black family. Tyrone Tanner wants to keep a black cat for a pet, but his mother won't let him. Later on, the "boss cat" saves the day when mamma is frightened by mice.

CITY IN THE WINTER, by Eleanor Schick. New York: Macmillan, 1973.

Positive portrayal of a little boy and his grandmother spending a winter afternoon together. Jimmy helps his grandmother with household chores on the day he stays home from school because there is a blizzard.

A FAMILY FAILING, by Honor Arundel. New York: Thomas Nelson, 1972.

The complicated relationships which lead to a separation of parents is explored in this title. When the father eventually moves out, the daughter is forced to reshape her view of both parents. (Faults with this title are explored in Children's Literature: an Issues Approach, by Masha Kabakow Rudman, pp. 51-52 [see Sources and Notes, No. 31]. Ms. Rudman explores the fact that many books about family problems portray the mother negatively, showing her absorbing most of the guilt for the parental conflicts.)

FRIDAY NIGHT IS PAPA NIGHT, by Ruth Sonneborn. Illus. by Emily McCully. New York: Viking, 1970.

Although viewed in a setting of poverty, the strengths and love of a Puerto Rican family are seen as the children wait for papa to come on Friday night. Papa works at two jobs far away from home, so he only comes home on Friday night. The children are worried when papa doesn't appear at the usual time. He arrives late because he took a sick

friend home. The children are happy to get their
sents but the best gift is to have papa home safe.

<u>I WOULD RATHER BE A TURNIP</u>, by Vera and Bill Cleaver.
    Philadelphia: Lippincott, 1971.

    As is typical, this writing pair offers a readable and
believable presentation of an atypical family situation. Annie
Jelks faces adjustment to having her illegitimate nephew come
for a visit. Annie has decided to hate Calvin upon his arrival, but her sympathies are aroused when others in the small
town taunt the warm and exceptional child. Annie's changing
attitude is affected by the Black maid, who is shown in a
warm relationship to the children.

<u>THEN AGAIN, MAYBE I WON'T</u>, by Judy Blume. Scarsdale,
    N.Y.: Bradbury, 1971.

    Thirteen-year-old Tony is worried about things like
nocturnal emissions and erections, but his major problem is
his view of the family. His father, having sold an electrical
invention, becomes a success and moves the family from
Jersey City to a big house on Long Island. Tony dislikes
the "keep up with the Joneses" attitude around him. His
questioning of the family's sense of values causes him acute
stomach pains. Because there is no physical reason for the
pains, Tony sees a psychiatrist, who begins to help him face
his conflicts.

<u>TROUBLE IN THE JUNGLE</u>, by John Rowe Townsend. Illus.
    by W. T. Mars. Philadelphia: Lippincott, 1969.

    The adventures of four English children temporarily
abandoned to live in an empty warehouse in a slum area.
Their survival is complicated by their irresponsible Uncle
Walter's involvement with a gang of criminals. Sequel to
this story is <u>Goodbye to the Jungle</u>, in which the family
moves to a development project. Walter, the ne'er-do-well
head of the family, finds himself in trouble with the police.
Kevin, 15, and Sandra, 14, assume responsibility for holding
the family together.

<u>WHERE IS DADDY? THE STORY OF A DIVORCE</u>, by Beth

Goff. Illus. by Susan Perl. Boston: Beacon, 1969.

As often happens in the case of a divorce, the little girl in the story blames herself for her parents' divorce. Her mother and grandmother help her to understand that the problem is between her parents, and is not her fault.

PART III

VIEWS OF THE WORLD

Man and the Environment

Religion and Politics

War and Peace

Celebration of Life and Death

INTRODUCTION

Children reach what is often called "the questioning stage" at about age 3-5. This is the period when the child is beginning to discover that there is so much in the world to know. Questions are asked about things, animals, people, the young and the old. Child psychologists caution adults to be aware that children's questions should be answered in a manner commensurate with their understanding.

Mass communication exposes children to an enormous amount of information, with which they are often not able, intellectually or emotionally, to cope. Within the barrage of facts and information with which they are faced, children seek for meaning.

In early childhood, psychologists have concluded, the distinctions made by young people are not the same as those made by adults. Children are interested in the moral and physiological distinctions and determinations of an event. When a child asks a question followed by the sometimes annoying repetitions of "why?" he is really trying to do some fact-finding on his own level. Some psychologists believe it is not bad to give answers based in fantasy at this early stage, particularly if that fantasy serves the child well until he can handle the truth. Others feel that the real truth can be told, but that one must be careful not to expose the child to so much truth that he becomes confused or frightened. There may be no need to give every young child complete biological explanations of subjects like sex, birth and death, because they will almost always be misunderstood. For instance, an answer to "Why do people die?" could be simply, "To make room for other people." Elkund (see Sources and Notes, No. 25) suggests that probably the best answers are those which are intellectually respectable but informative on the child's level.

Elkund also states that it is only at adolescence that

the child begins to test hypotheses against facts. Before this time hypothesis is often taken as fact, just as fantasy is integrated with reality. Separation of fact from fiction is sometimes difficult, even for adults, who may revert to early beliefs in magic, supernatural powers, etc. without even being conscious of it. Again, Elkund states that it is at adolescence that the young person has developed the ability to reason, to compare, and to establish mental ideals. Often these ideals are compared with his home situation and the latter is found wanting. The problem, as Elkund describes it, is that the young person establishes ideals but does not know whether these ideals are realistic or achievable. Often, too, the adolescent may form certain ideals but act just the opposite; for instance, the young person who continually expresses concern for the poor but spends all his money on trivia, never giving anything to causes of the poor. This lack of insight into their own behavior is transferred by adolescents to adults. Adults who don't live up to their idealistic views are considered cop-outs. Adolescents feel that when adults voice ideals they should be capable of putting them into practice. The adolescent constructs ideals of family, religion, society, and personalities. This is why adolescent "crushes" are so often shortlived, because nobody can match their romantic ideals. The adolescent's emotional involvement causes him to remove criticism from himself and place it on the adult. When more adult responsibilities are assumed, these attitudes in their exaggerated form gradually disappear.

If this assessment is accurate, even in a general way, this may be adequate reason for presenting in literature viewpoints that are not too romantic or idealistic. Presentation of realistic views of the world may offer the adolescent more choices for formulating his own ideals. Further ideas of ways to accomplish ideals may be offered. The credibility of certain positions can also be questioned.

The predominant theme in adolescent materials is a focus on self. Subjects such as peer influences, separation from family, and introspection about religion and politics are often operable only on the periphery. Many titles contribute to the non-objective critical view of adults already common among adolescents.

1. Man and the Environment

Traditional mythology explained the phenomena of life and the universe by placing responsibility largely in the hands of the Gods. Man's growing scientific knowledge has elucidated such problems as population growth, pollution in cities, and food production. The rape of nature's resources has become a growing concern. Human responsibility for the environment has become a social and political issue. Consumer education and studies in ecology are now part of many elementary schools' curricula. The disappearance of animals is now considered a human problem, not a natural process of nature. Man is being blamed for the lost species of the world, the shortage of natural resources, and the destruction of lands, trees, and water.

There is a growing wealth of non-fiction material portraying the mysteries and beauties of nature, and some that deal pointedly with subjects of environmental preservation. Few titles, however, deal with the human factors and other phenomena which aid in the destruction of the environment. A scattering of titles have appeared which direct themselves to the survival of one species or another. Most of the books directed toward children serve to challenge their consciousness about the problem. Few, however, detail evidence of environmental assault and offer possible solutions. More titles are needed which explore the economic systems as they affect nature. Many of these books will necessarily be non-fiction, but fiction, too, can serve as a medium for the exploration of such concerns.

Several of the books chosen for this section show children and young people developing an affinity for animal life. Some make more direct statements about the need to advocate changes which will aid in the preservation of the environment.

BEAVER POND, by Alvin Tresselt.   Illus. by Roger Duvoisin. New York: Lothrop, 1970.

An ecological tale about beavers who build a pond and about the animals who live nearby. The building of the beaver dam has formed a pond. The birds nest there and other animals come to drink. In winter the pond freezes and in spring the beavers rebuild the dam. When in danger, the beavers flee and there is no one to care for the dam. The dam breaks and the pond flows away. The cycle of nature continues when the beavers build a dam in another spot farther down the stream.

BIG BLUE ISLAND, by Wilson Gage. Illus. by Glen Rounds. Cleveland: World, 1964.

A lonely boy living with his great uncle on an island in the Tennessee River senses the beauty of the world as he watches a great blue heron. Eleven-year-old Darrell was sent to live with his uncle after the death of his mother. The eccentric old man is his only relative.

Darrell longs to leave the lonely island. He is angry, sulks and wants to run away. The island is a game reserve and, observing the great blue herons, Darrell is even more angry. He hates the independence of the birds, but he gradually becomes enraptured with them and begins to change his values. He develops a new respect for the old uncle, who has chosen to live his life in communion with nature.

BLESS THE BEASTS AND CHILDREN, by Glendon Swarthout. New York: Doubleday, 1970.

Five misfits in an Arizona boy's camp sneak out and save a herd of buffalo from hunters. The five boys, representing a variety of backgrounds, wealthy and poor, are residing in the Box Canyon Boys' Home, where it is hoped they will begin to make social adjustments. Problems within the camp are basic to the story, and one day the five boys steal a truck. They enter a buffalo compound and decide to free the buffalo. Some of the animals are to be shot in what is called a "thinning out" of the herd. Readers are provided with a view of boys facing developmental problems, but a statement is also made about useless slaughter, hunting and guns.

A CLEARING IN THE FOREST, by Carol and Donald Carrick. New York: Dial, 1970.

Man's ability to exist in communion with nature is the theme of this picture story. A man and a boy clear a space in the forest. They build a house and settle in. But the spirit of the forest is displeased. "We must rid the forest of these people," it says. So the rains come and drown the garden, a procupine chews the porch, a woodpecker hammers holes in the house, mice attack the cupboard, and so on. The man and boy are determined to stay. In winter when it is hard for the animals to find food, the man and boy feed them. The spirits are pleased and in spring the garden grows. Enough food is available for both the humans and the animals. The man and boy have not just received gifts from the forest; they have also shared.

THE FRIEND OF THE SINGING ONE, by E. C. Foster and Slim Williams. Illus. by Fermin Rocker. New York: Atheneum, 1967.

An appreciation of wolves is shown in this story of an Eskimo boy's friendship with a young wolf. Caught on the floating ice together, the boy and the wolf spend a summer of survival together, depending on each other and finally returning home.

GENTLE BEN, by Walt Morey. Illus. by John Schoenherr. New York: Dutton, 1965.

The son of a salmon fisherman befriends an Alaskan brown bear which has been mistreated, and then struggles to keep him as a pet. Gentle Ben is finally taken away.

This author has written other titles about animals interacting with humans. Gloomy Gus (Dutton, 1970) is about a bear cub who becomes the pet of a lonely boy, after the mother bear is shot. The boy's unfeeling father insists that the bear must go. Kavik, the Wolf Dog (Dutton, 1968) describes a wolf dog who receives kind treatment for the first time from a young boy of fifteen. The boy rescues the injured wolf after a plane crash.

HOAGIE'S RIFLE GUN, by Miska Miles. Illus. by John Schoenherr. Boston: Little, Brown, 1970.

In the Appalachian mountains men and animals relate as friends and enemies. Hoagie is good with guns, and one

day he and his brother set out to hunt for food. The boy
and a bobcat are after the same prey. Hoagie, fascinated
with the sight of Old Bob, the bobcat, is not ready when a
rabbit runs past. He shoots and misses, but the bobcat is
ready and kills the rabbit. Hoagie is so angry that he wants
to kill the bobcat, but his brother pleads for the life of the
wild animal. A statement is made for the quality of man
and animals in hunting for survival; but in the end, man is
master with the gun.

Other stories by this author present man in relation
to the animal world; for example, Eddie's Bear (Little, Brown,
1970), in which a boy has a face-to-face encounter with a
brown bear. He finds the bear very unthreatening. Later,
the brown bear's brother forages and damages the camp, and
the innocent bear is blamed.

HOOK A FISH, CATCH A MOUNTAIN, by Jean Craighead
George. New York: Dutton, 1975.

A plea for the preservation of wildlife is made through
the story of a young girl who catches a rare fish during a
visit to Wyoming. She is dismayed when her father won't let
her throw it back. The story evolves into a reasonably interesting adventure, although some parts are a bit overplayed
and therefore don't read well.

After the rare "cutthroat" has been caught and sent to
the taxidermist to be stuffed and hung, Spinner is very angry
with her father. She then goes with her cousin on a backpacking trip high in the mountains, to trace the origins of the
great fish. The two mountain climbers encounter hazards and
near death on the trip, but it is later that Spinner realizes
the answer to the mystery.

Feminists will probably not appreciate the portrayal of
the heroine as fearful of everything, including grasshoppers,
and as being used to perfumes, leotards and dance. After
the big adventure, she cuts her hair and decides to stay
awhile.

IF I BUILT A VILLAGE, by Kazue Mizumura. New York:
Crowell, 1971.

A picture book which presents a village that is a model
of ecological balance. This poetic statement says it can be
done: men can live in harmony with the environment.

IN THE SHADOW OF THE FALCON, by Ewan Clarkson.
   Illus. by David Stone. New York: Dutton, 1973.

   A conservation novel dealing with the life of falcons. Living alone on falcon island, a farmer determines to protect the falcons from hunters and poachers. The main body of the story follows the falcons as they learn to fly and hunt, and face the danger of being captured by humans. The predator in animal life is shown to be necessary to the balance of nature.

JULIE OF THE WOLVES, by Jean Craighead George; with
   pictures by John Schoenberr. New York: Harper and Row, 1972.

   A runaway Eskimo girl travels across Alaska, alone except for the wolves, which she learns to love and which eventually save her from the grizzly bear.
   The themes are ecology, survival, and a young girl facing decisions about her life. She faces conflicts regarding her heritage and her dreams of a new land.
   The appreciation of the wolves--their gentleness, and their help in Julie's survival--can aid in the development of new attitudes toward an animal species usually pictured as vicious and attacking human prey.

THE MIDNIGHT FOX, by Betsy Byars. Illus. by Ann Grifalconi. New York: Viking, 1968.

   A city boy, formerly indifferent to nature, spends a summer in the country. While there, he gets to know a black fox and protects it from being shot by his uncle.

THE MOON OF THE MOUNTAIN LIONS, by Jean Craighead
   George. Illus. by Winifred Lubell. New York: Crowell, 1969.

   A fictionalized story of a young mountain lion moving to the lower slopes of the mountain during the winter. This brief but lovely study in nature is part of a series, (Thirteen Moons) to which Ms. George has contributed, among others, The Moon of the Wild Pigs, The Moon of the Deer, The Moon of the Alligators and The Moon of the Gray Wolves.
   All the books present positive views of nature but

several, like <u>The Moon of the Alligators</u>, make strong pleas for conservation. In this title, the moon is in October, in the tropical Everglades. Through the alligator and other animal species, one is made acquainted with the complex balance of nature.

<u>THE MOUNTAIN</u>, by Peter Parnell. New York: Doubleday, 1971.

    The spoiling of the wilderness, after Congress designates a beautiful mountain area as a national park, is explored in text and pictures. The area filled with flowers and animals gradually changes for the worse. A road is built and people arrive, bringing their litter. Facilities for campers occupy once beautiful space. At the end, a flower is seen in the middle of the litter. This simple and strikingly illustrated book is designed for the very young, but the message is for everyone.

<u>OUTSIDE</u>, by Andre Norton. Illus. by Bernard P. Colonna. New York: Walker, 1974.

    This futuristic look at a time when man lives in sealed enclosures and eats only preserved foods might stir some thought, response and even responsibility toward the environment.

<u>ROAM THE WILD COUNTRY</u>, by Ella Thorp Ellis. Illus. by Bret Scheslinger. New York: Atheneum, 1967.

    An extremely well written story of three boys who drive a drought-endangered herd of horses to safety. This is not just a story of concern for animals but a portrayal of survival against the elements as the boys move through a hailstorm and encounter deadly animals along the way.

<u>THE SHEEP OF THE LAL BAGH</u>, by David Mark. Illus. by Lionel Kalish. New York: Parents Magazine Press, 1967.

    Set in India, this is a mild story concerned with machinery replacing the old ways. The text is accompanied by nice pastel water-color pictures.

THE STREET OF THE FLOWER BOXES, by Peggy Mann.
   Illus. by Peter Burchard. New York: Coward, 1966.

   On a city block, West 94th Street, a group of tough boys pulls up the flowers planted by a new family on the block. Later, the same group is seen leading a cleanup campaign to beautify the neighborhood. Although solutions to problems facing cities are not this simplistic, some insights can be gained from this small challenge to community responsibility.

TRUMPET OF THE SWAN, by E. B. White. Illus. by Edward Frascino. New York: Harper, 1970.

   Louis, a trumpeter swan, was born mute and is thus unable to court lovely Selina. Louis is saved by the creative thinking of his father, who steals a trumpet for Louis. Thus the mute swan is able to communicate and win Selina for his wife.
   This fanciful and charming story could be used to introduce children to endangered species. Valuable support for this cause is also found in Last of the Trumpeters by Rose E. Hutchinson (Chicago: Rand, 1967). In this poetic text, readers are introduced to the life of the trumpeter swan. Man's responsibility for the near extinction of the species is clearly established in the narrative which is accompanied by full-color illustrations.

WHITE BIRD, by Clyde Bulla. Illus. by Leonard Weisgard. New York: Crowell, 1966.

   Luke rescues a baby boy found floating down the river, and as the boy grows, Luke forbids him outside contacts. Finding a wounded albino crow and nursing it back to health provides sustenance for the lonely boy. A sensitive story about human relationships also shows how love for animals sometimes helps people maintain a measure of mental balance.

WHO REALLY KILLED COCK ROBIN? by Jean Craighead George. New York: Dutton, 1971.

   The town of Saddlesboro is very pollution-conscious. They have devised methods to clean the air and the water, and the mayor and residents are very proud of their community. Cock Robin is one of the most respected residents.

He lives in a nest built in a Stetson hat on the mayor's porch.
One day Cock Robin is found dead. If the town is free of
pollution, who then killed Cock Robin? Tony, a bird watcher,
and his friend Mary set out to solve the mystery. In the end
it is found that the bird died from parasites transmitted to the
town through the migration of the sparrows. The town of Saddleboro is part of the earth, of one ecosystem. They have
been affected by the lack of environmental measures in another
place. An interesting mystery is provided in this very pointedly message-oriented story.

WILD GEESE CALLING, by Robert Murphy. Illus. by John
    Kaufman. New York: Dutton, 1966.

  Another boy-animal companionship book portrays a
friendship between a lonely boy and a wounded Canada goose.
The boy nurses the goose back to health and attempts to keep
him as a companion.

THE WUMP WORLD, by Bill Peet. Boston: Houghton Mifflin, 1970.

  The grass-eating Wumps live in a peaceful world until
they are invaded by the Pollutians from the planet of Pollutia.
The Pollutians immediately begin to "improve" their new habitat. They build tall buildings and freeways. They pile up
trash and pollute the air and water. Soon their own destruction forces the Pollutians to move on to another planet.

Z FOR ZACHARIAH, by Robert C. Z. O'Brien. New York:
    Atheneum, 1975.

  In a peaceful valley, two survivors of an atomic holocaust are brought together. One is a young girl and the other
is a killer. The fact of the holocaust and the destruction of
the environment makes both an ecological statement and a
statement for peace. The rest of the story provides a close
look at the frailties of human nature, even when the evidence
of death and destruction is all around.
  In diary form, the girl, Ann, records the events of
her life before and after the man, John, appears. At first
the girl is happy to be in the company of another human.
She nurses John, who is weak from injury and exposure, back
to health. But soon the situation changes. Ann finds herself

almost slave to the man, doing all the work, planting and harvesting the food and then falling prey to John's physical advances. When she refuses to succumb to John's advances, the two fall into verbal and physical conflict, to the eventual point of a shooting by which John hopes to maim the girl so that she cannot escape. Ann has thoughts of killing in self-defense but she cannot, so she devises a plan to escape, hoping she will find other signs of life in another place. This is essentially a suspenseful story of human nature in conflict.

2. Religion and Politics

Martin E. Marty in an article titled "Religion Today and Tomorrow" (American Libraries, Feb. 1974, pp. 69-72) notes the impact of religion upon society. He quotes Paul Tillich: "Religion is the soul of culture and culture the form of religion." He delineates the pervasiveness of religion in social reform and in wars. Only a few children's books note such pervasiveness, although a particular author's religious ethic is often apparent in his or her portrayal of characters.

Implications of the impact of religion on the development of children's literature is apparent in the historical outline (see pages 5-22). Early fiction was saturated with religious concepts and dogma. Religious instruction was the primary concern, rather than religious understanding, tolerance and appreciation.

In modern societies, governmental conflicts and wars are still often based in religious beliefs. Young people's abilities to understand these phenomena will depend upon their access to information and varied views. Leo Pheiffer suggests that "An understanding and appreciation of the dynamics of interreligious relationships in the U.S. today requires some consideration of the background against which the religious groups act to each other and to the society of which they are a part" (see Sources and Notes, No. 79, pp. 33-41). His article also implies the direct relationship between religious bigotry and various political phenomena.

Most religions are defined around Gods with the possible exception of the Society of Ethical Cultures, which focuses on man's human relationships and survival as related to those around him. Included in this section are largely titles which consider religion as it affects the individual and prejudices based on religious beliefs. A few stories give a view of religion within the context of family and the community.

Politics

When interviewing young people, it was extremely hard to find many who seemed well informed about politics, although they all wanted "peace." Bibi Wein found this to be so while interviewing for her book Runaway Generation (see Sources and Notes, No. 97). She felt that their disillusionment with politics was the result of the Kennedy assassinations. The events of "Watergate" may have had a similar effect upon young people's interest in politics.

According to Dwight Macdonald (see Sources and Notes, No. 92), adult analysis of the political world is also often inept. He says, "Ask a dozen passersby, picked at random, whether they believe it is right to kill helpless people; they will reply 'of course not' (the 'of course' is ominous) and will probably denounce the inquirer as a monster for even suggesting there could be two answers to the question. But they will 'go along' with the government in World War III and kill as many helpless enemy as possible." Good and evil are regarded as platitudes rather than political. This is most often the case in children's books--political systems are dealt with by presenting stories full of pathos which move young people to tears, but ingredients for recognizing the problems and/or possible solutions are absent.

Aside from the adult novel, very little is available for young people in fiction which deals creatively with political themes, that is, politics on the level of government, social systems and structures and social problems as affected by politics. The Advise and Consent(s) for children have yet to appear. The titles chosen here have some element of politics in the plot. Several have been selected from the growing number of books dealing with political and social structures during World War II. A few adult titles recommended for young adults have also been noted.

AN AMISH FAMILY, by Phyllis Reynolds Naylor. Illus. by
    George Armstrong. Chicago: J. Philip O'Hara, 1974.

A positive view of Amish life as seen through the story of the Stolzfus family in Pennsylvania. Information is included about the community's methods of governing, the "Ordnung". Marriage and other customs are explained.

There is also an indication of the effects of outsiders on the group. Tourists unaware of Amish customs try to take pictures, without realizing that the people are not allowed to submit to any reproduction of their image.

<u>ARE YOU THERE GOD? IT'S ME, MARGARET</u>, by Judy Blume. Scarsdale, N.Y.: Bradbury Press, 1970.

Margaret talks to God about her problems even though she is of "no religion." She discusses her fears about moving, about wanting to grow and develop, about her crush on Philip Leroy and about wanting to get her period to be sure she's normal.

This is really a girl's story of moving into adolescence, but it might be considered for its appreciable insight to a view of religion held by a girl who has not been forced by her parents to make a decision in that regard.

"Are you there God? It's me, Margaret. Life is getting worse every day. I'm going to be the only one who doesn't get it. I know it God. Just like I'm the only one without a religion. Why can't you help me? Haven't I always done what you wanted? Please let me be like everyone else." (Quote from page 101.)

<u>AUNT AMERICA</u>, by Marie Halun Bloch. Drawings by Joan Berg. New York: Atheneum, 1963.

A simplistic view of the iron curtain is gained from this story from the Ukraine. Lesya is extremely excited when she learns that her great aunt from America will visit her family. Lesya had read in the history books about the city of Kiev, but she had never visited it. Now she is to have not only a chance to visit the great city but to meet there her Aunt from America.

The political ramifications of the story are at first exposed through Lesya's view of her father and her Uncle Vlodko. Uncle Vlodko has always had more than her own family because he knows how to deal with the authorities. Father on the other hand has had his problems with the government. Lesya doesn't understand it all, but when Aunt America visits the family Lesya notices the respect her aunt shows for her father in contrast to Uncle Vlodko. She overhears the adults in conversation about her father and mother having been sent to the labor camps when they refused to give information about the resistance. Other small items in

140 / Survival Themes

the story are informative about the "system"; for example, the people gather to listen in the square to the "public radio."
    Lesya remains naïve about all of this, being obsessed with the desire for a doll just like the one Aunt America brought her sister. She steals the doll and hides it under a bridge. This provides the basic conflict in the story as Lesya deals with her conscience. In the end she grows up a little and is somewhat politicized when she realizes that her Aunt may be in danger because of her plans to transport letters from the various families to the United States. Lesya, having overheard a conversation about the searching of baggage, rushes to Kiev to warn her Aunt. The letters are destroyed, Lesya confesses to having stolen the doll, and she has developed a new respect for her father.

THE BEARCAT, by Annabel and Edgar Johnson. New York: Harper, 1960.

    The Bearcat Mine in Montana is run by a crooked boss. Jeff Denver, a young boy, becomes involved in the struggle to improve the conditions of the miners. The reader is introduced to the hazards of the mining industry and through the workers' fight for their rights a view of the early stages of unions is seen.

BEING THERE, by Jerzy Kosinski. New York: Harcourt, 1971.

    This is an interesting political satire in which Chance, a gardener, is mistaken for a man of importance. He is transformed to Chauncey, diplomat and political advisor to important people in Washington, including the president. As a gardener, Chance had lived an isolated life, except for watching television. His statements about gardens are overheard and grossly misinterpreted. Simple garden information is assumed to be a profound approach to human and political problems. News reporters aid in projecting the image of Chance as a philosopher. Even when Chance is silent, it is assumed that this means something. In actuality, Chance is different from the norm. He has not conformed or become involved in the meaningless pursuits of those who now revere him.

THE ENDLESS STEPPE: GROWING UP IN SIBERIA, by

Esther Hautzig. New York: Crowell, 1968.

The time is 1941. In Poland, Esther Rudonic has little awareness of the seriousness of the war, which seems far away as she attends school and enjoys her family. But one day Esther's idyllic life is shattered and she and her family are suddenly taken from their homes and shipped to Siberia. Her father is a capitalist, considered a threat to the growing communist regime.

The narrative follows the family on their long train trip in a cattle car, across Russia to Siberia. Scenes of hunger and claustrophobic airless quarters are clearly drawn.

This is more than a story of political repression; it is the story of a family and their feelings for each other. The humor grows and is evident throughout, as is the sense of survival based on their strong family ties. They barter for food, for a space, for a bed. They live in conditions worse than any they have encountered before. But their spirit of cooperation remains strong. They find hope in themselves and in the new friends made along the way.

FRIEDRICH, by Hans Peter Richter. Translated from the German by Edith Kroll. New York: Holt, Rinehart and Winston, 1970. (Originally published under the title Damals War es Friedrich, 1961).

This is a gripping story of the growing ostracism of Jews in Nazi Germany. The story is poignant because it shows the quandary faced by Germans, former friends of Jews, who find themselves having to make decisions in a time of growing viciousness which affects them and annihilates their friends.

Friedrich, a Jew, is the best friend of the narrator of the story. A yearly chronicle portrays the lives of the two boys and their families as circumstances get worse for the Jews. The two families live in the same house. First, Friedrich's father is fired and then the family is asked to leave the apartment. They refuse to leave, but later the apartment is ravaged and the family is beaten. This scene exposes the viciousness which has swelled like a tide among the German populace.

In the tragic ending, Friedrich's mother dies, his father is killed, and finally Friedrich himself, barred from a bomb shelter because he is a Jew, is killed.

This is the story of the building of social systems upon which the horrors of destruction are often founded.

I WAS THERE, by Hans Richter. Translated from the German by Edite Kroll. New York: Holt, Rinehart and Winston, 1972. (Originally published in Germany under the title Wir Waren Dabei, 1962).

Through his experiences as a Hitler youth, the author chronicles the Nazi movement. The narrator of the story and Heinz and Gunther all approach the growing movement from a different perspective. Gunther is most resistant to the ideas of Nazism because his father is a communist. All the boys become caught up in the pomp and circumstance of the uniforms, the marching, and the rigid training. Scenes show them active in the collection of scrap metal, the routines of the organization, the taunting and beating of Jews, and finally in actual combat.

The spread of the movement through a community, mainly by indoctrination rather than information, is amplified. The story is followed by an appendix of notes about the Hitler era and a chronology of the Hitler years.

One of the most interesting and thought-provoking moments is when Gunther's father joins the fight, in spite of his stand against the Führer. He fights because he wants to save Germany.

There is little in this story about the horror faced by the Jews, except in the case of the beatings. The narrative is strictly from the point of view of a young German Nazi, unwittingly nationalized and viewing Hitler's gradual destruction.

JOURNEY TO TOPAZ, by Yoshiko Uchida. Illus. by Donald Carrick. New York: Scribner, 1971.

The story of one Japanese family, evacuated from San Francisco to detention camps during World War II, in America.

The trauma and disbelief of the family are vividly expressed as they are rapidly uprooted and moved. They must get rid of all their belongings, leave their friends and give up jobs and school.

The austere and frugal living conditions at the camps are described. Amid all this, the positives of family closeness and love are well portrayed. Yuki, the young girl in the family of four, meets a friend who lives in the next stall, and her friend's grandparents become part of the story.

Dust storms, sickness and death are some of the trials to which they are exposed, as the reader realizes it all happened in America.

Religion and Politics / 143

KATE, by Jean Little. New York: Harper and Row, 1971.

Kate is "half" Jewish, but it is unimportant in her life and relationships until she makes some discoveries about her father and mother and their past. These discoveries and her relationship with a little girl named Susannah help Kate to begin thinking and learning about herself. She learns of her father's alienation from the family because her grandfather rejected him for marrying a non-Jew.
Growing selfconsciousness causes a rift between Kate and her best friend, Emily. The split is healed only after Kate begins dealing with her Jewishness and realizing the strengths in one's need for a friend.
Strengths of family and the meaning of love are touched upon, and the problems of loving within cultural conflicts are exposed through the parent's story.

A KIND OF SECRET WEAPON, by Elliott Arnold. New York: Scribner, 1969.

Peter's father, Lars, operates an underground newspaper in the basement of his home in Denmark during the Nazi occupation. When Peter accidently discovers the press, his father and mother decide he is old enough to join their forces. Neither Peter nor his mother are aware of the depth of father's involvement in the underground.
Peter tells his story of fear, excitement, trauma and commitment as he learns there is more to the underground than the newspaper. His father is finally captured and killed, and the underground network helps Peter and his mother escape to Sweden.
This is a powerful story of a young boy, like many young people in critical times, forced to accept responsibilities beyond his years. The viciousness of the ruling power is not to be forgotten, but neither is the power of the people to resist, against seemingly inconquerable odds. All the characters are believable, each surfacing in his own place and his own way.

MENNONITE MARTHA, by Margaret Pitcairn Strachan. Illus. by Charles Geer. New York: Ives Washburn, 1961.

Set in Pennsylvania, 1884, this is a family story backgrounded by the mores and religion of the Mennonites. Young Martha sometimes has dreams of buying some bright pink material for a dress, because all of her life she has worn either brown or gray. Mother is saving her egg money to furnish the parlor. Meanwhile, papa reads in the news about a new piece of machinery, a reaper, which would help him produce more on the farm. Grandpa, the local minister, considers the possible purchase a wasteful extravagance. The story details how these elements are worked out to the satisfaction of all.

Set well in religion and culture, this story exposes family problems, love, and humor.

<u>THE MOUNTAIN OF TRUTH</u>, by Dale Carlson. New York: Atheneum, 1972.

An intriguing story of religion and mysticism, set in a remote Tibetan lamasery. The story is told through Peter's memories as the parents of lost children have come to search for them. Peter has been a part of the group and aids in the search for Michael and the rest. Michael has found his mystic destiny by leading the children into hiding to found a new religious order in which they will strive to develop mental capacities which will help them construct a new order in society. A special story, sometimes slow moving but compelling enough to maintain interest.

<u>MY ENEMY, MY BROTHER,</u> by James Forman. New York: Hawthorn, 1969.

Dan and his father, Polish Jews, survive the concentration camp and return to Poland after the war. What is the promise of the future? Dan dreams of going to Israel, while his grandfather feels he must live his last years where they began.

Dan decides to travel to Israel with several other young people, one of whom is Hannah, the only girl in the group. The experiences of their travel to Israel include the death of one of the group, capture and separation. But Dan escapes and finishes the trip. He is overwhelmed with happiness when he finds Hannah and the others already there.

The final arrival in Israel and assignment to a kibbutz arouse mixed emotions in David. He wonders if he has made the right decision.

Later, David trains to be a shepherd and accidently discovers and befriends a young Arab, Said. The human conflicts of politics and war are exposed through David and Said, brothers and enemies. Their conflicts are not resolved, but many compelling questions arise from their friendship and subsequent alienation.

The characters are well drawn, each with his own background and needs, and each facing a new life, in his own way.

NIGHT WATCHMEN, by Helen Cresswell. New York: Macmillan, 1970.

This is an allegory portraying the struggle for individual freedom in a conforming society. Henry is bored when he has to spend three weeks away from school to recuperate from an illness. Then he meets (or dreams about) a pair of tramps, Josh and Caleb. He is intrigued by their life of freedom, their social observations and their methods of survival. After Henry becomes thoroughly familiar with this alternative system of survival, the two leave--or did it all really happen?

AN OLD TALE CARVED OUT OF STONE, by A. Linevski. Translated from the Russian by Maria Polushkin. New York: Crown, 1973.

Ancient tribal rituals and customs are viewed through this story of a young boy who becomes shaman of his people. At seventeen the responsibility of interpreting the spirit voices which control life and death in this Neolithic community falls upon Liok. His own survival and his mother's at stake, Liok, realizing he hås no supernatural powers, relies upon his imagination to develop schemes which result in the provision of food, etc. However, the tribe is suspicious of his unconventional methods and when he loses a symbolic necklace, he flees in fright and finds an advanced tribe which has developed weapons. Liok is adopted by the tribe and takes a wife, but again he finds himself in trouble when he treads upon forbidden grounds. His wife is sacrificed and he returns to his original tribe, hoping he can share some of the wisdom gained in his travels.

A POCKET FULL OF SEEDS, by Marilyn Sachs. Illus. by Ben Stahl. New York: Doubleday, 1973.

Nicole and her sister have lived in a foster home

because their parents could not afford to keep them. Nicole leaves the foster home to return to her family when she is eight years old. Nicole's parents are French Jews and she falls victim to hostile treatment from her classmates and some adults. Eventually her parents are taken by the Nazis and Nicole goes again to foster parents, but she is not safe there. Concerned for Nicole's safety, a sympathetic teacher takes her in as a boarding student.

Following Nicole's life from eight to adolescence, one learns about the social and political pressures imposed upon countries like France as a result of the Nazi victimization of Jews.

A PROMISE, A PROMISE, by Molly Cone. Illus. by John Gretzer. New York: Houghton, 1964.

Some insights into the Jewish faith are revealed through this story of Ruth Morgan, who is growing in her own knowledge and understanding of her religion. As she prepares for her Bas Mitzvah, one views the customs and rites of the faith.

PROUD TO BE AMISH, by Mildred Jordan. Illus. by W. T. Mars. New York: Crown, 1968.

This is perhaps one of those cases of too many facts for fiction. The theme is also the well-used one of children in a strict religious environment longing for worldly things. Katie Zook envies Gloria, who is Lutheran and who owns a red dress. She also feels guilty about other worldly thoughts and the radio she secretly listens to and shares with her little brother. The radio and her thoughts are kept hidden from her parents, until she finds out that they and other adults are sometimes tempted by modern inventions and conventions.

Similarly, in Plain Girl by Virginia Sorensen (Harcourt, 1955), Esther, a young Pennsylvania Mennonite girl, attends public school after her father is forced by law to enroll her. Seeing how the other children live and dress, Esther begins to question her own life.

THY FRIEND, OBADIAH, by Brinton Turkle. New York: Viking, 1969.

One of a group of titles picturing a small Quaker boy.

In the first, <u>Obadiah the Bold</u>, the boy is introduced. In the next <u>Thy Friend Obadiah</u>, the boy is followed around by a seagull. He tries to rid himself of the pesky bird, until one day the seagull doesn't appear and he realizes that he misses it. In <u>Adventures of Obadiah</u>, the boy takes a wild ride at the sheep sheering squantum. In these picture stories, language, customs and habits common to Quakers are introduced through incidents and illustrations.

<u>THE WITCH OF BLACKBIRD POND</u>, by Elizabeth Speare. Boston: Houghton Mifflin, 1958.

This is the story of a young girl who dares to be different in a rigid puritanical community. Kit dresses flamboyantly and makes friends with Hannah, a suspected witch. Her independence of choice ends in her arrest on charges of witchcraft. In spite of her uncle's defense and the testimony of a lonely child she has befriended, it seems that Kit will be hanged. However, in the end, her beau, a strong-minded seaman, manages to free her.

Detailing the story, Kit sails from Barbados to the Connecticut colony in 1687, meeting Nathaniel Eaton, the first mate, and John Holbrook, who is about to study for the ministry. First indications of Kit's independent nature are apparent when she jumps overboard to rescue a child's doll.

Arriving at her aunt's home, she is surprised at the austere life of her mother's sister and family. She meets her cousins, Judith and Mercy, and is fascinated and questioning. She also tries to understand the politics involved in the preservation of the Connecticut charter, with which her uncle is actively concerned.

She begins teaching at the Dame school and meets Hannah Tupper, considered a witch because of her lonely existence and her Quaker beliefs. Her relationship is encouraged by Nat, who has known Hannah for some time and understands her needs and basic goodness. Ignoring the warnings of her uncle, Kit continues to visit Hannah. Then comes the eventual arrest, and her narrow escape.

Life, politics, and religion in these times are interwoven against the background of Kit and her new family.

3. War and Peace

In an interesting article titled "Love and Power, the Psychological Signals of War" (see Sources and Notes, No. 76), David McClelland analyzes literature to predict the nation's readiness for war. He predicts that in the seventies the American nation is leaning more toward war than at any period since 1825.

He believes that children's stories, along with other materials, reflect the people's attitudes toward such things as achievement, need for power and need for affiliation.

He also speculates that periods of strong reform movements and of strong religious movements seem to ferment war: for instance, the Abolitionist Movement, leading to the Civil War; the 19th- and 20th-century crusades for social justice, followed by World War I; the New Deal, followed by World War II. In the case of the two world wars, Americans were not the aggressors, but their reformist zeal may have led to American participation. This may also be true of Vietnam, and could lead to greater intervention in the Middle East.

High need for power and a low need for affiliation, according to McClelland's analysis, seem to be controlling factors apparent in literature which deals with war.

Following is an article noting some of the developments in writings about World War II for children and young people. Along with others, some of the titles are further reviewed in the pages that follow. War-related titles with an emphasis on politics are included in the preceding section, "Religion and Politics." At the end of this section is a reprinted list of titles with an emphasis on peaceful coexistence.

CHILDHOOD'S ISLAND RECEIVES GIFT OF MYRRH:

A Study of Children's Books with World War II Settings

by Marcia Shutze and M. Jean Greenlaw

An interest in literature for children that encompassed the settings and emotions of war led to a search of the literature for books that dealt with World War II. Research revealed that few books using World War II as a setting were published during the war years (1940-1945). Books with this setting began to appear during the late fifties, increased in abundance during the sixties, and seem to have peaked as we move into the seventies. Curiosity concerning this pattern triggered a desire to investigate the possible influences that created this phenomenon.

Children's literature during the past decade has been going through a period when more realism has been encouraged in stories. Children's writers have taken a new attitude toward children and realism in their literature. As Constantine Georgiou points out in Children and Their Literature, the nineteenth-century attitude was that children's literature should be a character-building experience, and, therefore, it was preachy and moralizing. However, today the attitude is that children's literature should mirror for the young readers our complex world as it is. "Good does not always triumph and evil is not always punished."[1]

Another principle strongly operating since the nineteenth century was what Selma Lanes in Down the Rabbit Hole terms the "Peter Pan Principle." This principle has been apparent until recently and is based on the adult's attitude that he does not want "to ruffle that blanket of primal innocence with which all children enter the world."[2] A champion of this principle was the French scholar and romantic Paul Hazard, who saw "childhood as a fortunate island where happiness must be protected."[3]

Ms. Shutze is a graduate student in the School of Journalism at the University of Georgia and a first grade teacher in Athens, Georgia. Dr. Greenlaw is an associate professor of reading in the College of Education at the University of Georgia. This article is reprinted by permission of the American Library Association from Top of the News, January 1975, pp. 199-209.

Today childhood's island is vastly different from the nineteenth century's version, or for that matter, the mid-twentieth century's version. The critical political, social, and economic issues that face the world today are so intertwined and interrelated that they have woven a highly complex web around today's world, and have cast their ensnaring, gossamered shadow over childhood's island. As Jane Yolen points out, the mass media have brought all of the issues confronting society into the immediate sight and sound perception of almost everyone, including children. Television is in approximately 95 percent of American homes. Also, more people know how to read today than ever before, including children, and consequently the print media have a larger readership than ever before.[4]

With our changing attitude toward children and realism in their literature due to the decreasing adherence to the "Peter Pan Principle," the supersaturating effect of the mass media, and the refurbishing of our educational philosophy, the libraries and bookstores on childhood's island are making more and more room for realistic fiction.

Several of the authors writing realistic children's literature have expressed how they feel about the new realism and why they write it. As Erik C. Haugaard, author of <u>The Little Fishes</u> (1967), stated:

> I wanted to tell not only what happens to the victims of war but also how in degradation he could refuse to be degraded. Our history books tell about the victories and defeats of armies; I wanted to tell about the defeat and victory of human beings.[5]

Emily Neville, children's author, expressed her attitude toward the new realism in yet a different way. She sees her mission as a writer

> ... to show the reader, not how great a hero he could become, because I don't think most people are going to become heroes but simply how hard it is to be a plain decent human being.... The values that I write about will not lead to greater heroics; only I hope to fuller humanity.[6]

The authors of this new realism have a specific message for their readers, often quite different from the messages contained in other books such as history books. These authors have expressed a faith that today's realism in children's literature will give young people a deeper sensitivity and insight in solving society's problems in the future--a "fuller humanity."

Books with World War II settings have been increasing in number since the late fifties. There seems to be a strong relationship between the increasing number of books with a World War II setting and the more permissive attitude toward realism in children's literature during this same period. If children's literature is truly reflective of the world, then most certainly war would be a topic for children's authors today. This country has been involved either directly or indirectly in war since December 7, 1941--World War II, the Cold War, the Korean War, the Vietnam War, and the Arab-Israeli War, among others. What are children--especially American children, who have been spared much of the direct cruelties and horrors of war--being told about war? How are the authors of the new realism trend presenting their views as compared with what authors wrote about war during the war and postwar years of World War II?

War and Postwar Years

Three books that were published during the war and postwar years are Marie McSwigan's Snow Treasure (1942), and Claire Huchet Bishop's Pancakes--Paris (1947) and Twenty and Ten (1952). In both Snow Treasure and Twenty and Ten children are placed in dangerous wartime situations, but all ends well. In Snow Treasure the Norse children smuggle their country's gold supply to safety via their sleds while under the Nazis' observation, bringing it to a waiting ship. In Twenty and Ten twenty French children successfully hide ten Jewish children from the Nazi soldiers. In these two stories, both based on factual events, war is presented realistically--the fear of being caught and punished by the Nazis for smuggling a gold supply out of a country or hiding Jewish children; the material shortages of war; and the inconsiderate and arrogant attitude that some Nazis displayed in dealing with people. However, the strength and realism of these two authors' anti-war statements are not as keen or as sharp as are the anti-war statements of those authors writing since the later fifties.

All three of these books are enjoyable and have very worthwhile messages about war. It is important to remember

that these three books were written primarily for younger
children, while many of the later books have been written
for older readers. Also, as is pointed out in A Critical
History of Children's Literature,

> It is natural that the war stories of the late fifties and
> the sixties should have more perspective than the earlier ones. The overtones of many of them are mature,
> giving them meaning for older boys and girls.[7]

In addition to the increased perspective of the later books,
the trend toward more realism in children's literature was
not yet underway.

World War II Stories Since the Late Fifties

A second finding was that the authors' war statements
become increasingly stronger and more realistic as time
takes us further away from World War II. The authors of
a second group of books, twenty titles published since the
late fifties, make much stronger statements about war, in
more poignant and powerful settings. This is evident when
the twenty books are broken down into two subgroupings:
(1) those books published in the late fifties and early sixties,
and (2) those published since 1965.

The books included in the first subgroup are Meindert
DeJong's The House of Sixty Fathers (1956), John Tunis' Silence
over Dunkerque (1962), Hilda Van Stockum's The Winged Watchman (1962), James Forman's The Skies of Crete (1963), Margaretha Shemin's The Little Riders (1963), and I Never Saw Another Butterfly (1964). In all six of these books war is portrayed
very vividly and realistically.

The authors of these books point out war's horrors
and tragedies more strongly by making clearer and more
realistic anti-war statements than those authors in the war
and postwar years' group. However, in each case, despite
separations, material shortages, and other cruelties, everything works out favorably in the end. Tien Pao in The House
of Sixty Fathers is reunited with his family; Sergeant Williams
and his companion in Silence over Dunkerque not only return
safely to England but also bring with them a Nazi prisoner
captured in the English Channel; Johanna in The Little Riders
helps to save the lead figures on the town clock from being
made into munitions; and the Verhagen family in The Winged

Watchman survive the Nazi occupation of Holland to rebuild their country and their lives.

The Skies of Crete, the fifth book in this subgroup, also conforms to the vivid and realistic characteristics of the other four. However, unlike the other four, the ending is not completely happy in that only Penelope and her mother escape from Crete, leaving behind her cousin, father, and grandfather, who safely return to their village. The fact that these stories end on mostly happy notes is not bad, but there were war victims for whom everything did not end happily.

I Never Saw Another Butterfly, inasmuch as its publishing date places it in the first subgroup, is an exception to the finding noted previously that as time takes us further away from World War II, authors' war statements become stronger and more poignant. The poets and artists contributing to this anthology were some of the 15,000 children who passed through Terezin, Czechoslovakia, a stopping-off point for Jews being sent to the gas chambers in the east. Only about 100 of these children survived the war. It is a book that is beautiful and gripping in the simplicity of its harsh and cruel realities, and its wonderful and imaginary fantasies. It cuts right to the bone of war. These children, all under fifteen,

> ... saw and heard everything that the grown-ups did: the endless queues, the funeral carts and the human beings harnessed to pull them, the executions, and the shouts of the SS-men. But they saw other things too: the green meadows, the bluish hills beyond the village gates, the animals, the birds, the butterflies. ... And ... princesses with coronets, wizards and witches, insects with human faces, a land of happiness with cookies, candy and soda pop.[8]

It is a very special and unique book, and is certainly an exception to this subgroup.

The second subgroup of books comprises those published since 1965. Out of this subgroup the strongest war statements are made in those books which do not always end on a happy note, but this does not mean a hopeless note. In John Tunis' His Enemy, His Friend (1967), the story concludes with the main character, a Nazi officer, being shot. The officer had returned to the Normandy village where he

154 / Survival Themes

supposedly had given the command to execute six of its citizens during World War II and while there he is shot by the mentally disturbed son of one of those who had been executed. As May Hill Arbuthnot noted, "If the conclusion seems somewhat contrived, it certainly underscores the theme that love is stronger than hate, and that love alone is the hope of the world."9

Return to Hiroshima (1970) by Betty Jean Lifton is a nonfiction book that is a pictorial and prose documentary of Hiroshima, Japan, showing the effects of the atomic bomb that was dropped on the city on August 6, 1945. This is a book in which there is no way to escape the realities of war --the realities of war that are as real today as they were thirty years ago. The atomic bomb left in its aftermath survivors who suffer and die from leukemia due to the radiation, mentally retarded children who were born shortly after the bombing, orphans, scarred and disfigured people, and those socially outcast, for genetic reasons, with little hope of marriage and family because they are children of survivors. In the midst of all these painful reminders there is still hope-- hope for peace. One of the best summations of this hope is engraved on the base of the Children's Monument in Peace Park, which was built by the children of Hiroshima in memory of a young survivor who later died from leukemia: "This is our cry, this is our prayer: peace in the world."10

Of all the fiction books of this period, James Forman's Ceremony of Innocence (1970), which was based on factual events, made the strongest statement in the most realistic of situations. Hans and Sophie Scholl and two close friends, all students at Munich University during the war, wrote and published the White Rose leaflets denouncing Hitler and Nazism. They were fully aware of what would happen if they were discovered. They were not extraordinary youths; they had no desire to be martyrs. They were members of warm, happy families and they were young, with their futures before them. However, their action was a matter of conscience, and the following is a description of the irrevocable results:

> They entered (Hans and the soldiers). A black hose lay uncoiled on the floor. There were puddles of water, and in the center of the room stood the squat black engine with its long neck. It was smaller than he had imagined from pictures he had seen of the French Revolution. He closed his eyes. They were tying him down, and he held himself rigid so

that it might end without his ever uttering the great
cry that was tearing him apart. Then he was flat
down. He heard the sound of rollers, and at the
last there burst from his throat a cry, uttered in
a great voice, a voice that combined anger, reproof,
and an overwhelming conviction for which he was
willing to die.

'Long live freedom!'

Then the greased blade fell. His teeth met
through his tongue, and it was over.[11]

All four youths were guillotined. However, their memories
and what they died for are still very much alive today in
Germany and, thanks to Mr. Forman, in the minds of many
young readers.

Not all of the books in this second subgroup show the
cruelties and horrors of war by ending in death and destruction. Some end with people surviving the war to rebuild a
new life in what everyone hopes will be a better and peaceful world. Esther Hautzig's The Endless Steppe: Growing
Up in Siberia (1973) tells of how a Polish family survived five
bitter years in Siberia to return to Poland to begin anew. A
similar book is When Hitler Stole Pink Rabbit (1972) by Judith
Kerr. Anna's Jewish family encountered many cruelties and
kindnesses in their odyssey from Germany to Switzerland to
France to England in search for a safe place to live and for
her father to publish anti-Nazi pieces. In A Kind of Secret
Weapon (1969) by Elliott Arnold, Peter Andersen and his
mother escaped from the Gestapo in Denmark, after his father was killed by the Nazis, to begin a new life in Sweden.
They carried with them the fervent hope of returning after
the war to help rebuild a free and peaceful Denmark and new
lives for themselves.

In Erik Haugaard's The Little Fishes, the main character, Guidio, very realistically portrays a picture of a war
victim's life. He does not allow himself to become trapped
in the horrors and tragedies of war, and tries to objectively
analyze the what, the why, and the effect of war. Guidio refuses to be defeated by the degradation and the hate that war
breeds.

At least in this second subgroup the discussion of the
realities of war does not always end on a happy note; hopeful,

yes, but not necessarily happy. This is more realistic and adds strength to the anti-war message.

The Maturing Effect of War

In all of the books mentioned, young children during wartime conditions assumed responsibilities and found themselves in situations where they had to make decisions which matured them beyond their years. War took from them something that could never be recaptured--their childhood. One of the best examples of war's maturing effect on all different types of children is found by looking at James Forman's six novels with World War II settings and their main characters: Penelope and Alexis in The Skies of Crete, Nicholos and Angela in Ring the Judas Bell (1965), Hans and Gretchen in Horses of Anger (1967), Paul in The Traitors (1968), Daniel in My Enemy, My Brother (1969), and Hans and Sophie Scholl in Ceremony of Innocence. In all six novels the reader meets young people who, through their experiences in war, leave whatever childhood they had remaining behind them in the ashes and rubble of war. Penelope and Alexis in The Skies of Crete and Hans and Sophie in Ceremony of Innocence have been discussed.

Nicholos and Angela, the main characters in Ring the Judas Bell, lived through World War II, losing their mother to a Nazi execution squad. As the story begins, they are caught in the midst of the civil war that raged in postwar Greece. Kidnapped by the Andarte, the Communist guerrillas, and deported to Albania, they escape from prison with twelve other children, all younger than they, encountering hunger, cold winter weather, and people looking for them because there is a price on their heads. After leaving some of the children in Yugoslavia, and Angela quitting the troop in the mountains, Nicholos leads the rest of the children home--a very maturing experience for a young boy not more than fifteen.

In Horses of Anger the reader meets Hans, a young German patriot as the story opens, who is willing to die for Führer and the Fatherland. At fourteen he is at home, in school, and still very much a typical young boy; but at fifteen he is helping to man an anti-aircraft tower near Munich, wondering how long it will be before he will be killed. When Gretchen, a refugee who has been assigned to live with Hans' family, arrives, she has already matured beyond her years by the unspeakable shocks of war. She has lost family, home, and childhood to a stray bomber that accidentally dropped a bomb on her house.

In The Traitors Mr. Forman introduces the reader to another young German boy, Paul. Unlike Hans or his brother, Kurt, he cannot commit himself to Hitler and his madness. What he finally does commit himself to, after witnessing five long years of Nazi cruelty and destruction, is subversive work against the Reich in the last days before the Allies come, in order to save his town from complete destruction by the Nazis.

"Like Forman's heroes in Ring the Judas Bell and Horses of Anger ... Daniel Baratz in My Enemy, My Brother is no mewling teenager with niggling concerns but a boy coping with questions as broad as mankind."[12] Daniel is sixteen and a survivor of a Jewish concentration camp at the end of World War II when the story begins. For him childhood has ended before this story ever begins. As one reviewer noted when writing about this book, "Every one of Mr. Forman's teenage novels is a taut, searing document about moral choices in war torn places. There are never easy answers and completely happy endings...."[13] They are examples of childhood gradually and completely pulverized through five years of war.

Books by two additional authors reflect the maturing effect so aptly shown in Forman's books. Summer of My German Soldier (1973) by Bette Greene and The Upstairs Room (1972) by Johanna Reiss are powerful books, each of which has received national acclaim.

Summer of My German Soldier differs from the other books discussed in that the setting is the United States and it explores the effects of war on a child in Arkansas. Patty is a twelve-year-old beset by many problems. An awkward, forthright, bright Jewish child, her parents neither understand nor like her. This is compounded by her younger sister, Sharon, who is pretty and adored by all. The only person who cares about Patty is Ruth, the black housekeeper. Her entire world changes when Anton, a German prisoner-of-war, escapes. She protects and hides him and through him comes to believe that she is, indeed, "a person of value." All the seething and petty hatreds of a small town are ably described and the book ends realistically with Patty sent to a girl's reform school for her crime of protecting a war criminal.

158 / Survival Themes

There is hope, however, and one closes the book believing that Patty will rise above her plight and be a stronger person.

Set in Holland, The Upstairs Room chronicles the life of Annie, a Jewish child, from 1938, when she was six, through 1945, when the war ended. We see the inexorable progress from vague war threats to the breaking up of the family and their being hidden in various homes of non-Jews. The everyday problems of the terror of hiding make the experience even more vivid as seen through the eyes of a child.

Yes, for all of these youths, no matter what context the reader meets them in, he sees young people maturing and accepting awesome responsibilities in times of war. As Hanus Hachenburg, one of the young Terezin poets who perished in Oswiecim, wrote:

> I was once a little child,
> Three years ago.
> That child who longed for other worlds.
> But now I am no more a child
> For I have learned to hate.
> I am a grown-up person now,
> I have known fear.
> ...
> Somewhere, far away out there, childhood
>   sweetly sleeps. [14]

Objectivity and Lack of Moralizing

In writing about war it would be very easy for an author to moralize and to preach to the young reader. However, in the twenty-two books discussed the impression gained is that none of the authors resorted to this in their writings. Repeatedly, in review after review of several of the books mentioned, the objectivity and lack of moralizing were pointed out.

Three different reviews of A Kind of Secret Weapon noted this point. A reviewer in Commonweal wrote, "The book is extremely well executed; a gripping tale of courage and loyalty told without sentimentality...."[15] It was described in Young Readers' Review as "a serious book with moments of humor to relieve the tension, but it is not a 'preachy' kind of book."[16] Sidney D. Long in The Horn Book

Magazine noted that "Many questions--of patriotism, of men's actions in war, of forgiveness and revenge--are raised in the book, but each reader will have to answer for himself."[17]

Another interesting case in point is Return to Hiroshima. One reviewer felt that "Mrs. Lifton is all for remembering everything and dwells rather too relentlessly on horrors...."[18] However, this is what Mrs. Lifton intended to show in this book--the far-reaching and unbelievable horrors of war, with everyone having as an objective a peace-filled world. Selma Lanes noted that "Low key text and photographs combine to tell it as it was, is, and will be for the survivors of Hiroshima. A whisper more eloquent than most shouts against war."[19]

Recognized Quality of Books

The books discussed here are all quality books. All are well written, with well-drawn characters, for the most part; and the plots are quite realistic and believable. Each was reviewed in at least one journal, and in some cases there were as many as five reviews.

A second basis indicating the quality of these books is the fact that one was a nominee for the National Book Award, another a Newbery Honor Book, and several received the Spring Book Festival Award and were cited on such selective lists as The Horn Book Magazine "Honor Roll," Library Journal's and Publishers Weekly's "Best Books of the Year" lists, and the American Library Association's "Notable Book List."

Conclusions

Five conclusions are proposed about the twenty-two books discussed here:

1. The books written during the war and postwar years were not as strong or as powerful in their statements about war as compared with the books published since the late fifties.

2. Authors' statements about war become increasingly stronger and more realistic as time takes us further away from World War II. No matter how strong the statement about war is and how realistic the situation

is, there is always that element of hope present that
  the situation will get better. This hope is an expression of faith in living and surviving to see the coming
  of a better world.

3. The young people in these books matured beyond their
   years in these war situations. Childhood is forever
   lost in the ruin and rubble of war.

4. The authors of these books did not preach about their
   war beliefs with didactic sentimentalism. Rather,
   they tried to present an accurate and realistic picture
   of war, allowing the reader to draw his own conclusions.

5. The books were accepted as quality books. Reviews
   in several noted journals and magazines illustrated
   this point. Also, a number of the books read received
   awards in recognition of their quality.

Whatever any future studies would show, children today have available to them an excellent collection of quality books with World War II settings, which make very sensitive statements about the harsh realities of war and what it does to people. Paul Heins, in one of The Horn Book Magazine's Christmas editorials, compared different types of children's books to the qualities of gold, frankincense, and myrrh, the gifts of the Magi. "Myrrh--a bitter spice, medicinal in property--reminds us of life's more than occasional bitterness."[20] What we have happening to children's literature with World War II themes is very timely. The Magi, such authors as Forman, Lifton, Hautzig, Van Stockum, Tunis, Arnold, Greene, and the perished poets and artists of Terezin, are visiting childhood's island with their gifts of myrrh: Ceremony of Innocence, Return to Hiroshima, The Endless Steppe: Growing Up in Siberia, The Winged Watchman, His Enemy, His Friend, A Kind of Secret Weapon, Summer of My German Soldier, and I Never Saw Another Butterfly.

References

1. Constantine Georgiou, Children and Their Literature (Englewood Cliffs, N.J.: Prentice-Hall, 1969), p. 360.
2. Selma G. Lanes, Down the Rabbit Hole (New York: Atheneum, 1972), p. 78.
3. Ibid.

4. Jane Yolen, "Peter Rabbit ... Says Good-bye to Snow White," Publishers Weekly 199:79 (Feb. 22, 1971).
5. "The Booklist," The Horn Book Magazine 44:144 (Feb. 1968).
6. Emily Neville, "Social Values in Children's Literature," in Sara Innis Fenwick, ed., A Critical Approach to Children's Literature (Chicago: Univ. of Chicago Pr., 1967), p. 52.
7. Cornellia Meigs and others, A Critical History of Children's Literature (London: Macmillan, 1969), p. 508.
8. Hana Volavkova, ed., I Never Saw Another Butterfly: Children's Drawings and Poems from Terezin Concentration Camp 1942-1944 (New York: McGraw-Hill, 1964), book cover.
9. May Hill Arbuthnot, Children's Reading in the Home (Glenview, Ill., 1969), p. 180-81.
10. Betty Jean Lifton, Return to Hiroshima (New York: Atheneum, 1970), p. 46.
11. James Forman, Ceremony of Innocence (New York: Hawthorn, 1970), p. 236.
12. Jane Manthorne, "Outlook Tower," The Horn Book Magazine 45:328 (June 1969).
13. "The Traitors," Young Readers' Review 5:2 (Nov. 1968).
14. Hanus Hachenburg, "Terezin," in Volavkova, ed., I Never Saw Another Butterfly, p. 22.
15. Laura Polla Scanbon, "A Selected List of Children's Books," Commonweal 203: 301 (May 23, 1969).
16. "A Kind of Secret Weapon," Young Readers' Review 5: 1778 (March 1969).
17. Sidney D. Long, "Summer Booklist," The Horn Book Magazine 45:407 (Aug. 1969).
18. "Book Review: Children's Books," The New York Times, May 24, 1970, Section 7, Part II, p. 4.
19. Lanes, Down the Rabbit Hole, p. 228.
20. Paul Heins, "Gold, Frankincense and Myrrh," The Horn Book Magazine 44:655 (Dec. 1968).

Bibliography

Arnold, Elliott. A Kind of Secret Weapon. New York: Scribner, 1969.
Bishop, Claire Huchet. Pancakes--Paris. New York: Viking, 1947.
_____. Twenty and Ten. New York: Viking, 1952.
DeJong, Meindert. The House of Sixty Fathers. New York: Harper, 1956.

Forman, James. *Ceremony of Innocence*. New York: Hawthorn, 1970.
———. *Horses of Anger*. New York: Farrar, 1967.
———. *My Enemy, My Brother*. New York: Hawthorn, 1969.
———. *Ring the Judas Bell*. New York: Farrar, 1965.
———. *The Skies of Crete*. New York: Farrar, 1963.
———. *The Traitors*. New York: Farrar, 1968.
Greene, Bette. *Summer of My German Soldier*. New York: Dial, 1973.
Haugaard, Erik C. *The Little Fishes*. Boston: Houghton, 1967.
Hautzig, Esther. *The Endless Steppe: Growing Up in Siberia*. Boston: G. K. Hall, 1973.
Kerr, Judith. *When Hitler Stole Pink Rabbit*. New York: Coward, 1972.
Lifton, Betty Jean. *Return to Hiroshima*. New York: Atheneum, 1970.
McSwigan, Marie. *Snow Treasure*. New York: Dutton, 1942.
Reiss, Johanna. *The Upstairs Room*. New York: Crowell, 1972.
Shemin, Margaretha. *The Little Riders*. New York: Coward, 1963.
Tunis, John. *His Enemy, His Friend*. New York: Morrow, 1967.
———. *Silence over Dunkerque*. New York: Morrow, 1962.
Van Stockum, Hilda. *The Winged Watchman*. New York: Farrar, 1962.
Volavkova, Hana, ed. *I Never Saw Another Butterfly: Children's Drawings and Poems from Terezin Concentration Camp 1942-1944*. New York: McGraw-Hill, 1964.

BORIS, by Jaap Ter Haar. Translated by Martha Mearns. Illus. by Rien Poortvleit. New York: Delacorte, 1970.

The horrors of war are viewed as people face starvation and death during the nine-day siege of Leningrad during World War II. But this is also a story of human compassion which sometimes transcends commitment to war. Boris and Nadia leave their Russian camp to hunt for potatoes and they are discovered by a German soldier. The children fear for their lives but the soldier returns the two children to their camp.

Although some Russians are outraged, Boris remembers this kindness and later shares a bit of his food with a German prisoner.

DAWN OF FEAR, by Susan Cooper. Illus. by Margery Gill. New York: Harcourt Brace Jovanovich, 1970.

Nine days in the lives of Derek, Peter, and Geoff, English boys living in an area just outside London during World War II.
The routines of war are evident to the children as they hear the sirens and run for shelter. But it is all still very much a game, watching the planes, imagining the workings of the army, etc. They build a camp, a secret hiding place, which is destroyed by a neighborhood gang. During a retaliatory fight, the younger boys get a view of violence as they observe a fight between two older boys, Tom Hicks and Johnny Wiggs.
That evening, the bombing, which has gradually been getting worse, hits directly and Peter and his whole family are killed. The reality of war is now very evident and for the first time the children know fear.

FOR THOSE I LOVED, by Martin Gray and Max Gallo. Boston: Little, Brown, 1972.

Peace and happiness never come for a survivor of a Nazi death camp. When the author was 14 years old in September 1939, he lived in the Jewish ghetto in Warsaw. He reports his life there and his attempts to hide out in a cupboard. He describes his later capture and the cattle-truck ride to the concentration camp. He escapes and becomes a soldier in the Red army. The next move is to the United States, then later to France. He is now a grown man with a family but has not found peace.

THE FORGOTTEN SOLDIER, by Guy Sajer. Translated from the French by Lily Emmet. New York: Harper, 1971.

There is no romanticizing of war in this World War II novel. Men's feelings of pain, exhaustion, terror and despair are portrayed in a story of the Germans' entry into Russia. The story is told by a young man who at sixteen is impressed with the uniforms of the soldiers, but by the time he is eighteen he longs to forget war. He joined the Wehrmacht, a year after Hitler's assault on the Soviet Union. For two years, battles in Poland, Kiev, Kharkov, etc. are chronicled. From this German soldier's viewpoint, the bitterness of battles and defeat is shown.

IF I DIE IN A COMBAT ZONE, BOX ME UP AND SEND ME HOME, by Tim O'Brien. New York: Delacorte, 1973.

The morality of war is questioned by a former foot soldier in Vietnam who served reluctantly. He reports the daily life of the foot soldier and his near attempt to desert and flee to Canada. Instead he fought and was later honorably discharged, having earned several medals; but he still objected to the war.

THE LONG ESCAPE, by Irving Werstein. New York: Scribner, 1964.

Set in 1940, this book demonstrates the horrors of war through the story of Justine Raymond, a nurse at La Maison des Enfants de Heyst, a rest home for poor children recovering from illnesses.

Justine and the children are followed through the German invasion of Belgium, the evacuation to Dunkerque and the trip to England, when Dunkerque was hit.

Based on a true story, the tragedies of war--the terror, the running and hiding, and death--are viewed as Justine and the children make their long escape.

THE PUSHCART WAR, by Jean Merrill. Illus. by Ronnie Solbert. Reading, Mass.: Addison-Wesley, 1964.

Beginning with the "daffodil massacre," March 15, 1976, the Pushcart War is declared. What follows is a full-scale campaign by the pushcart owners in New York City to defend themselves from the trucks.

With humor, the story details the simple elements of a war campaign: politics, warring factions, citizens and local politicians join the fight.

In spite of the humor, this story presents serious implications about war and peace.

SILENCE OVER DUNKERQUE, by John R. Tunis. New York: Morrow, 1962.

The story of Sergeant Edward Henry George Williams, an English prisoner of war in German hands during World War II. The sergeant was with one of the first British contingents to France. Instead of getting the leave he was expecting, the sergeant becomes embroiled in battle, is separated from his troop, and moves toward Dunkerque, hoping to be evacuated there by ship.

Meantime, the sergeant's twin boys hide away on a boat sailing across the channel to Dunkerque, hoping to locate their father. They return safely, realizing the situation is more critical than they had imagined.

The sergeant eventually finds passage on the British warship, H.M.S. Wakefield, but it is hit in a minefield. He manages to save himself and another soldier, and they are later rescued by a 14-year-old French girl, Giesel. She takes them to her farm, to hide out from the Germans. The story follows the mystery and intrigue of their hiding out and their eventual return home through enemy territory.

The real story of bombings, fear and death, the realities of war, is told here.

SLAUGHTERHOUSE-FIVE; OR, THE CHILDREN'S CRUSADE, by Kurt Vonnegut, Jr. New York: Delacorte, 1969.

The hero of this striking and sometimes bitter novel is Billy Pilgrim, a survivor of prison and the fire bombings of Dresden in World War II. A chronical against war and the society which promotes it is built around Billy, who comes unstuck in time. His life shuttles between the past, where the incidents of war are viewed; the planet of Tralfamadore, where he is exhibited in the zoo; and the future, where he remembers the terrible destruction of Dresden and cries.

UNCLE MISHA'S PARTISANS, by Yuri Suhl. New York: Scholastic, 1973.

The dangers faced by youths assuming an active role in the resistance during World War II are credibly viewed in this sensitive story of a twelve-year-old Ukrainian boy whose family was killed by the Nazis. Modeled after the actual experiences of a group of resistance fighters, the story of Motele is told. After being orphaned by the Nazis, Motele joins the group and he is later sent on a very dangerous mission. His skill at playing the violin is used as a decoy. The mission is successful and Motele feels he has revenged the death of his family.

PEACE:

A Publishers for Peace Bibliography

This selective list of new children's books centers on the fact that people can and must learn to settle their differences peacefully. This is not an issue new to books for children, but because the newest children's books are always the hardest to find, our committee confined its selection to recently published titles, with very few exceptions. Publishers were invited to submit suggested titles from their current and recent back-lists. We chose 50 books that through direct statement or skillful, amusing indirection, press the serious point that peaceful coexistence is and always has been possible, that peace is the strongest, wisest course in the lives of men and nations today.

Preschool and Primary

BAKER, Betty. The Pig War. Illus. by Robert Lopshire. Harper. 1969. $2.50; PLB $2.57.
An I Can Read History of the 1859 incident between the United States and British Canada that began with an intrusive pig and nearly escalated to a full-scale war; an easy-to-read demonstration of the idiocies that can grow into international conflict.

This bibliography is a specially annotated version of a list of children's books prepared for Publishers for Peace by a committee chaired by Lillian N. Gerhardt of the SLJ Book Review. Others on the committee: Mary Jo Howard, Nassau Library System, N.Y.; Trevelyn Jones, Garden City Public Library, N.Y.; Aileen O'Brien Murphy, New York Public Library; Gail Sage, Brooklyn Public Library. This article is reprinted from School Library Journal, Oct. 15, 1970, pp. 104-5, 112, by permission of the R. R. Bowker Co., a Xerox company.

BOLOGNESE, Don. <u>Once Upon a Mountain.</u> Illus. by author.
   Lippincott. 1964. $2.95; PLB $2.82.
A shepherd calls for help and hears laughter. Convinced his
town is being ridiculed by the mountain village opposite, he
prepared for war only to discover that the "hee-ha-haw" had
come from a donkey. Disarmingly amusing, and deceptively
simple.

COWLEY, Joy. <u>Duck in the Gun.</u> Illus. by Edward Sorel.
   Doubleday. 1969. $2.95.
Continuing commitment to life rather than death is central to
this story of a war prevented when a duck, with the help of
obliging soldiers, nests in the one cannon of a besieging army.

FITZHUGH, Louise & Sandra Scoppettone. <u>Bang Bang You're
   Dead.</u> Illus. by Louise Fitzhugh. Harper. 1969.
   $3.95; PLB $3.79.
An obvious anti-war lesson in words and pictures tracing the
increasingly violent actions of some children who began a
game of playing at war.

FOREMAN, Michael. <u>Two Giants.</u> Illus. by author. Pantheon. 1967. $3.95; PLB $3.74.
Two happy giants fall out over the ownership of a seashell
and gradually discover how ridiculous it is for the equally
powerful to fight each other.

HUTCHINS, Pat. <u>Tom and Sam.</u> Illus. by author. Macmillan. 1968. $4.50.
A small war between two small boys starts to escalate when
their sense of property leads them to attempt to steal from
each other, and they recognize in time that their rivalry
could cost a pleasant friendship. A transparent moral buoyed
by humor.

KIRKPATRICK, Oliver. <u>Naja, the Snake and Mangus, the
   Mongoose.</u> Doubleday. 1970. $4.50.
A Jamaican parable of the re-thinking of roles and the peaceful solutions discovered by habitual enemies, the snake and
mongoose, when they find out that they take pleasure in each
other's cleverness and company.

LA FONTAINE, Jean de. <u>The Lion and the Rat.</u> Illus. by
   Brian Wildsmith. Watts. 1964. $4.95.
The internationally famous fable of mutual reliance and of
how the concept of relative size is meaningless in the account
of a rat's ability to save the king of beasts by gnawing away
a net trap.

LOBEL, Anita. Potatoes, Potatoes. Illus. by author. Harper. 1967. $2.95; PLB $2.92.
Two brothers, soldiers in opposing armies, meet to do battle on their own potato field, a situation which nearly kills their mother; it's an early childhood stunner about the vainglory of war and its toll in innocent victims.

TURKLE, Brinton. Fiddler of High Lonesome. Illus. by author. Viking. 1968. $3.50; PLB $3.37.
Not about peace per se, but a plea for the right of all to life in this story of a backwoods boy Lysander, whose violin can make the animals dance, and his refusal to ever again use his music to thus set them up for his hunting cousins.

UDRY, Janice M. Let's Be Enemies. Illus. by Maurice Sendak. Harper. 1961. $2.50; PLB $2.57.
A small book with a big idea--in which two determinedly contrary little girls discover the futility of their arguing, negotiate their differences, and settle down to be friends.

VARGA, Judy. The Magic Wall. Illus. by author. Morrow. 1970. $3.95; PLB $3.78.
Adapted from a medieval Austrian folktale, the author/illustrator recreates the dilemma of good King Frederick, who brings trouble and bad feeling to his cordial kingdom when he accepts bad advice and barricades his territory with unnecessary defense measures.

WEZEL, Peter. The Good Bird. Illus. by author. Harper. 1966. PLB $3.27.
Anything can be read into this textless series of pictures which follow the course of an unlikely friendship between a wild bird and a goldfish in a bowl. The committee decided that it emanated a feeling of peace (which just goes to show how wide a selection net can be cast over any subject).

WIESNER, William. Tops. Illus. by author. Viking. 1969. $4.50; PLB $4.11.
Two gentle giants make friends, and their example brings peace to two evenly matched countries at war.

WIESNER, William. Tower of Babel. Illus. by author. Viking. 1968. $3.95; PLB $3.77.
This retelling of the biblical legend can be used to show the chaos that attends on lack of communication and an unwillingness to learn to understand one another.

WONDRISKA, William. Mister Brown & Mr. Gary. Illus.
    by author. Holt. 1968. $3.95; PLB $3.59.
Two pigs sent by their king to define "happiness" repair to
separate islands--one to amass great material wealth, the
other to provide his family with simple comfort. A simple
message to the effect that "most" and "biggest" do not necessarily mean "strength" or "best."

Middle Grades

BABBITT, Natalie. Search for Delicious. Illus. by author.
    Farrar. 1969. $3.95.
An amusing satiric fantasy centering on the way rumors and
viciously manipulated information can lead to violence and
war.

FEHRENBACH, T. R. United Nations in War and Peace.
    Random. 1968. $1.95; PLB $2.88.
An up-to-date outline of how the Security Council and General
Assembly operate to keep or restore peace.

GOODWIN, Harold. Magic Number. Illus. by author. Brad-
    bury. 1969. $3.95.
A misguided scientist attempts to force peaceful coexistence
on the wild creatures inhabiting his garden, and, although the
animals do eventually arrive at peace, their clever arrangements are reached despite, rather than because of, the dic-
tatorially bumbling professor.

GREEN, Wade. Disarmament: the Challenge of Civilization.
    Coward. 1966. $2.80.
An anecdotal record of the various international disarmament
agreements pursued between 1924 and 1965.

HARRISON, Deloris, ed. We Shall Live in Peace: the
    Teachings of Martin Luther King, Jr. Illus. by Ernest
    Crichlow. Hawthorn. 1968. $3.95.
Excerpts from the speeches and writings of America's fore-
most advocate of nonviolence.

HOUSTON, James A. White Archer: an Eskimo Legend.
    Illus. by author. Harcourt. 1970. $3.50; PLB $3.54.
Vigorous drawings enhance this tale of an Eskimo boy, bent
on revenging his parents, who learns the futility of "an eye
for an eye, a tooth for a tooth."

I Never Saw Another Butterfly. McGraw. 1964. $3.95.
These poems and beautifully reproduced drawings by children later killed in Nazi concentration camps speak powerfully against the tragic waste of lives in war.

JONES, Weyman. Edge of Two Worlds. Illus. by J. C. Kocsis. Dial. 1968. $3.95.
Romantic in essence, unsentimental in execution, this finely detailed historical novel exemplifies, through the enforced mutual reliance of an aged Indian and a 15-year-old white boy crossing the Texas plains, the resolutions possible to problems of generational, racial, and territorial enmities.

KELEN, Emery. Peace Is an Adventure. Meredith. 1967. $3.50.
The work of the many agencies of the United Nations is made vivid through these accounts of the men and women working for the UN around the world.

KIPLING, Rudyard. Miracle of the Mountain. (Orig. title: The Miracle of Purun Bhagat.) ed. by Aroline B. Leach. Illus. by Willi Baum. Addison-Wesley. 1969. $4.95.
The dignity of all life, animal as well as human, is made amply clear in this Kipling story especially adapted for younger children.

KRUMGOLD, Joseph. Henry Three. Illus. by Alvin Smith. Atheneum. 1967. $4.75. PLB $4.37.
Two young boys keep their heads while all about them are losing theirs in a suburban panic to build air raid shelters at the threat of war.

LANIER, Sterling E. War for the Lot: a Tale of Fantasy & Terror. Illus. by Robert Baumgartner. Follett. 1969. $3.95; PLB $3.99.
Woodland animals under the threat of invasion by marauding rats are temporarily able to submerge their own differences and work together. Patterned on human strategies of war, the story subtly presses for the need for constant vigilance in maintaining good relations.

LAYCOCK, George. Never Trust a Cowbird. Norton. 1966. $3.95; PLB $3.69.
Profiles of 18 familiar wild animals illustrate the ways in which so-called natural enemies accommodate themselves to each other and share their diminishing wild territory.

LEICHMAN, Seymour. The Boy Who Could Sing Pictures.
  Illus. by author. Doubleday. 1968. $3.50.
The responsibility of rulers to support the aspirations of
their subjects is demonstrated through this story of a gifted
singer who averts rebellion through the social reforms insti-
gated by his songs to his king.

MERRILL, Jean. Black Sheep. Illus. by Ronni Solbert.
  Pantheon. 1969. $3.95; PLB $3.89.
An amusing animal fable for our times about a herd of sheep
who find out the hard way that the herd is enriched by the
presence of nonconformity and dissent.

NORTON, Andre. Star Man's Son: 2250 A.D. Illus. by
  Nicholas Mordvinoff. Harcourt. 1952. $3.50.
One of the oldest titles on this list, this is still one of the
best sci-fi novels promoting world peace through an adven-
turous plot and well-sustained suspense.

PATTERSON, Lillie. Martin Luther King, Jr.: Man of
  Peace. Illus. by Victor Mays. Garrard. 1969. PLB
  $2.49.
A biography geared to the vocabularies of middle grade readers which also outlines the principles of non-violent civil dis-
obedience.

PEOPLE OF DESTINY Series. Childrens. ea. vol. PLB
  $4.50.
Biographies of three 20th-Century crusaders for peace and
mutual respect for life among all peoples: Dag Hammer-
skjold by Norman Richard (illus. by Hollis Assoc., 1969);
Albert Schweitzer by Kenneth Richards (1968); and Gandhi by
Don Torgersen (illus. by Hollis Assoc., 1969).

SAINT-EXUPERY, Antoine de. Little Prince. Tr. by Kath-
  erine Woods. Illus. by author. Harcourt. 1943.
  $4.25; PLB $4.28.
It was overweening pride that drove the Little Prince away
from the serenity of his kingdom.... Adults find that they
can read any number of meanings into the multifaceted international favorite, so it should come as no surprise on a list
that promotes the idea of peace.

WAHL, Jan. How the Children Stopped the Wars. Illus. by
  Mitchell Miller. Farrar. 1969. $3.75.
Set in the Middle Ages, this describes the successful crusade

of a band of children who march to the wars in the hope that the adults will stop fighting.

Junior High School and Up

CARR, Albert Z. Matter of Life and Death: How Wars Get Started--Or Are Prevented. Viking. 1966. $4.50. PLB $4.13.
An absorbing analysis of the underlying causes of three American wars, the economic and psychological pressures that led to them, and the ways in which these can be recognized and resisted today.

FORMAN, James. Horses of Anger. Farrar. 1967. $3.50.
A splendid evocation of time, place, and atmosphere through the story of teenager Hans Amann's experience of war in Hitler's Germany--from super-patriotism, through dreary disenchantment, to stunning, empty destruction.

FRANK, Anne. Anne Frank: Diary of a Young Girl. Rev. ed. Tr. by B. M. Mooyart. Intro. by Eleanor Roosevelt. Doubleday. 1967. $4.95.
A powerfully moving journal of the two years Anne, her family, and other Jews were hidden from the Gestapo during the German occupation of Holland; it pinpoints the stupidity and tragic waste of life and talent inherent in any war.

GREEN, Diana. Lonely War of William Pinto. Atlantic Monthly Pr. 1968. $4.75.
Based on historic characters, this competently written novel explores the crisis of conscience for one boy, a lonesome pacifist among war-happy brothers, during the American Revolution.

HUNT, Irene. Across Five Aprils. Follett. 1964. $3.95; PLB $4.17.
Spanning the five Aprils of 1861-65, this explores through the character of Jethro (10 years old when the Civil War began) the initial fascination and eventual disillusion that war holds for boys.

LAWSON, Don, ed. Youth & War: World War One to Vietnam. Lothrop. 1969. $4.50; PLB $4.14.
An anthology of 11 personal essays by, and about the experiences of, young men in 20th-Century wars--their reaction to

the reality of battles after the first surge of patriotic motivation.

LIFTON, Betty Jean. Return to Hiroshima. Photogs. by Eikoh Hosoc. Atheneum. 1970. $5.95; PLB $5.69.
"Return here through the pages of this book and learn of the city--Of the old have they forgotten? Of the young, do they remember? Of the wounded, have they been healed?" Strong photographs with spare, moving text.

PAULI, Hertha. Toward Peace: The Nobel Prizes and the Struggle for Peace. Washburn. 1969. $3.50; PLB $3.24.
A history of the Nobel Peace Prize with sketches of its winners and their contributions.

SCHECTER, Betty. Peaceable Revolution. Houghton. 1963. $3.75.
This traces the impact of passive resistance on history through accounts of the lives and ideas of such men as Thoreau, Gandhi, and Martin Luther King, Jr.

STILES, Martha B. Darkness Over the Land. Dial. 1966. $3.95.
Through the skillful delineation of family and public life in Hitler's Germany, this novel examines the citizen's share in an aggressor nation's collective guilt.

TUNIS, John. His Enemy, His Friend. Morrow. 1967. $3.95; PLB $3.78.
On the surface, this is a novel about championship soccer, but essentially it is about the continuing negative effect of war on ordinary people through the story of the German soccer star who must return to France to play against the son of a man he had ordered shot during the German occupation.

UNTERMEYER, Louis, ed. Time for Peace. Illus. by Joan B. Victor. World. 1969. $3.95; PLB $3.86.
Quotations on the subject of peace from the King James Version of the Bible with an introductory essay by the distinguished editor in which he further supports the theme through quotations from several poets.

4. Celebration of Life and Death

The word celebration brings to mind "joy." Joy implies exuberance and delight. Children commonly display joy in their relations with each other, or even as they play alone. Adults sometimes place limits on these expressions, not realizing the child's need for this process. Not only does joy relax a person physically but it contributes to emotional balance.

Some cultures still provide systematic group-processes for the expression of joy and celebration. Religious rituals, visits from strangers, installation of governmental leaders, and birth and death are occurrences for celebration. In Western cultures many of these opportunities for celebration have disappeared. Some children find few occasions for this type of emotional outlet.

Since joy appears to be a physical type of expression, it is hard to consider it in relation to reading materials. Perhaps poetry is the literary form most often used to express submerged feelings of celebration and to communicate the meaning of these feelings to children and others. Fiction titles with an element of humor promote joyous responses. Since children, like adults, gravitate toward materials which are joyful rather than painful, most popular listings for children include many books of humor, light adventure and uncomplicated mysteries. The difficult area for the writer seems to be the ability to express joy and celebration amidst pain. Yet it is probably man's ability to celebrate living in spite of turmoil which provides the greatest resources for survival.

Some titles listed in earlier sections are examples of an author's ability to celebrate life through fiction. Listed here are a few additional titles chosen as purely joyful expressions or as stories which present problem situations with joyful approaches to solutions. A number of picture books have been included because one of the values of this type of literature is often the joy expressed in the language and artistic design.

ABBY TAKES OVER, by Phyllis La Farge. Illus. by Glo
    Coalson. Philadelphia: Lippincott, 1974.

    Mama takes a much needed vacation and Abby, aged nine, helps her father look after the younger children. She also helps with the cooking. The very humorous scenes that result from Abby's efforts are a joy to the reader.

APT. 3, written and illustrated by Ezra Jack Keats. New
    York: Macmillan, 1971.

    Two boys, Sam and Ben, go from door to door in their tenement building, searching for the lovely music they have heard. Finally they find a blind man in Apt. 3. At first they are frightened when the man invites them in, but when he volunteers to play them some "secrets" on the harmonica they realize they have found the source of the music. The setting is bleak, but there is joy in the friendship formed.

BOYS AND GIRLS, GIRLS AND BOYS, by Eve Merriam. Illus.
    by Harriet Sherman. New York: Holt, 1972.

    Popular for its non-sexist portrayal of children, this is a joyful picture book in which boys and girls are shown exploring, being active and enjoying life uninhibited by the usual sex roles.

BUBBLES, by Eloise Greenfield. Washington, D.C.: Drum
    and Spear, 1972.

    A young Black boy is indeed bubbling over with joy when he learns to read. He reads to his mother and he reads to his sister when his mother is busy.

CITY RHYTHMS, by Ann Grifalconi. New York: Bobbs,
    1965.

    On a hot summer day in New York City a small boy is aware of the rhythm of the city as he hears the sound of subway, the people, the market, the pigeons, etc.

176 / Survival Themes

COME ALONG, by Rebecca Caudill. Illus. by Ellen Rankin. Holt, 1969.

    Haiku poetry and beautiful illustrations combine in a celebration of nature.

DON'T YOU REMEMBER? by Lucille Clifton. New York: Dutton, 1973.

    Tate, a four-year-old Black girl, is very frustrated when nobody seems to remember her birthday. She is not prepared for the joyful surprise the family has prepared for her.

I'M GLAD I'M ME, by Elberta H. Stone. Illus. by Margery W. Brown. New York: Putnam, 1971.

    A small Black child expresses the joy of being himself, in the midst of an inner city atmosphere.

JUBA THIS AND JUBA THAT, by Virginia A. Tashjian. Illus. by Victoria de Larren. Boston: Little, Brown, 1969.

    The air of jubilance expressed by children at play is found in this collection of stories, riddles, games and songs.

THE LOLLIPOP PARTY, by Ruth Sonneborn. Illus. by Brinton Turkle. New York: Viking, 1967.

    The story begins by showing the problems of children whose mothers have to work, but ends in celebration. One day Tomas's mother doesn't come home at the usual time. At first he feels alone and frightened, but then his teacher visits unexpectedly. He and she have a "lollipop party."

LORDY, AUNT HATTIE, by Ianthe Thomas. Pictures by Thomas di Grazia. New York: Harper, 1973.

    On a summer vacation, Jeppa Lee celebrates country living with her Aunt Hattie. They pick huckleberries, go fishing, and just sit drinking cool lemonade.

MADELINE, by Ludwig Bemelmans. New York: Viking, 1939.

The popularity of this title and the others in the series about a young girl in a French orphanage is indicative of the author's ability to provide a mood of celebration and adventure, even as Madeline has an appendix operation. In Madeline's Rescue, Madeline and the other girls struggle to keep a dog at the orphanage and they end up finally with one for each girl.

MA 'N DA LA, by Arnold Adoff. Illus. by Emily McCully. New York: Harper, 1971.

This delightful title is based on a Buddhist symbol of the universe. Ma is for mother, Da is for father, La is for singing, Ha is for laughing, Ra is for cheering, Na is for sighing, and Ah is for feeling good. The feeling of celebration is most apparent when this rhythmic text is read aloud. The vibrant pictures complement the text.

MARTIN'S FATHER, by Margrit Eichler. Chapel Hill, N.C.: Lollipop Power, 1971.

Problems and joys are expressed as a father and his small son handle all the chores of running a house.

MY SPECIAL BEST WORDS, by John Steptoe. Illus. by the author. New York: Viking, 1974.

In this story, Bweela, a little girl, is the narrator. She gives clues to her feelings about her family, her little brother who isn't toilet trained, and the special words that she and her brother use.

Steptoe is expert at presenting the sense of balance with which children approach life; adults might often handle similar situations negatively. The word for Steptoe's books is "SPECIAL!"

NEW LIFE: NEW ROOM, by June Jordan. Illus. by Ray Cruz. New York: Crowell, 1975.

The author captures the humor and joy of a family

facing the crisis of too little room for their growing clan. As poets often do, Ms. Jordan is able to portray in her writing that sense of joy that sometimes helps people through difficult situations. There are already three children--Rudy, nine, ten-year-old Tyrone, and Linda, who is six. And there is a new baby coming. Linda doesn't want to move into the room with her brothers and they don't want her. But partitioning, arranging and painting their new room is such fun as they work out a compromise.

NOISY NANCY NORRIS, by Lou Ann Gaeddert. Illus. by Givia Fiammenghi. New York: Doubleday, 1965.

Noisy Nancy banged, jumped, shouted, ran, laughed, etc. until the landlady threatened eviction. She became so quiet that the landlady became worried. She baked the now sad Nancy some cookies and asked her to make just a little noise.

RAIN, RAIN RIVERS, by Uri Shulevitz. New York: Farrar, 1969.

Watching the rain from inside her cozy room, a little city girl celebrates the rain with thoughts of a child's all-time favorite, splashing in puddles.

UMBRELLA, by Taro Yashima. New York: Viking, 1958.

Momo can't wait for the rain so she can wear her new boots and carry her umbrella to nursery school. The little Japanese girl's pleasure is felt as she walks to school straight as an adult when the rain finally comes. The joyful sound of the rain is simulated by the Japanese syllables bon po lo, bon po lo, etc.

Closely related to the celebration of life should be the celebration of death. Because of the way death is handled by parents and the media, however, children have little understanding or confrontation with the whys of death until it touches them. Death is often magnified beyond belief in the child's mind, and fears of it can be the most destructive process in a child's life.

Wickes (see Sources and Notes, No. 66) indicates that some children are keenly aware of the undercurrents affecting their lives and those around them. Fears of such undercurrents should not be allowed to grow into troublesome fantasies. For instance, Wickes gives an example of a patient haunted by fears from her childhood. Once she had suddenly been seized by fear of a funeral procession. After this she would run blindly whenever she saw one. Her parents and other adults, unconscious of her need to deal with the mysteries of death, assured her that there was nothing to be afraid of. But this did not resolve her fear, and vague and symbolic figures of death haunted her at night.

Death has always stood out in man's consciousness, for it is not only counter to the urge to live but is pointed up in the regressive elements of ourselves. Mythology and early literature for children contain many indications of an obsession with death. Some historians feel that this is because children in the past faced death at an early age more often than in modern cultures.

The child is most often so caught up in the business of living and discovery that fears of death are not overwhelming, but when these fears arise, it is important to realize that they cannot be reduced by dismissing them as simple folly. The child then feels odd because no one seems to understand, as in the case of the young woman noted earlier. The symbols are often too vague for adults to realize the actual fear in the child.

Some experts suggest that the important thing is to offer the child some type of security--in our companionship and in conveying our acceptance of death as an extension of life. It is imperative that positive values be built to meet these fears. Most of all, in order to deal with the child's fears the adult must come to grips with his or her own feelings.

Hurlock (see Sources and Notes, No. 21) believes that religious instruction fosters in children unrealistic concepts about death which must be dismissed or almost always revised at adolescence. Some cultures attempt to maintain a sense of balance about death by recognizing the personal loss, but by also providing an atmosphere of celebration at the point of death. Gypsy funerals, for instance, are active, with dance, singing and drinking.

180 / Survival Themes

In any case, all children have some experience with death, whether it be an animal, a friend, a relative, or someone else's friend or relative. Although healthy views of death in literature will not spare anyone the feelings of personal loss, they may help individuals revamp their perspectives positively.

Some titles in preceding sections present the incidence of death as part of the story. The following titles concentrate on feelings about and reactions to death.

ANNIE AND THE OLD ONE, by Miska Miles. Illus. by
    Peter Parnell. Boston: Little, Brown, 1971.

    Young Annie lives a good life in her Navajo world. She helps watch the sheep, carries pails of water to the cornfield, and goes to school every day on the school bus. Most of all, she enjoys the time spent with her grandmother, "the old one."
    One evening grandmother tells the family, "My children, when the new rug is taken from the loom, I will go to mother earth."
    Annie begins to think of ways to stop the finishing of the rug, so as to delay her grandmother's death. Her mother has explained that the old ones sometimes know the time of death because they are close to the animals and to the earth.
    When grandmother realizes what Annie is trying to do, she describes to Annie the cycle of life and death in nature. Annie begins to understand and her fears gradually subside. She accepts that the inevitable will happen.
    Positive images of the relationship between old and young are presented. Positive explanations of life and death are bolstered by the wisdom and character of "the old one" and the innocent strength of the child.

THE FIRST SNOW, by Helen Constant. Pictures by Vo-Dinh.
    New York: Knopf, 1974.

    A beautiful and simple story exploring the Buddhist concept of death. Lien, a young Vietnamese girl, faces her first New England winter and the fact of her grandmother's death. Melting snow on Lien's palms symbolizes the continuation of life. As melted snow continues to exist as water, so life and death are but two parts of the same thing.

The beautiful illustrations by Vo-Dinh, Constant's husband, use pencil, print and collage techniques.

GROVER, by Vera and Bill Cleaver. Illus. by Frederic Marvin. Philadelphia: Lippincott, 1970.

When Grover's mother becomes ill, he fears that she will die, but neither he nor his father suspects that death will come in the way that it does.

After his mother's death, the story covers the differences in the demonstrations of grief by Grover and his father. Grover is disappointed because his father is unable to handle his mother's apparent suicide. Father retreats from the world and from the support of his family and friends. He isn't able to handle the situation as Grover's mother had suggested before she died.

Grover suffers questioning and pain, but most painful is watching his father's reaction. The central question is whether his mother should have faced the pain and suffering of terminal illness or whether suicide was her right.

This is a very intense book, with heavy questions and strong emotional reactions. In one scene, after being taunted about his mother's suicide, Grover seeks revenge by chopping the neck off his teaser's pet turkey. Grover's experiences and questions should provoke deep thought in all readers.

HOME FROM FAR, by Jean Little. Boston: Little, Brown, 1965.

One of a set of twins is killed in a car accident, after which the family adopts two foster children. The surviving twin girl feels that her dead brother is forgotten. She finds no outlet for her grief among the family. Eventually it is revealed that her mother's reason for never mentioning the dead brother is to keep her daughter from dwelling on the dead as had happened to her once in the past.

MAY I CROSS YOUR GOLDEN RIVER? by Paige Dixon. New York: Atheneum, 1975.

Jordan learns soon after his eighteenth birthday that he has a degenerative disease which will result in his death. The story describes his and his family's reactions to this fact. Many details of his thoughts are included as he interacts with friends and family. It is apparent that the support of his family helps him to come to terms with himself. He then prepares himself and them for his death.

THE MULBERRY MUSIC, by Doris Orgel. Pictures by Dale Payson. New York: Harper, 1971.

In this story a young girl adjusts to the death of her grandmother. Liza's parents have tried to keep the impending death of grandmother hidden. Liza's confusion and trauma when she learns the truth are made evident. The eventual message is one of love transcending death as Liza suggests that grandma's favorite music be played at the home memorial services. She realizes grandma will always live in her memory.

MY GRANDSON LEW, by Charlotte Zolotow. Illus. by William Pène DuBois. New York: Harper and Row, 1974.

Simple and moving story of thoughts about a loved one who has died. At six years old Lewis remembers all the nice things about grandfather, who died when he was two. The author makes one believe this story, although one has to wonder whether a two-year-old would retain such a sense of loss for four years.

SQUIB, by Nina Bawden. Philadelphia: Lippincott, 1971.

In a boating accident, Kate is saved but her father and her brother Rupert are drowned. This story covers Kate's discovery and later involvement with a young boy called "Squib," whom she believes might be her brother. She speculates that her brother did not drown, but was rescued and never returned to her family.

The plot begins with Kate and her associates in the park commenting about the sad and unusual child, Squib. They have learned that he lives in the tower of a house for the aged, with a weird old woman. Stories are told that she keeps him in a basket and doesn't allow him many associations.

By the time Squib disappears from the park, Kate has decided that the pictures found in her home verify that Squib is her brother. Gradually, as the plot evolves, the children become involved in a search and chase to rescue Squib from the old woman.

The true story about Squib is later revealed, but Kate would still like her mother to adopt the boy. Her mother refuses, understanding Kate's guilt at being the one saved in the drowning accident. Squib's adoption would form an unhealthy replacement in Kate's mind. However, Squib is adopted by a nearby family and Kate is the first to open up communication with him.

A rather strange story revealing a child's trauma resulting from death.

A TASTE OF BLACKBERRIES, by Doris Buchanan Smith. Illus. by Charles Robinson. New York: Crowell, 1973.

Jamie is a prankster, but he is special and everyone likes him, including the boy telling the story. The focus remains on Jamie as the first-person narrator tells about the day Jamie was stung by a bee. The boy ignores Jamie's pleas for help, thinking he is pulling another stunt. He is shocked when Jamie is later sent to the hospital, where he dies.

Feelings surrounding the death--guilt, sorrow, and questioning--are well handled. A short simple book, with great impact.

THE TENTH GOOD THING ABOUT BARNEY, by Judith Viorst. Illus. by Erik Blegvad. New York: Atheneum, 1971.

A boy tries to think of ten good things to say at the funeral for his dead cat, Barney. Some may consider this a somewhat contrived and overly cute method of dealing with death, even of a pet.

WHERE THE LILIES BLOOM, by Bill and Vera Cleaver. Philadelphia: Lippincott, 1969.

Set in the Appalachian mountains, this is the story of four motherless children, who bury their dead father in secret, because they want to stay together. If their father's death is discovered they will probably be sent to foster homes. The second oldest girl has no time to deal with grief as she struggles to help the family survive during the bitter mountain winter.

Death is the central theme, but customs of community and of marriage are disclosed as the story proceeds. The girl, in the end, releases her pent-up grief and realizes that promises to the dead cannot always be kept.

PART IV

SOURCES AND NOTES

Sources and Notes

Included here are background materials and primary sources for the development of this text. Articles are included which offer criticisms of many of the books discussed earlier. Some offer additional suggestions in the subject categories chosen. In selected cases explanatory notes are given in some detail as an indication of the value of the item in relationship to the text. Several bibliographies are listed as resources for expanding an investigation of titles in the various categories.

1. AMERICAN INDIAN AUTHORS FOR YOUNG READERS: a selected bibliography. New York: Association on American Indian Affairs, 1973.
   A list of books for young people by American Indian writers in which the authenticity is noted. The introduction to the list discusses past and present treatment of Indians in literature, citing examples of common stereotypes.

2. AMERICAN LABOR: THE TWENTIETH CENTURY, by Jerold S. Auerbach. New York: Bobbs Merrill, 1969.

3. AND JILL CAME TUMBLING AFTER: SEXISM IN AMERICAN EDUCATION, edited and introduced by Judith Stacey, Susan Bereaud and Joan Daniels. New York: Dell, 1974.
   A collection of articles dealing with the sociological and psychological influences of stereotypes on male and female development.

4. ANGER AND THE ROCKING CHAIR: GESTALT AWARENESS WITH CHILDREN, by Janet Lederman. New York: Viking, 1973.

5. ASIA: A GUIDE TO BOOKS FOR CHILDREN. From Asia Society, 112 East 64th Street, New York, N.Y. 10021

6. "ASIAN IMAGES--A MESSAGE TO THE MEDIA," Bridge Magazine 3:2 (April 1974), 25-30.
   Within a historical context, the Asian image in children's books is examined, stating that children's books do nothing to counter existing stereotypes. Listed and discussed are popular negative approaches to Asians used in the media. A list of important dates in Asian history is added.

7. THE BEST IN CHILDREN'S BOOKS, 1966-72, edited by Zena Sutherland. Chicago: University of Chicago Press, 1973.
   A selection of titles from those reviewed in the Bulletin of the Center for Children's Books.

8. "BIOGRAPHY: THE BAD AND THE BOUNTIFUL," by Patrick Groff. Top of the News (April 1973), 210.
   This article is included because so many images of heroes and heroines are presented to children through biography. Although many of these titles are on library shelves in the biography section, many are nevertheless primarily fiction.
   Groff notes some of the ways in which children have been cheated through biographies written especially for them. He questions the positive effects such biographies can have on children. He believes first of all that biographies written about adults may not have any effect on very young children because they cannot make image associations with adults. In general, he believes that biographies for children are not faithful to the biographee, because authors tend to eliminate weaknesses and other negatives.
   Groff criticizes the way biographies for children are often written: many authors are involved in rewrite paste-ups which they believe are acceptable to children. He cites cases of authors who blatantly borrow passages from other materials. He questions the inclusion of too much detail, but also warns against "jumping across the iceberg of someone's life."

9. THE BITTER CRY OF THE CHILDREN, by John Spargo. Introduction by Walter Trottner, and an introduction to the 1906 edition by Robert Hunter. New York: Quadrangle Paperbacks, 1968.

10. THE BIZARRE IN CHILDREN'S PICTURE BOOKS, by Coleen C. Salley and Karen H. Harris, Top of the News 31:1 (November 1974), 95-100.
    A discussion of the historical development of children's literature from early Puritan works which contained threats of hell and damnation, to 18th-century materials which were highly moralistic and nostalgic, to a current trend which the author feels plays upon the subconscious fears of children. Titles cited which display this emphasis on terror are:
    The Beast of Monsieur Racine and No Kiss for Mama (described as a "mean book), both by Tomi Ungerer;
    The Inspector, The Hunter, and Tick and the Gumberoo, all by George Mendoza;
    Through the Window, by Charles Keeping.

11. THE BLACK AMERICAN IN BOOKS FOR CHILDREN, ed. by Donnarae MacCann and Gloria Woodard. Metuchen, N.J.: Scarecrow Press, 1972.
    After an introduction presenting some basic issues regarding the treatment of Blacks in children's materials and the problems of selection, a series of articles is included. Authors of the materials presented are largely from the library, educational and publishing worlds. The five general subject headings are: "Black Perspectives: The Basic Criterion"; "Racism in Newbery Prize Books"; "More Modern Examples"; "Some Early Examples," and "Racism and Publishing."

12. BLACK BOOKS BULLETIN. Published by The Institute of Positive Education, 7850 South Ellis Avenue, Chicago, Illinois, 60619.
    The Bulletin publishes a variety of articles from the Black perspective. Prominent Black authors and educators present views of the Black experience in America and elsewhere. Also included are notes on Africa. Reviews and listings of materials for reading and study are included in each issue. It is especially helpful in keeping up-to-date on materials from minority

publishing houses and serves as a clearing house for many publications useful in Black studies. Reviews of children's materials are also included.

13. BOOKS, CHILDREN AND MEN, by Paul Hazard. 4th ed. Boston: Horn Book, 1960.
    In a historical context, Hazard makes a valiant plea for children's books which portray "universal morals," that are not didactic, that are fresh and full of candor and that inform and inspire. He describes with verve and humor the development of children's literature in England, France, Germany and the United States. He expects that children will continue to fight for what they want and need.

14. "BOOKS FOR SPECIAL EXPERIENCES," Top of the News 32:3 (April 1976), 239-267.
    This series of articles by various experts in children's literature includes:
    "Maybe This Will Help," by Laurel Goodegon, in which it is suggested that books help children in special situations by bringing them to the realization that they are not alone. Themes of the books discussed include death, divorce, a trip to the hospital, adoption, moving, and a new baby.
    "Leisure in Children's Literature," by M. E. Kingsbury--a discussion of the transmission of values that aid the child in handling a culture which offers more leisure time.
    "Didacticism in New Dress, a Look at 'Free' Stories," by June M. Bingham and Grayce Scholt, which proclaims that literature is the device through which children learn social roles. The article also studies the current use of books in social movements. A warning against formula writing is offered.
    "The Child's World of the Fictional Deaf," by Patrick Groff, in which the question of representation of deaf children as characters in children's fiction is presented.

15. BOOKS FOR THE MULTI-RACIAL CLASSROOM: a select list of children's books showing the backgrounds of the Indian sub-continent and the West Indies. 2nd rev. ed., compiled by Judith Elkin. (Pamphlet no. 17)

190 / Survival Themes

London: Library Association, Youth Libraries Group, 1976.

One of a series of lists published by a section of the British Library Association. This one is of special interest because few resources, including children's materials, are available from the Caribbean. Included are several titles not found in popular listings of children's materials. Available from Miss L. Hopkins, Central Children's Library, Paradise, Birmingham B3 3HQ.

16. "BOOKS, READERS AND THE INDIVIDUAL," by Marjorie Sullivan. Top of the News (April 1971), 292-298.

A discussion of books as a source for the development of the "individual." Sullivan proclaims that in post-industrial societies, "instead of the individual" there has been the group and the "tube," listening, looking and reacting together. She notes the loss of identity and the alienation of the young.

After asserting that books can turn the person into an individual, she lists the following as examples of titles that can help one make that turn:

Coming of Age in Mississippi, by Ann Moody
My Life, My Music, by Ravi Shankar
Elephant Boy, by Leonard Wibberly
Anti politics in America, by John H. Bunzel
Got to Stop Draggin that Little Red Wagon Around, by Robert Paul Smith
Good Times, Bad Times, by James Kirkwood
Dawn, by Elie Wiesel
The House of Tomorrow, by Jean Thompson

An appended bibliography lists items which give insight to problems of youth, America, reading and libraries.

17. BRIDGE OF CHILDREN'S BOOKS, by Jella Lepman. Translated from the German by Edith McCormick. Chicago: American Library Association, 1969.

Shows how children's books were used to help restore Germany after the war.

18. BRIDGES OF UNDERSTANDING, by Charlotte Matthews Keating. Tucson, Ariz.: Palo Verde Publishing Co., 1967.

A list of books dealing with various minority groups

which the author feels help make the child more sensitive to the unique values of various groups.

19. BRITISH CHILDREN'S BOOKS IN THE TWENTIETH CENTURY, by Frank Eyre. New York: Dutton, 1973.
    The author traces the trends of didacticism and the change which brought about more imaginative works. Period covered is from 1900 to 1970.

20. "THE CHANGING WORLD OF SCIENCE AND THE SOCIAL SCIENCES," by Mary K. Eakin. Top of the News (November 1970), 23-31.
    Particulary interesting in this article is a section called "Do Not Disturb," in which Ms. Eakin projects that we are "imbued with the idea that childhood is and must be kept a carefree time." She indicates that facts for children about the social sciences and science have been carefully selected to exclude ideas which might disturb the child. Such selection deprives children of the opportunity to look questioningly and critically at the world. She makes a plea for controversy as a factor in children's science and social studies books. She asks that they be allowed to examine controversial issues so that they can understand all the facets of problems with which they may one day be faced.

21. CHILD DEVELOPMENT, by Elizabeth Bergner Hurlock. 5th ed. New York: McGraw-Hill, 1973.

22. CHILD DEVELOPMENT: PHYSICAL AND PSYCHOLOGICAL DEVELOPMENT THROUGH ADOLESCENCE, by Marian E. Breckenridge and E. Lee Vincent. 5th ed. Philadelphia: W. B. Saunders, 1965.

23. THE CHILD FROM FIVE TO TEN, by Arnold Gesell and Frances L. Ilg. New York: Harper, 1946.

24. THE CHILD FROM 9 TO 13, THE PSYCHOLOGY OF PREADOLESCENTS AND EARLY PUBERTY, by Reuven Kohen Raz. Chicago: Aldine, 1971.
    The period of life which Dr. Kohen Raz discusses

and analyzes is called the culmination of childhood and the threshold of adolescence. The physiological and psychological development of males and females during this period of growth are speculated upon. The author sees this period as one often overlooked in books on growth and development.

In his concluding statements, the author acknowledges that his findings are not all definitive at this stage but are worthy of consideration because of the apparent importance of this period as a time of integration and preparation. (Quotations from this volume are included in other parts of this text.)

25. CHILDREN AND ADOLESCENTS, INTERPRETIVE ESSAYS ON PIAGET, by David Elkund. New York: Oxford University Press, 1970.

In the preface the author indicates that this book was not meant to be a text on Piaget, but supplementary reading for courses in educational psychology and child development. He has attempted to digest Piaget's major findings without distortion.

In the first chapter the author presents a general view of Piaget and his findings regarding the child's stages of development:
   a) The first stage is termed the sensory motor period and is concerned with the gradual development of the ability to construct and reconstruct objects. Reasoning is accomplished without the aid of language, by use of mental images.
   b) The second stage is called the pre-operational stage. The gradual acquisition of language represents the elaboration of symbolic functions--language represents things, dreams, night terror, symbolic play and first attempts at drawing things.
   c) The third stage is the stage of concrete operations when the child begins to process in his head those things done before only in concrete action.
   d) During the fourth and last stage, there gradually emerge "formal operations" wherein the adolescent constructs and reasons realistically. Understanding of complex symbolism, language and contrary-to-fact propositions is apparent.

Also presented is Piaget's theory that language is not an adequate measure of development. Language, he believes, is stimulated more by environment than by thought.

Chapter II deals with children's questions, in which the thesis is presented that in today's world, more than ever, the child is exposed to ideas that he or she cannot handle emotionally or intellectually.

"How the Mind Grows: Two Paths of Mental Development" is the third chapter, in which the growth of thought from egocentric to sociocentric (highly personalized to socially accepted and tested) is discussed. The two paths taken by mental growth are substitution and integration, both leading gradually to more objectivity, reciprocity and relativity.

Chapter IV discusses egocentrism in children and adolescents--the gradual process by which the child develops new mental systems which should, by the end of adolescence, allow him to relate his feelings and thoughts to others and to integrate feelings of others with his emotions.

In "Cognitive Structure and Experience in Children and Adolescents," Chapter V, it is presumed that every experience, sensation, and/or feeling or emotion presupposes some kind of cognitive structuring. For instance, to label emotions requires some capacity to discriminate among many emotions. Some phenomena, such as prejudice and class-associated cliques, rarely appear before adolescence because the child in earlier stages lacks the cognitive structures upon which to build such experience.

From 5 to 7 is known as the age of reason--children begin to communicate, make comparisons, make judgments about truth and falsehood, reality and appearance.

The adolescent is capable of combinatorial logic which allows him to see a variety of alternatives to a question.

In chapter VI, "Piaget and Education," warning is given that Piaget is not an educator but a philosopher, although his theories have had a notable impact on educational practices. Piaget's influence on education probably results from his unique view of children and their developmental processes. The author projects that probably the most important thing to remember about Piaget's findings regarding motivation and learning is that learning should be conceived in broader terms than the mere ability to absorb the curricula. What the child learns about himself may in the long run be more important. We must also recognize learning as an ongoing process. Once we realize that children are learning something all the time, we can broaden our options for teaching.

Chapter VII presents parallels and differences in the theories of Piaget and Montessori. Both take a biological approach to study of the child. The norms in aspects of the child's development are emphasized by both, rather than the individual differences. Both have a genius for "empathy with the child." One major difference is that Montessori was concerned with the child's welfare, while Piaget studied the child with concern for information.

Chapter VIII, "Two Approaches to Intelligence," presents Piaget's theories in relation to popular psychological theories regarding intelligence. The differences seem to be largely in the approaches to intelligence rather than in views of the nature of intelligence. Piaget's theories offer no general support to the importance of pre-school instruction or to the use of motivational methods and materials. It is apparent in his findings that motivational tools, in and of themselves, will not arouse motivation.

The last chapter discusses reading logic and perception, one of the least known areas of Piaget's research. According to Piaget, in the early stages the child's perception is centered and becomes increasingly decentered. Experimental reading exercises are offered, based on Piaget's theory of perceptual growth.

26. CHILDREN AND BOOKS, by May Hill Arbuthnot and Zena Sutherland. 5th ed. Glenview, Ill.: Scott, Foresman, 1977.

Revision and reorganization of the earlier title designed for the study of children's literature. The new version contains some notes and references concerning current issues in children's book selection. A long list of sources and adult references is appended.

27. CHILDREN AND LITERATURE: VIEWS AND REVIEWS, by Virginia Haviland. Glenview, Ill.: Scott, Foresman, 1973.

Essays, statements and articles of criticism covering areas important to students of children's literature. The first chapter contains articles written as early as 1803. Many of the writers are also authors of importance, some of whom are listed in the historical outline earlier in this volume; e.g., Sarah Trimmer, Charlotte Yonge, Mary Mapes Dodge. Several articles cover realism and the modern period.

28. CHILDREN AND POLITICS, by Fred I. Greenstein. Rev. ed. New Haven: Yale University Press, 1970.

29. CHILDREN ARE PEOPLE, by Judy Brunger-Dhuyvetter. Cartoons by Bülbül; photos by Eileen Mazer. 1974.
    An annotated bibliography with introduction. Order from P.O. Box 2428, Stanford, California 94305.

30. CHILDREN ARE PEOPLE: THE LIBRARIAN IN THE COMMUNITY, by Janet Hill. New York: Crowell, 1974.
    Originally published in England, this title discusses the job of the children's librarian in today's societies. Pertinent to the discussion of themes in children's literature is "Attitudes toward Children's Books," in which the author warns against "crudely prescribing books like pills for specific situations."

31. CHILDREN'S LITERATURE, AN ISSUES APPROACH, by Masha Kabakow Rudman. Lexington, Mass.: D.C. Heath, 1976.
    Ms. Rudman selects the following issues for discussion: Siblings, Divorce, Death and Old Age, War, Sex, The Black, The Native American, and The Female, all of which become chapter headings. The issues are discussed in relationship to selected titles, with some suggestions for ways of furthering the discussion. A helpful list of background materials is included in each chapter. Chapter 10 presents methods of Using Children's Books in a Reading Program. Three appendices include Publishers' Addresses, Selected Children's Book Awards and Other References for Children's Literature.

32. CHILDREN'S LITERATURE IN THE ELEMENTARY SCHOOL, by Charlotte S. Huck. 3rd ed. New York: Holt, 1976.
    A detailed survey of children's literature (783 pages) with sections on Books of Yesterday and Today, Picture

Books, Traditional Literature, Modern Fantasy, Historical Fiction, etc. Part Three contains three chapters on the uses of materials and the learning environment. Suggested learning experiences also accompany each of the earlier chapters surveying various categories of books. The several appendices include a pronunciation guide.

33. THE CHILD'S CONCEPTION OF THE WORLD, by Jean Piaget. Translated by Joan and Andrew Tomlinson. Totowa, N.J.: Littlefield, Adams, 1969.

34. A CHILD'S RIGHT TO EQUAL READING, by Verne Moberg. Washington, D.C.: National Educational Association, 1973.
    Pamphlet. Includes notes on the importance of adult role models in child development.

35. "COMMUNAL SEX AND COMMUNAL SURVIVAL; INDIVIDUALISM BUSTS THE COMMUNE BOOM," by Laurence Veysey. Psychology Today (December 1974), 73-78.
    Veysey briefly analyzes the historical development of communal living in the U.S. He feels generally that today's group processes are different from those in the past, because the group today is used as a vehicle for the formulation of individual insights rather than, as in the past, the expectation that the individual will conform to the group. Veysey is author of The Communal Experience (Harper & Row, 1973).

36. THE CONSPIRACY AGAINST CHILDHOOD, by Eda J. Leshan. New York: Atheneum, 1967.
    The author theorizes about the individual differences of children, which are often unacknowledged in programs and educational activities. Emphasis is placed on the meaningless tasks which children are forced to perform. The author also explores the child's psychological and physical need for play, and suggests that today's child needs more help than ever before in coming to terms with free choices, because social and moral standards are presently in a state of upheaval.

37. "COUNTERING OLD MYTHS," by Georgess McHargue. American Libraries (March 1975), 166-67.
    Note on myths about American Indians which are perpetuated in children's books.

38. A CRITICAL APPROACH TO CHILDREN'S LITERATURE, by James Steel Smith. New York: McGraw-Hill, 1967.
    Looking at children's books from a critical and literary standpoint.

39. A CRITICAL APPROACH TO CHILDREN'S LITERATURE, ed. by Sara Innis Fenwick. Chicago: University of Chicago Press, 1967.

40. A CRITICAL HANDBOOK OF CHILDREN'S LITERATURE, by Rebecca J. Lukens. Glenview, Ill.: Scott, Foresman, 1976.
    In the preface the author states that this book grew out of her conviction that children's books differ from those for adults only in degree, not in kind. She offers a structure for effectively evaluating children's books based on literary criteria.

41. A CRITICAL HISTORY OF CHILDREN'S LITERATURE, by Cornelia Meigs and others. Rev. ed. New York: Macmillan, 1969.
    One of the more exhaustive historical approaches to children's literature.

42. "A DECADE OF TEEN AGE READING IN BALTIMORE, 1960-1970," by Linda Lapides. Top of the News (April 1971), 278-298.
    A survey of materials teenagers chose to read for themselves indicating changes in reading interests from 1960-1970. In 1960 some top choices were: Mrs. Mike; Anne Frank, Diary of a Young Girl; To Hell and Back; Seventeenth Summer; The Nun's Story; On the Beach; Jane Eyre; The Ugly American and Exodus. Classics included: A Tale of Two Cities; Ivanhoe; Poe's Tales; David Copperfield; Les Misérables; The Adventures of Tom Sawyer; and Twenty Thousand Leagues Under the Sea.

In 1970 the survey revealed interest in such titles as: <u>Joy in the Morning</u> by Betty Smith; <u>Mr. and Mrs. Bo Jo Jones</u> by Ann Head; <u>Gone with the Wind</u>; <u>Jane Eyre</u>; <u>Catcher in the Rye</u>; <u>Manchild in the Promised Land</u>; <u>To Kill a Mockingbird</u>; <u>Nigger</u>; <u>To Sir with Love</u>; and <u>Black Like Me</u>.

Ms. Lapides concluded that the survey showed teenagers' interest in "real" situations and issue-oriented materials. (The 1970 survey is available on order from the Enoch Pratt Library, Baltimore, Maryland.)

43. DESCHOOLING SOCIETY, by Ivan Illich. New York: Harper and Row, 1972.

    Magnificent plea for the disestablishment of schools, proclaiming that we learn the most out of school.

44. A DIFFERENT KIND OF COUNTRY, by Raymond F. Dasmann. New York: Macmillan (Collier Books), 1970.

45. DISCUSSING DEATH: A GUIDE TO DEATH EDUCATION, by Gretchen Mills et al. Palm Springs, Calif.: ETC Publications, 1976.

    Presents guidelines and resources for adults who may be involved with children in discussion of the subject.

46. DOWN THE RABBIT HOLE, ADVENTURES AND MISADVENTURES IN THE REALM OF CHILDREN'S LITERATURE, by Selma G. Lanes. New York: Atheneum, 1972.

    A commentary on children's literature that presents discussion of the adult romanticization of childhood which results in "sunshine-saturated" and "curruption-free" books "devoid of living substance." There is also discussion of illustrations, books in series and publishing in general. Some opinions about the presentation of images are offered with an analysis of <u>Little Black Sambo</u>.

    The book's appendices include lists of titles in several categories, including: For the Home Library; First Books; Sickbed Specials; Manners; Family Life; Sibling Rivalry; Anti-War Books; On Old Age; On Death; Seeing the World; etc.

47. EMERGING HUMANITY, MULTI-ETHNIC LITERATURE FOR CHILDREN AND ADOLESCENTS, By Ruth Kearney Carlson. Dubuque, Iowa: William C. Brown, 1972.

    Suggestions for the use of multi-ethnic materials in the classroom.

48. EXPLAINING DEATH TO CHILDREN, edited by Earl A. Grollman, with an introduction by Louise Bates Ames. Boston: Beacon Press, 1969.

    Contains information related to children and their understanding and/or reaction to death, from the points of view of religion, psychology, sociology, anthropology, biology and children's literature.

    A bibliography of source materials, including folktales, is given. The following are listed in a bibliography of books discussed as appropriate for the older child: Little Women and Little Men, by Louisa Alcott; Miss Hickory, by Carolyn Bailey; The Cat Who Went to Heaven, by E. Coatsworth; Meet the Austins, by M. L'Engle; Roller Skates, by Ruth Sawyer; The Bronze Bow, by E. Speare; Charlotte's Web, by E. B. White, and others.

49. "A FEMINIST LOOK AT CHILDREN'S BOOKS," prepared by the Feminists on Children's Literature. Library Journal (January 15, 1971), 235-240.

    After citing negative sexist implications in prepared reading lists, the collective says what it would like to see in children's books, including: encouragement of girl readers to develop physical confidence and strength without fear of loss of "femininity"; elimination of references to tomboys; encouragement for girls to find satisfaction and fulfillment in work, and laying aside the myth that this proves her inability to love a man; fewer depictions of women as castrators.

    Books listed as presenting positive images included: A Wrinkle in Time, by Madeleine L'Engle; Island of the Blue Dolphins, by Scott O'Dell; Strawberry Girl, by Lois Lenski; The Mixed-up Files of Mrs. Basil E. Frankweiler, by E. L. Konigsburg; Where the Lilies Bloom, by Vera and Bill Cleaver.

    Secondary recommendations included: Alice in Wonderland; Anne of Green Gables; and Rebecca of Sunnybrook Farm.

    The article concludes that present books reinforce

sex roles as imposed by the society. The group hopes that in the future there will be no need for a list of books especially for girls.

50. FEMINIST RESOURCES FOR SCHOOL AND COLLEGES: A GUIDE TO CURRICULUM MATERIALS, ed. by Carol Ahlum & Jacqueline M. Fratley. Old Westbury, N.Y.: Feminist Press, 1974.

51. FROM PRIMER TO PLEASURE IN READING: an introduction to the history of children's books in England with an outline of some developments in other countries, by Mary F. Thwaite. 1st American edition. Boston: Horn Book, 1972.
    History of children's book publishing in England, with helpful details about authors and publishers. Illustrations from major titles are included, and also notes on hornbooks, chapbooks, picture books, books of poetry, etc. Appendices and bibliographies are extremely helpful.

52. "GINGERROOT AND GINSENG TEA: THE WORLD OF THE ASIAN NOVEL," by Violet Harada. Top of the News (Jan. 1975), 167-171.
    The author presents an analysis of four novels by and about Asians which deal appropriately with the "universal concerns inherent in the human condition": The Life of Keshav, by Rama Mehta; The Sound of Waves, by Yukio Mishima; The Man in the Box: A Story from Vietnam, by Mary Lois Dunn; and To Beat a Tiger, by Elizabeth Foreman.

53. GOOD BOOKS FOR CHILDREN, ed. by Mary K. Eakin. Chicago: University of Chicago Press, 1967.

54. THE GREEN AND BURNING TREE: on the Writing and Enjoyment of Children's Books, by Eleanor Cameron. Boston: Little, Brown, 1969.
    A series of articles rewritten by the author from former magazine articles. The essays include comments about her own methods of writing as well as her perspectives about children's literature and its meaning.

She comments at one point that beneath the surface of the story there is much to be felt--tenderness, wisdom and sadness, but more often wit and humor. Within these essays, she analyzes many authors' books for children, discussing their wit, artistry and skill as writers. She concludes that often it is an author's perspective, retreat to, or recapturing of his or her own childhood which sparks the thesis of their writing for children. In the last essay she relives her own past and its meaning in regard to her writing.

55. A GUIDE TO NON-SEXIST CHILDREN'S BOOKS, compiled by Judith Adell and Hilary Dole Klein. Edited by Waltraud Schacher. Introduction by Alan Aida. Chicago: Academy Press, 1976.

The list is divided into three categories: Pre-School through Third Grade, Third Grade through Seventh Grade, and Seventh through Twelfth Grade. Aida, in the introduction, suggests that books are like dreams and dreams can be rehearsals for reality where children are concerned.

56. GUIDING YOUR CHILD TO A MORE CREATIVE LIFE, by Fredelle Maynard. New York: Doubleday, 1973.

Useful and specific suggestions for parents who seek resources for aiding their children in developing creatively. Chapter 8 is entitled "In the Beginning Is the Word: Books and the Growing Child" (pages 262-358). It's suggested that a child reads for the "deepest and most urgent reasons: to understand, to be reassured, to know and experience more, to escape, and above all to become more independent, more grown up."

Following are notes concerning children's responses to books: a) children respond most to books that contain elements of both warmth and security of family and of individual rebellion; b) children identify with characters who suffer in fairy tales and fiction; c) children are not innocent spirits; they know pain, fear, and confusion. They know mothers and fathers are not all kind and reliable; d) truly artistic materials that help children explore language are important; e) children should be offered books that present a sense of right and wrong, but not books that set out to improve character.

Part III, "Special Kinds of Reading," considers

classics, reality in books, poetry and comic books.
Part IV, "The Noisy Arts," deals with the effects of noise, media, parent management, etc. Suggests making the most of all media and art.
A selected list of books is appended.

57. HIP POCKET BOOKS--THE BAYA READING INTEREST REPORT, by Regina Minudri and Joni Bodart, <u>School Library Journal</u> 20 (November 1973), 70-71.
BAYA (Bay Area Young Adults) is a group of librarians in the San Francisco area which meets regularly to discuss teenage books and problems. This group conducted an informal survey of what Bay Area teenagers including teens in junior high and high schools, really read for fun. They also tried to learn the topics of interest to teens. Among the top ten titles were: <u>I Never Promised You a Rose Garden</u> (mentally troubled teenager); <u>Go Ask Alice</u> (premarital sex, drugs); <u>My Darling My Hamburger</u> (premarital sex); <u>Mister and Mrs. Bo Jo Jones</u> (premarital sex); <u>Bless the Beasts and Children</u> (alienation and loneliness); <u>The Outsiders</u> (alienation and loneliness); <u>That Was Then, This Is Now</u> (alienation and loneliness).
Few classics or books published earlier than 1964 were selected. Also discussed is the rejection of award-winning titles. The authors further indicate the most popular subjects and the most popular subject interests.

58. THE HISTORY OF CHILDHOOD, ed. by Lloyd DeMause. Foreword by William L. Langer. New York: Harper, 1974.
Throughout history, children have suffered abuse, neglect, even brutal killings. This title shows how various societies have considered and dealt with children from early to modern times. To fully understand how children are dealt with in literature one needs a background on the views of children within the society. The evidence is presented here from journals, diaries, notes, etc. The picture is not pretty; however, as is noted in the foreword, there have always been parents who have cared.

59. HORN BOOK REFLECTIONS ON CHILDREN'S BOOKS

AND READING, selected from eighteen years of the Horn Book Magazine, 1949-1966, ed. by Elinor Whitney Field. Boston: Horn Book, 1969.

60. HOW CHILDREN SEE OUR WORLD, by Jella Lepman. New York: Avon, 1975.

   Jella Lepman, founder of the International Youth Library, records the responses from children in 40 countries to subjects such as family, school, books, and mass media.

61. IMAGE OF THE BLACK IN CHILDREN'S FICTION, by Dorothy Broderick. New York: Bowker, 1973.

62. IMAGES OF THE NEGRO IN AMERICAN LITERATURE, ed. by Seymour L. Gross and John Edward Hardy. Chicago: University of Chicago Press, 1966.

   A series of articles about the presentation of Black images in well-known books. Covers materials from colonial times to the present.

63. "IN THE COUNTRY OF TEENAGE FICTION," by Richard Peck. American Libraries (April 1973), 204-207.

   Discussion of the problems faced by writers of fiction for teenagers. The author suggests that adults feel there must be a book to answer every specific problem. Too few books for young people, he says, reflect their need to grow independently. Young people seek retreat from the tyranny of their peers.

   Books for teens fit into two extremes: sex and violence or fantasy. There is no middle ground. The most popular books explore the personal problems of the young with the adult world in the background.

   Recommended as providing answers and good writing are: The Outsiders, by S. E. Hinton; Vibrations, by George Wood; The Skating Rink, by Mildred Lee Seabury; Dinky Hocker Shoots Smack, by M. E. Kerr; Lottery in Lives, by J. M. Couper; Leap Before You Look, by Mary Stolz; Pistol, by Adrienne Richard; No More Trains to Tottenville, by Hope Campbell.

   Richard Peck is author of Don't Look and It Won't Hurt and Dreamland Lake, both published by Holt Rinehart & Winston.

64. "INCREASING CHILDREN'S FANTASIES: HOLD HIGH THE CARDBOARD SWORD," by Jean T. Freyberg. Psychology Today (February 1975), 63-4.

    Ms. Freyberg discusses the adult (parent or educator) serving as catalyst to a child's imagination. She believes that imaginative play can provide gains in attention span, self control, and in the ability to interact and communicate with other children. She believes that imaginative play is important to older children, but is particularly so to the child under six. She recommends storytelling as one of the tools, along with pretend games, changing voices, role playing, etc.

65. INFORMATION CENTER ON CHILDREN'S CULTURES, 331 East 38th St. New York, N.Y. 10016. Write for lists and materials on various cultures including: Africa: an annotated list of printed materials suitable for children, and Latin America.

66. THE INNER WORLD OF CHILDHOOD, A STUDY IN ANALYTICAL PSYCHOLOGY, by Frances G. Wickes. Introduction by Carl Jung. Rev. ed. New York: Appleton Century Croft, 1966.

    Influences of parental difficulties upon the child are delineated, among other things. Thoughts and feelings in the child develop slowly. Children remain creatures of sensation and intuition for some time, while weaving for themselves strange explanations of the discovered world. The child doesn't understand the parental problems but intuits strength, courage, honesty, or fears and cowardice from them.

    Warning is given that no child should be allowed to fail continuously. Also, adults are warned against the misuse of love: "Childhood is life, not preparation for life."

    Adolescence is cited as a marked stage in a person's development. Teens should be left free to find their own life and comrades, leading them to the understanding that modern world problems are their responsibility. Adults should be ready with standards, values and some place where the unknown can be weighed and appraised.

    Presented is an interesting thought about homosexuality--that the practice results from an overemphasis on a normal desire, which has been thwarted in its attempts to find true and natural expression.

A complex book, but well worth the struggle to interpret and understand.

67. INTERRACIAL BOOKS FOR CHILDREN. Published by Council on Interracial Books for Children, 1841 Broadway, New York, N.Y. 10023.

Studies, articles, listings, commentaries on racism, sexism and other issues affecting children's book publishing. The Council, in association with the Foundation for Change, now sells reprints, packets, lesson plans, etc. Some special issues of the Bulletin are available in reprint. Of particular interest are Volume 7, Nos. 2 & 3, Asian Americans in Children's Literature; and Volume 7, No. 6, Ageism in Children's Books.

68. "IS TOMORROW A FOUR-LETTER WORD?" by Jean Karl. School Media Quarterly (Winter 1973), 104-110.

A discussion of realism in children's materials, in which Ms. Karl proclaims that elements of realism exist in some of the earliest children's publications. She discusses such materials as Jingling ABC's, published in 1826, The Poor Little Rich Girl, David Copperfield, Railway Children, Linnet on the Threshold, and The Hundred Dresses. She says that these titles and others were forerunners in presenting the unpleasant side of life, as well as the good things. Authors write in a specific time, she says, and their books in one way or another represent the spirit of that time.

Books recently published which she believes present problems and symbols of our times are: A Nice Fire and Some Moonpennies; In the Night Kitchen; The Planet of Junior Brown, and His Own Where.

The article concludes by indicating that although adults write for children, children are free to accept or reject what they are given.

69. ISSUES IN CHILDREN'S BOOK SELECTION: a School Library Journal/Library Journal Anthology, with an introduction by Lillian Gerhardt. New York: Bowker, 1973.

Twenty-nine articles on subjects applying to selection of children's books. Following are notes on selected articles.

"Moral Values and Children's Literature," by Dorothy Broderick, presents notes from Lawrence Kolberg's theories on how children absorb moral values. Ms. Broderick suggests that such theories might have implications in evaluating children's books.

Several articles on minority images include recommendations and criticisms of titles. Authors include June Jordan, Mavis Wormley Davis, Dr. Kenneth Goodman, and Ray Mickinock.

"Sexuality in Children's Books" is discussed by Josette Frank and Barbara Wersba. Titles mentioned positively are: I'll Get There: It Better Be Worth the Trip, by John Donovan, and Up a Road Slowly, by Irene Hunt.

"The Maturation of the Junior Novel from Gestation to the Pill" considers such novels as Too Bad about the Haines Girl, by Zoa Sherburne, which applys the common formula for teen novels; Mr. and Mrs. Bo Jo Jones, by Ann Head, and My Darling, My Hamburger, by Paul Zindel. The author feels that new books do not reflect the new adolescent culture, but the same old ideas, against a new backdrop.

70. LABOR IN AMERICA, by Foster Rhea Dulles. 3rd rev. ed. New York: Crowell, 1968.

71. LALUZ, NATIONAL REVIEW OF LALUZ. Subscription Dept., 360 S. Monroe, Denver, Colorado 80209.

This magazine publishes articles about and for the Spanish-speaking. In the March-April, 1975 issue, articles and criteria are reprinted from The Interracial Book Council. Also in this issue, a column called "Minority Review of Books" is announced. Publishers and reviewers are encouraged to send information, notices and books to be reviewed.

72. LATIN AMERICA: AN ANNOTATED LIST OF MATERIALS FOR CHILDREN. Selected by a committee of librarians, teachers, and Latin American specialists, in cooperation with the Center for Inter-American Relations. Published by the Information Center on Children's Cultures-U.S. Committee for Unicef, 1969.

Recommended and rejected materials are both included. Latin America, Central America, Panama and

Mexico, and the Caribbean Islands are assessed in terms of representative materials for children.

Addresses of publishers and dealers, including some listings from minority and foreign publishers and booksellers, are given in an appendix.

73. "LEST WE FORGET: BOOKS ON THE HOLOCAUST," by Sara Farkas. School Library Journal (May 1975), 37-38.

Books for children from fourth grade to high school concerning the period of history in which the Nazis aimed at the mass destruction of Jews. Some titles listed are discussed in this text under the subjects "Religion and Politics" and "War and Peace."

74. LITERATURE FOR ADOLESCENTS, SELECTION AND USE, ed. by Richard A. Meade and Robert C. Small, Jr. Chicago: Merrill, 1973.

A collection of articles designed to serve as a text for the study of adolescent materials. Some of the articles deal directly with book materials, others serve to challenge the reader to think seriously about this area of literature. One article from each section has been selected for comment, to give an impression of the overall value of this volume and also because of the ideas related to previous chapters.

From Section I--"Literature and the Schools," by Arthur Daigon. The author examines the processes of literature study in classrooms, suggesting that in general, little of worth happens to the student for the following reasons: 1) Students can only become sensitive to literature if the protagonist is sensitive to the "stuff of their students" and somehow bring them together. 2) Students follow the pattern presented by many teachers, of being only concerned with what will be required in the future, rather than with reading for appreciation and insight. 3) Promoters of reading are often not well read; they struggle to push a product which they reject themselves. 4) Materials are forced on passive, unimpressed students under the guise of exposure. This kind of negative exposure may serve to make students reject reading rather than learn from it. 5) Literature teachers have to be able to show the adolescent the relatedness of materials taught (even classics) to the world as they know and understand it. Daigon further analyzes the study of literature and concludes that literature and the human experience are in no way separate. It is the literature teacher's effectiveness in aiding young people in participating in (experiencing) a variety of human experiences and learning from them that will make these classes more successful.

From Section II--"Literature for Adolescents: Pap or Protein?" by Frank G. Jennings. Jennings concludes that most of the materials which fall into the category of the junior novel and are on popular reading lists for this group are not worthwhile, because they fail to challenge young people to think and grow. He feels that most of these books are false in their presentation of the realities of living. They are written in a manner to be absorbed and digested rather than dealt with critically. Jennings agrees that most of the writing is clear and in familiar language, but content, style, and consequential plots are lacking. It is easy, he says, for anyone to do a good cheap selling job and to elicit a response, "that's a good book." A teacher can make a very dull and uninteresting story come alive. This aliveness is often far beyond the scope of the material itself. Teachers must assume a more active role as critics of children's literature.

Jennings describes many career books as "two-dimensional cutouts masquerading as characters." He looks critically at animal stories, mysteries and love stories, and suggests that they are like cookie cutouts in their similarity of theme and approach. "Sex never rears its curly head in these antiseptic volumes," he proclaims; the adolescent is left with syrupy narratives and "faint-hearted" portrayals of misunderstandings between father and son and mother and daughter. He suggests that the adolescent wants to know what it is like to hope and fail, to suffer, to die and to love wastefully, and concludes that reading is the source of much that insures the humanizing of the world.

Section III--"For Everything There Is a Season," by G. Robert Carlsen. Mr. Carlsen concludes that most English Literature courses have not produced avid readers; rather, in many cases, they have turned the adolescent from reading for life. He suggests that among the reasons for this is teachers' general lack of acquaintance with the themes with which young people are concerned. He believes that adolescents find satisfaction in books written especially for them. Carlsen recommends books by authors such as John Tunis, Ann

Emery, Mary Stolz, Adrien Stoutenberg, Margaret Maize Craig and James Kjelgaard as a beginning, with the popular adult novel as the next step. Following this will come an appreciation of the classics, but not too long before full maturity. Each generation, he says, has literary idols, found first by college students and then filtering back to high school. Young people reject books because of their lack of content on the human experience; they are not interested in aesthetic value and subtle implications. When asked why they like a book, in general the response has to do with what the book is about, not with the way it is written.

The content areas which Carlsen feels are important are: a) The search--books in which individuals are looking for direction in their lives; b) Problems of the social order--books that deal with social injustices, economic deprivation and political tyranny; c) The bizarre, the offbeat, the unusual human experience--dealing with the fringes of human life; d) The transition-- the movement of the adolescent into adult life. Titles are suggested for each of the four areas, as follows:

THE SEARCH: Catcher in the Rye; The Razor's Edge; Of Human Bondage; A Burnt-out Case; April Morning; A Separate Peace.

PROBLEMS OF THE SOCIAL ORDER: Advise and Consent; Black Like Me; Fail Safe; The Ugly American; 1984; To Kill a Mockingbird.

THE BIZARRE, THE OFF BEAT, THE UNUSUAL IN THE HUMAN EXPERIENCE: Metamorphosis; The Loved One; The Secret Sharer; The Nun's Story; Crime and Punishment.

THE TRANSITION: Sarah; Maggie; Arrowsmith; Of Human Bondage; Great Expectations; The Way of All Flesh; Joy in the Morning.

Section IV. This author surveyed librarians and teachers for titles which they considered popular and well-written for this age group. She then applied criteria for writing fiction upon which recognized critics agree. From a list of thirty titles, 16 qualified as good literature. The findings were as follows:

GOOD LITERATURE:

Brink	Caddie Woodlawn
Bro	Sarah
Caudill	Tree of Freedom
Chute	The Innocent Wayfaring

210 / Survival Themes

Chute	The Wonderful Winter
Clark	Santiago
Edmonds	Wilderness Clearing
Forbes	Johnny Tremain
Gray	Adam of the Road
James	Smoky the Cow Horse
Knight	Lassie Come Home
Krumgold	And Now Miguel
Rawlings	The Yearling
Richter	The Light in the Forest
Street	Goodbye My Lady
Walker	Winter Wheat

MARGINAL:

Annixter	Swiftwater
Benary Isbert	The Ark
Cavanna	Going on Sixteen
Daly	Seventeenth Summer
Fuller	The Loon Feather
Gipson	Old Yeller
Medearis	Big Doc's Girl
O'Hara	My Friend Flicka
Seredy	The Chestry Oak
Ullman	Banner in the Sky
Yates	Patterns on the Wall

NON LITERATURE:

Catton	Banners of Shenandoah
Kelly	The Trumpeter of Krakow
O'Hara	Thunderhead
Stolz	Ready or Not
Stuart	Hie to the Hunters

Section V--"Literature for the Average Student," by Robert Miles. Miles makes a plea for literature and courses designed for the average student. He asserts that much attention has been given to the gifted student and to the "culturally deprived" but that the average student has been forgotten. He suggests that the materials must have the following qualities: be intelligible to the student; be within the range of the student's maturity; be pleasurable; be emotionally and intellectually significant, not just stimulating superficial teen-age concerns. Titles suggested are:

West Side Story; The Light in the Forest; The Call

of the Wild; A Raisin in the Sun; Inherit the Wind; Of Mice and Men; The Caine Mutiny; Adventures of Huckleberry Finn; The Ox-Bow Incident; Crash Club; Black Like Me; Babbitt; Death of a Salesman; The Hidden Persuaders; The Jungle; The Rabbit Trap; Thunder on Sycamore Street and Black Boy.

Section VI consists of one article--"What Does Research Reveal about Attitudes toward Reading?" by James R. Squire. Attitudes, situations, economics, race, place, age and quality of the material all affect reading. Squire points out some of the research which may be of value to those involved in planning literature curricula. Also included is research regarding the effect and effectiveness of literature for the young adult.

75. THE LIVES OF CHILDREN: THE STORY OF THE 1ST STREET SCHOOL by George Dennison. New York: Random House, 1969.

Difficulties in the schooling of children are explained in this book. Disasters resulting from "grouping" are noted. One interesting comment is made about the use of books; "We own a lot, although there are few that aren't racist, judgmental, stupid, or irrelevant."

76. "LOVE AND POWER: THE PSYCHOLOGICAL SIGNALS OF WAR," by David McClelland. Psychology Today 8:8 (January 1975), 44-48.

McClelland makes associations between love and power as manifested in literature and national movements as clues to national appetites for war.

His research points to the fact that war may be predictable. Conclusions were drawn from collecting motivational data from the literature of England and the United States for several years. Findings were that when "the need for power is high, and higher than the need for affiliation, war tends to result about ten years later."

Reform movements promote wars, which open up the door for subsequent reforms.

Children's stories were collected from around the world and scanned for motivational content. In one country, stories emphasized achievement. In another country, the same tale would be used to show the fun in cooperation or working together. The same story in another country would emphasize the power need, making the child the hero or leader. Findings convinced researchers that materials like children's stories reflect the motivational tendencies of a nation.

A chart is presented for the period from 1785 to 1965, showing the correlation between need for power (when greater than need for affiliation), social reform, and actual war and peace.

77. MENTAL HEALTH. The Hartford Courant, Hartford Connecticut 06115.
    Free pamphlet containing information on current adolescent sexual attitudes and other topics such as violence in cities.

78. "A MINORITY NOBODY KNOWS," by Helen Rowan. The Atlantic (June 1967), 47-52.
    Problems regarding Mexican Americans.

79. MINORITY PROBLEMS: A TEXTBOOK OF READINGS IN INTERGROUP RELATIONS, ed. by Arnold Rose and Caroline B. Rose. New York: Harper and Row, 1965.
    A large volume of essays and articles on minority problems. Through these articles, racial tensions can be traced historically and socially.

80. MONTESSORI, A MODERN APPROACH, by Paula Polk Lillard. New York: Schocken Books, 1972.
    An analysis of Montessori theory and programming.

81. THE MORAL JUDGEMENT OF THE CHILD, by Jean Piaget and seven collaborators. Translated by Marjorie Gabain. New York: Free Press, 1932.

82. MULTI-ETHNIC MEDIA, SELECTED BIBLIOGRAPHIES IN PRINT, by David Cohen, Coordinator Task Force on Ethnic Materials Information Exchange, Social Responsibilities Roundtable. Chicago: ALA, Office of Services to the Disadvantaged, 1975.
    An annotated listing of bibliographies and articles covering several ethnic groups. A very useful listing for those seeking ethnic image materials. Several

other listings are available through the Office of Service to the Disadvantaged, American Library Association.

83. MYTHS, REALITY AND SHADES OF GRAY: WHAT WE KNOW AND DON'T KNOW ABOUT SEX DIFFERENCES, by Eleanor Emmons Maccoby and Carol Nagy Jacklin. Psychology Today 8:7 (December 1974), 109-112.

   The authors deal with some of the prominent sex stereotypes still perpetuated in books and other media. Some of the myths are: girls are more social than boys, girls have lower self esteem than boys, girls lack motivation to achieve, girls are better at rote learning and simple repetitive tasks. Boys are better at high-level tasks that require them to inhibit previously learned responses, boys are more analytic than girls. Girls are more affected by heredity and boys by environment; girls are auditory and boys are visual.

   Differences which these researchers feel are fairly well established are: males are more aggressive than females, girls have greater verbal ability than boys, boys excel in visual-spatial ability, boys excel in mathematics.

   Some of the questions to which answers are still ambiguous are: Are there differences in tactile sensitivity? Are there differences in fear, timidity and anxiety? Is one sex more competitive than the other? Is one sex more compliant than the other? Are females more passive than males?

   The authors conclude that sex myths will disappear as more evidence is presented to refute them.

84. "A NEW LIST OF BOOKS FOR FREE CHILDREN," Ms. Magazine, 5:3 (Sept. 1976), 95-97.

   The list includes recommended titles "reflecting new values and rejecting old stereotypes." The books were reviewed by readers ranging in ages from 10 to 36. (Order for 25 cents and self-addressed envelope from: Books for Free Children, Ms. Magazine, 370 Lexington Ave., New York, N.Y. 10017.

85. A NEW LOOK AT CHILDREN'S LITERATURE, by William Anderson and Patrick Groff; with a bibliography

compiled by Ruth Robinson. Belmont, Calif.: Wadsworth, 1972.

86. "OUR FOREBEARS MADE CHILDHOOD A NIGHTMARE," by Lloyd Demause. Psychology Today (April 1975), 85-88.
   Article about the historical treatment of children. Noted are common mistreatments and sexual abuse. The author says that through the study of the history of childhood, adults can gain insights to the personality traits upon which our adult society rests.

87. "THE PLIGHT OF THE NATIVE AMERICAN," by Rey Mickinock. School Library Journal 18 (September 1971), 46-49.
   Notes about the misconceptions, half truths and stereotypes presented in literature about American Indians. Children's books are some of the worst offenders, says Mickinock. For instance: in The Indians Knew, by Tillie S. Pine, hairstyles are incorrectly portrayed by the artist; in Cats for Kansas, by Le Grand Henderson, illustrations are inaccurate, warriors are depicted wearing the bonnets of the chief. He recommends several authors and titles:
   The Battle of Little Bighorn, by Mari Sandoz
   The Horsecatcher, by Mari Sandoz
   These Were the Sioux, by Mari Sandoz
   Half Breed, by Evelyn Lampman
   The Battle of 1000 Slain, by Peter C. Payne (abridged from Our Indian Heritage: Profiles of 12 Great Leaders, published by Chilton)
   The Long Death, by Ralph K. Andrist
   Custer Died for Our Sins, by Vine Deloria, Jr.
   Walk the World's Rim, by Betty Baker
   Killer of Death, by Betty Baker
   Raven's Cry, by Christie Harris
   Once upon a Totem, by Christie Harris
   Our Cup Is Broken, by Florence Means
   Walk in My Moccasins, by Mary Warren
   The Story Catcher, by Mari Sandoz
   When the Legends Die, by Hal Borland
   Little Big Man, by Thomas Berger
   Stay Away Joe, by Dan Bushman (Stay Away Joe Publishers)

88. POWER AND INNOCENCE, A SEARCH FOR THE SOURCES OF VIOLENCE, by Rollo May. New York: Norton, 1972.

89. PREJUDICE AND RACE RELATIONS, ed. with an introduction by Raymond W. Mack. New York: Watts, 1970.
    A series of essays exploring some of the major issues in race relations in this country. Included are an analysis of those physical and anthropological factors affecting race separation, including Jensen's controversial theory of the genetic factor in I.Q.; the reasons for the crisis in our cities as it applies to Blacks and others; the impact of institutions on prejudice; the viewpoints of Black leadership; and a discussion of options pursuant to separatism and to integration.
    Perhaps the concluding sentence of Bayard Rustin's essay sums up the views, questions, speculations and answers presented by the authors: "The very practical choice now before them [public officials] and the American people is whether we shall have a conscious and authentic democratic social revolution or more tragic and futile riots that tear our nation to shreds" (page 266).

90. THE PROOF OF THE PUDDING, by Phyllis Fenner. New York: John Day, 1957.

91. THE PSYCHOLOGY OF THE CHILD, by Jean Piaget and B. Inhelder. Translated by Helen Weaver. New York: Basic Books, 1969.

92. RADICAL PERSPECTIVES ON SOCIAL PROBLEMS: READINGS IN CRITICAL SOCIOLOGY, ed. by Frank Lindenfield. 2nd ed. New York: Macmillan, 1973.
    A series of essays dealing with social problems and human values. Section headings are Social Science and Human Values; Education for What?; Sex and the Family; The City as Social, Physical and Psychological Environment; Obedience, Crime and the Law; Work and Leisure; Poverty and Racial Equality; Power, Economy and the Warfare State; The Mass Society--Politics and Social Change; The New Left--Toward a Radical Ideology; Utopian Practices and Perspectives.

216 / Survival Themes

        The editor indicates that the articles are chosen for the general reader, not for the specialist, in hope that readers will be better able to deal with the social changes in the world around them.
        Of particular interest are the several articles which deal with the subject areas chosen for discussion in the previous chapters, i.e., family, sex, environment, race, and war. As a sample of the inclusions, Barrington Moore, Jr., in an article titled "Thoughts on the Future Family," hypothesizes the coming of an institutional bureaucratic system of child rearing, replacing the former unit family. An article by A. S. Summerhill discusses freedom for children, in getting an education, establishing values, etc. Melford Spiro offers an analysis of the formation of the kibbutz, including information about child care, family structure and education.

93. REACHING CHILDREN AND YOUNG PEOPLE THROUGH LITERATURE, ed. by Helen Painter. Kent, Ohio: Kent State University, International Reading Association.
        Articles, mostly based on papers presented at a convention of the International Reading Association in May 1970.

94. READING LADDERS FOR HUMAN RELATIONS, by Virginia M. Reid. 5th ed. Washington, D.C.: American Council on Education, 1972.
        List of titles pertinent to human relations, and how to use them.

95. "REVIEWING IN AN AGE OF CHANGE," by Peggy Sullivan. Top of the News (April 1973), 235-238.
        A discussion of the reviewing of teen-age novels for today's readers and selectors. Should reviewers quote passages and words, Sullivan asks, which may be considered controversial, in order to alert those who use reviews as a measure for purchase. She believes that such titles do belong in libraries but that librarians have a special responsibility to publicize the very different content of teen-age books today and to assist parents and other adults in realizing this so that they are not shocked by the contents of new books for the young.

96. "THE ROLE OF THE FEMALE IN CHILDREN'S BOOKS
--DISPELLING ALL DOUBTS," by Mary Ritchie Key.
<u>Wilson Library Bulletin</u> 46:2 (October 1971), 167-175.

97. THE RUNAWAY GENERATION, by Bibi Wein. New
York: David McKay, 1970.
    Includes interviews with young people aged 12-16 who ran away from home. The young people speak frankly about their lives and families, the use of drugs, and their feelings about sex and school.
    The homes of these children were not all broken or outwardly unhappy, but the children still had feelings of tension. Some did not blame their parents at all but said they left home because they felt bad most of the time, and that drugs helped them to feel better. One young man reported that the use of drugs and later going straight had helped him. For the first time he could confront his parents about his feelings and needs. In the appendix, Ms. Wein synthesizes the interviews under subject categories.
    School: She found the militant dopers and runaways ready to talk about school, but the hippies and street kids considered school irrelevant. Most of them felt that they were getting nothing out of school--even the good students felt this way. Many reported having enjoyed school in the elementary grades but felt it got increasingly boring.
    Personal Experiences and Attitudes: Many could recall some one good thing that had happened to them, but many also felt that nothing good had ever happened. Some wanted to change superficial things about themselves, especially looks in the case of the girls. Other things they mentioned that they would like to change were memory, bad temper and intolerance. The change in the world most often wanted was peace. They also commonly reported their feeling that the American dream was a myth.
    Politics: The interviewing began in Summer 1968, after the death of President Kennedy. Probably because of their disillusionment, most of them expressed little interest in politics, the civil rights movement or peace demonstrations.
    Religion: The young people generally rejected the term religion, but responded to "God," "spirit" and "soul." Religion was generally defined as a deep belief in man.

Freedom: Most of the young people had no definition of freedom, particularly in terms of themselves.

Culture: Most of them did not read and had little respect for the written word, although some reported interest in such titles as <u>Summerhill</u> and <u>The Autobiography of Malcolm X</u>. Music and radio were the prominent media in their lives.

Drugs: The majority reported having used drugs. In answering how drugs had affected their lives, many said that they used them just for the feeling or the "high." Most of them "turned on" socially. It appeared that only the hard dopers turned on alone. Most did not feel that everyone should use drugs, and many still felt that dope was bad. Almost all reported someone that they knew who had had a bad experience with dope.

Sex: Attitudes about sex had been primarily influenced by their friends. They had learned little from their parents. The boys had broader experiences than the girls. There was consistency in the thought that sex should be combined with a meaningful relationship.

Parents: Evidence of complete alienation was apparent in conversations about parents. Most of the young people simply did not want to talk about them. There seemed to be more sympathy for mothers than for fathers, and almost all felt that their parents were unhappy. Many wanted to have families of their own, but felt that they would have more openness and communication with their children than their parents had with them.

98. "THE SCHOOL AS SURROGATE CONSCIENCE," by Henry Steele Commager. <u>Saturday Review</u> (January 11, 1975), 54-57.

Commager notes ills of the society as they relate to the educational system. He states that the changes in the educational process in America came so fast that the system has not been able to keep up with them.

He implies that schools have been asked to perform a miracle, in that they are expected to help young people to understand the world when we have developed such a complex society that none of our institutions are sure of their direction.

He offers as a solution the enlistment of all educational agencies in an enterprise of education that shall "embrace the whole society."

Sources and Notes / 219

99. THE SECRET OF CHILDHOOD, by Maria Montessori. Translated and ed. by Barbara Barclay Carter. New York: Ballantine, 1972.

100. SELECTED MEDIA ABOUT THE AMERICAN INDIAN FOR CHILDREN, K-3, by Suzanne S. Cane, Carol A. Chatfield, Margaret C. Holmes and Christine C. Peterson. Department of Education, Division of Curriculum and Instruction, Bureau of Curriculum Innovation. Commonwealth of Massachusetts. 8M 1-71-048585. December 1970.

    Although all of the compilers of this list are admittedly non-Indians, they indicate in the foreword that they did a lot of research and studying to prepare this listing. The list is prefaced with comments by W. W. Keeler, Principal Chief of the Cherokee Nation.

    This is an annotated listing, directed toward teachers, but could be helpful to anyone seeking positive materials about American Indians. As indicated in the title, the selections, including books and other media, are directed to the very young child. Background reading for the adult, a list of additional sources and bibliographies and a list of publishers and addresses are included.

101. "SEX, SOCIETY AND THE FEMALE DILEMMA: A DIALOGUE BETWEEN SIMONE DE BEAUVOIR AND BETTY FRIEDAN," Saturday Review (June 14, 1975), 12.

    This and other articles on the role of women are included in this special issue marking International Women's Year.

102. SEXISM AND YOUTH, ed. by Diane Gersoni-Stavn. New York: Bowker, 1974.

    Includes articles from various publications which amplify problems of sexist roles in literature. Examples are: "Negative image of women in children's literature," by Dan Dolan, reprinted from Elementary English, April 1972; "Women in children's literature," by Aileen Face Nilson, reprinted from College English, May 1971; "Sex-role socialization in picture books," reprinted from the American Journal of Sociology, May 1972; and "Someday my prince will come," by

Marcia R. Lieberman, reprinted from College English, December 1972.

103. SEXISM IN AWARD-WINNING PICTURE BOOKS, by Suzanne M. Czaplinski. Pittsburgh: Know, Inc., 1973.

Survey and analysis of some award-winning picture books with sexist implications. Charts and graphs show the periods of history in which more materials portraying females in text and pictures were published. Examples of sexist titles are noted. Also listed are books showing equal treatment of the sexes. In conclusion the author suggests that children do absorb attitudes from books and stories.

104. THE SEXUAL ADOLESCENT: COMMUNICATING WITH TEENAGERS ABOUT SEX, by Sol Gordon. Belmont, Calif.: Wadsworth, 1973.

105. "SEXUAL STEREOTYPES START EARLY," by Florence Howe. Pittsburgh: Know, Inc., n.d.

Available for purchase for forty cents, this article outlines the problems of sex role identification.

106. STARTING OUT RIGHT: CHOOSING BOOKS ABOUT BLACK PEOPLE FOR YOUNG CHILDREN, PRESCHOOL THROUGH THIRD GRADE, ed. by Bettye Latimer. Washington, D.C.: Day Care and Child Development Council of America, 1972.

The authors of this title offer four chapters at the beginning giving reasons and background for the listing. Chapter I, "The Child's Book World: From Segregation to Token Integration," presents information regarding the historical gap in the production of materials by and about Blacks. Chapter II, "Criteria for Judging Books Involving Black People," asks the following questions: Is the book written from the Black perspective? What dimensions of Blackness are included? Does the author deal responsibly with the issues? Are the Black characters portrayed as human beings? Are the characters recognizably Black?

Chapter III, "Syndrome Patterns in Books Involving Black People," suggests avoiding the following syndromes: Romantic syndrome--glorifying situations on the one hand and ignoring or glossing over realities on the other. Avoidance syndrome--a denial of the harsh circumstances which have affected Blacks. Bootstrap syndrome--virtue brings reward. Oasis syndrome--the token Black in a sea of whites, as is particularly evident in picture books. Ostrich in the sand syndrome--dealing flirtatiously with issues of racism and injustice.

Chapter IV, "Bright April: A Critique of a Classic," examines this title in the light of the foregoing items, and concludes that the book should not be recommended.

Some of the titles on this list could be considered for "Images." Others fall into one or more of our selected categories:

> All About Us (views of the world, feelings)
> The Big Pile of Dirt (celebration)
> Bronzeville Boys and Girls (celebration)
> City Rhythms (celebration)
> Families Live Together (groupings, families)
> Father Is Big (families)
> Goggles (groupings, pairings)
> Hooray for Jasper (families)
> Hush Jon (families)
> Josephina February (families)
> People Are Important (views of the world)
> Playtime in Africa (views of the world, joy, celebration)
> A Ride on High (groupings)
> Sam (families, feelings)
> Sia Lives on Kilimanjaro (views of the world, families)
> Sunflowers for Tina (celebration, families)
> Sweet Pea (families, communities)
> This Is the Way (religions)
> This Is the World (views of the world)
> Where Does the Day Go (celebration)
> Your Hand in Mine (fear, loneliness)

107. SUFFER LITTLE CHILDREN: REFLECTIONS ON AMERICAN EDUCATION, by Max Rafferty. New York: Devin-Adair, 1962.

The author deals with what he calls the "era of nonsense," in which we rationalize with worn out theories of life adjustment and socialization when actually we are in a race for our lives.

108. TEXTBOOKS AND THE AMERICAN INDIAN, ed. by Jeanette Henry. Indianapolis: Indian Historical Society, 1970.
   Gives criteria for judging textbooks about the American Indian, with consideration given to cultural validity, contributions, etc.

109. "THAT'S ONE GOOD INDIAN: UNACCEPTABLE IMAGES IN CHILDREN'S NOVELS," by Laura Herbst. Top of the News 31:2 (January 1975), 192-198.
   The author discusses the stereotyped images of Indians presented in children's books. Not only is the individual stereotyped but the culture is presented in a negative way. The following titles are listed as unacceptable because of the depiction of white superiority in relation to Indian characters; lack of respect for Indian culture; and the presentation of the Indian as inferior or childish.
   Blood Brothers (Doris Anderson)
   Wagon Scout (Jane and Paul Annixter)
   Do Not Annoy the Indians (Betty Baker)
   O Children of the Wind and Pines (Laura Nelson Baker)
   The Sea Pair (Patricia Beatty)
   Squaw Dog (Patricia Beatty)
   Caddie Woodlawn (Carol Brink)
   Eagle Feather (Clyde Bulla)
   Riding the Pony Express (Clyde Bulla)
   Children of the Covered Wagon (Mary Jane Carr)
   Young Mac of Fort Vancouver (Mary Jane Carr)
   Medicine Man's Daughter (Ann Clark Nolan)
   Golden Horseshoe (Elizabeth Coatsworth)
   Indian Mound Farm (Elizabeth Coatsworth)
   Daniel Boone (James Daugherty)
   The Matchlock Gun (Walter D. Edmonds)
   Buffalo Trace (Virginia Eifert)
   Awani (Mary Jane Foltz)
   Kit Carson: Trail Blazer and Scout (Shannon Garst)
   Trading Post Girl (Lynne Gesner)
   Marie Tangle Hair (Dorothy Heiderstadt)
   The Burning Glass (Annabel and Edgar Johnson)
   Rifles for Watie (Harold Keith)
   Cayuse Courage (Evelyn Sibley Lampman)
   Navaho Sister (Evelyn Sibley Lampman)
   River Dragon (Daniel Carl Lane)

<u>They Were Strong and Good</u> (Robert Lawson)
<u>Bayou Suzette</u> (Lois Lenski)
<u>Valley of the Hawk</u> (Ruth Loomis)
<u>Captured by the Abnakis</u> (Clement Philbrook)
<u>The Buffalo Box</u> (Janet Randall)
<u>White Thunder</u> (Nancy Sharmack)
<u>Bear Teeth for Courage</u> (Florence D. Scull)
<u>Buffalo Knife</u> (William Steele)
<u>Flaming Arrows</u> (William Steele)
<u>Year of the Bloody Seven</u> (William Steele)
<u>The Apache Gold Mystery</u> (Eileen Thompson)
<u>Walk in My Moccasins</u> (Mary Warren)
<u>Little House on the Prairie</u> (Laura Ingalls Wilder)

110. TODAY'S WORLD. Bulletin 19a. Washington, D.C.: Association for Childhood Education International, 1967.

Seven authors write from various viewpoints about the child in today's world. Problems included are:

"Five Revolutions in American Life," by Max Lerner, discusses trends, technology, cultural changes, etc. as they may affect the child's development.

"Helping the Child's Heart and World," by Paul L. Adams, details issues of the society which affect the psychiatrist's approach to children--poverty and affluence, war and peace, segregation and integration, and changes in family. Adams suggests that at the same time that psychiatrists are trying to learn more about affecting change in children, they must also try to change the society in which children live.

"For Every Child: Health," by Brock Chisholm, says that health, after World War II, is defined as applying to a person's whole being.

"Nutritional Well-Being: Our Goal for All Children," by Elizabeth D. Munves, deals with problems of children's well-being, internationally, as based on nutritional balances or deficiencies.

"Essential Conditions in the Development of Self," by Charles Moustakas, discusses the evidence of creative energies and the expression of self which exists even in the newborn child. Elements such as confirmation, belonging and being are discussed in relation to the adult's responsibility to provide resources for the child's positive development in these areas.

"Some Recent Concepts of the Physical Growth of Children," by Frances E. Johnston, discusses hereditary and environmental influences on the child's growth.

"To Every Man a Chance," by Gertrude Noar, says that chances for children and democracy lie in education and in the involvement of children in decision-making.

111. THE TRAGIC MODE IN CHILDREN'S LITERATURE, by Carolyn Kingston. New York: Teachers College Press, 1974.

The author takes a look at novels which offer views of tragedy. Over 50 titles are included.

112. THE UNRELUCTANT YEARS, by Lillian Smith. New York: Viking, 1953.

113. "VERA AND BILL CLEAVER KNOW THEIR WHYS AND WHEREFORES," by Patricia J. Cianciolo. Top of the News 32:4 (June 1976), 338-350.

Ms. Cianciolo discusses writings by this excellent writing team and concludes that theirs are among the best novels dealing with the realities of the human situation for young people. These two authors have the talent to include knowledge and sensitivity about the human condition in stories which still are pleasurable reading. Titles discussed are: The Mock Revolt, Delpha Green and Company, Where the Lilies Bloom, The Mimosa Tree, Grover, Me Too, Ellen Grae, I Would Rather Be a Turnip, The Why's and Wherefores of Littlebelle Lee and Dust of the Earth.

114. WE CAN CHANGE IT, by Susan Shargel & Irene Kane. Change for Children, 2588 Mission St., Rm. 226, San Francisco, California 94110.

After spending some time working with teachers and parents developing methods for approaching non-racist and non-sexist education, the authors developed this list. After the bibliography for children, some background materials for adults are included, along with a list of alternative publishers. Notes concerning "adult intervention" and "classroom situations" are added, with the suggestion that the books alone will not accomplish desired ends, but materials must be accompanied by appropriate adult "role models" and adult child interplay.

This group has also published a photo-packet of "Women at Work" in atypical jobs.

115. "WHAT IS REAL? ASKED THE RABBIT ONE DAY," by Patricia Merla. Saturday Review (November 4, 1972), 43-50.

The author surveys some recent materials for children and contrasts them with some popular items written for adults, concluding that the trend is toward stark realism in children's books while adults are turning to fantasy. She analyzes several titles, indicating their plots and the reasons for interest in these subjects. She concludes that young and old are reading the "strangest books" because their real question is "What is real?"

For a more extensive bibliography readers should send a self-addressed envelope to Fantasy/Reality Bibliography, Saturday Review of the Arts, 450 Pacific Avenue, San Francisco, Ca. 94133.

116. WRITTEN FOR CHILDREN, AN OUTLINE OF ENGLISH-LANGUAGE CHILDREN'S LITERATURE, by John R. Townsend. Philadelphia: Lippincott, 1974.

Brief readable critical survey of the developments in English fiction for children from early times to date. Many personal notes about early authors are included.

In the chapter called "Looking Forward," Townsend states that he can't worry about children reading only what we consider good literature, but he challenges adults to offer children better materials.

117. YOUR CHILD'S READING TODAY, by Josette Frank. New and rev. ed. New York: Doubleday, 1969.

Comments, suggestions and analysis of problems in writing and selecting materials for children in the modern world.

Part I, "Parents, Children and Books," discusses problems such as conflicts between media and reading, how to help motivate children to read, and gives suggestions for selecting or determining a good book.

Part II, "What Do Children Like to Read?"

suggests for preschoolers, picture books portraying the real world. For first readers, fantasy, animal stories, fairy and folk tales. For the busy boys and girls aged 8-12, adventure, people and events or the past, horses, cowboys, etc.

INDEX

Abbot, Sidney and Barbara Love 75
Abby (adoption) 121
Abby Takes Over (humor) 175
Abe Lincoln Grows Up 20
Abortion 70
Abortion Facility Inventory 71
About Sex [film] 66
Across Five Aprils 172
Adams, Paul L. 223
Adam's World: San Francisco (Black family) 121
Adell, Judith 201
Adoff, Arnold 177
Adventures of Obadiah (Quakers) 147
Adventures of Samboe, The 14
Adventures of Tom Sawyer, The 17
Aesop's Fables 6
Age of Enlightenment, The 10
Age of Reason, The 7
Ahlum, Carol 200
Albert Schweitzer, People of Destiny Series (peace) 171
Alcott, Louisa May 17
Aldrich, Thomas Bailey 17
Alexander, Martha 47-48
Alice's Adventures in Wonderland 1, 16
All-of-a-Kind Family, series (Jewish family) 110
All-of-a-Kind Family Uptown (Jewish family) 110
Aloneness (feelings) 29-30
Aloneness and loneliness, "young people speak for themselves" about 28
Alternative, The (communal living) 70
Amblin [film] (sexuality) 67-68
American Friends Service Committee 70
American Indian Authors for Young Readers 186
American Indians see Native Americans
American Labor: The Twentieth Century 186
American Universal Geography 12

Amish Family, An (Amish religion and culture) 138-139
Anaya, Rudolfo A. 41-42
And Jill Came Tumbling After: Sexism in American Education 186
Andersen, Hans Christian 15
Anderson, Lonzo 36
Anderson, William 213
Andy (aloneness) 36-37
Angelita (images, Puerto Rican) 82
Anger 48
Anger and the Rocking Chair: Gestalt Awareness with Children 186
Annie and the Old One (celebration of death) 180
Antonio (feelings, longings) 41
Anything You Want to Be [film] (sex roles) 77
Apt. 3 (celebration of life, tenement) 175
Arbuthnot, May Hill 154, 194
Ardizzone, Edward 38
Are You There God? It's Me, Margaret (religion, peers) 139
Arilla Sundown (images, integrated marriage) 86
Arkin, Alan 38
Arnold, Elliott 143, 155
Arundel, Honor 122
Asia: A Guide to Books for Children 187
"Asian Images--A Message to the Media" 187
Asian novels, list 200
Ask Beth: You Can't Ask Your Mother (sexuality) 64
Ask Me If I Love You Now? (sexuality) 78
At the Back of the North Wind 17
Atomic bomb aftermath 154
Auerbach, Jerold S. 186
Aunt America (politics, iron curtain) 139-140
Authors of children's literature, attitudes toward children 149

Babbitt, Natalie 47, 169
Bad Fall (peers, friendship) 96
Baker, Betty 166
Baker, Elliott 78
Baker, Margaret 115-116
Bang Bang You're Dead (peace) 167
Barbauld, Anne Letitia 11
Bawden, Nina 182-183
Be Nice to Josephine (families) 121-122
Bearcat, The (mining industry, unions) 140
Bear's House, The (families 110

Beaver Pond (ecology) 128-129
Becoming Partners: Marriage and Its Alternatives 70
Being There (political satire) 140
Bemelmans, Ludwig 177
Benjie on His Own (feelings) 46
Bereaud, Susan 186
Berenstain, Stan and Jan 84
Besant, Mrs. 16
Best in Children's Books, 1966-72, The 187
Better Than the Birds, Smarter Than the Bees (sexuality) 64
Big Blue Island (ecology) 129
Bingham, June M. 189
Biography, criticism of 187
"Biography: The Bad and the Bountiful" 187
Bird, Caroline 76
Birthday Wish, The (friends) 104
Bishop Claire Huchet 151
Bitter Cry of Children, The 18, 188
"Bizarre in Children's Books, The" 188
Black American in Books for Children, The 188
Black Beauty 17
Black Books Bulletin 188
Black Sheep (peace) 171
Blacks
   books for preschool children, list 221
   distorted images of 79
   portrayal of in literature 80, 188
   positive images of 83-89
   selecting books about 220-221
Blake, William 12
Blanzaco, M. D. 74
Bless Me, Ultima (feelings, Mexican-American family) 41-42
Bless the Beasts and Children (ecology) 129
Bloch, Marie Halun 139-140
Blue, Rose 118
Blue Backed Speller 11
Blue Fairy Book, The 18
Blue Willow 20
Blum, Ralph 77
Blume, Judy 123, 139
Bobbsey Twins, The 2, 19
Bodart, Joni 202
Bodies (sexuality) 61
Bolognese, Don 167
Book for Boys and Girls, A 8
Book of Courtesye 6

230 / Survival Themes

Book of Martyrs 9
Book of Nurture 7
Books (see also Children's book production)
   development of the individual, list 190
   production trends 21
Books, Children and Men 1, 189
"Books for Special Experiences" 189
Books for the Multi-Racial Classroom 189
"Books, Readers and the Individual" 190
Boreman, Thomas 10
Boris (Siege of Leningrad, W. W. II) 162-163
Borland, Hal 87
Born Female: The High Cost of Keeping Women Down 76
Borrowers, The 22
Boss Cat (Black family) 122
Boston Women's Health Collective 76
Boy Who Could Sing Pictures (peace) 171
Boys and Girls, Girls and Boys (celebration of life) 175
Brace, Charles 16
Braden, William 77
Bragdon, Elspeth 35-36
Breasted, Mary 63
Breckenridge, Marian E. 191
Brenner, Barbara 61
Bride Wore Braids, The (sexuality) 78
Bridge of Children's Books 190
Bridges of Understanding 190
British Children's Books in the Twentieth Century 191
Broderick, Dorothy 203, 206
Brooke, Leslie 19
Brooks, Gwendolyn 29-30
Brothers, Dr. Joyce 76
Brothers Systems for Liberated Love and Marriage 76
Brunger-Dhuyvetter, Judy 195
Bubbles (celebration) 175
Bulla, Clyde 134
Bunting, Eve 105
Bunyan, John 8
Burchard, Peter 22
Burnett, Frances Hodgson 18, 19
Burns, Helen 64
Butterfly's Ball, The 14
Byars, Betsy 44, 133

Caines, Jeanette 121
Caldecott, Randolph 17

Call It Courage (aloneness) 30
Calvinism 7
Cameron, Eleanor 200
Campbell, Hope 77
Cane, Suzanne S. 219
Carlsen, G. Robert 208
Carlson, Dale 144
Carlson, Natalie Savage 115
Carlson, Ruth Kearney 199
Carr, Albert Z. 172
Carrick, Carol and Donald 129
Carroll, Lewis 16
Cat Across the Way, The (friends) 104
Caudill, Rebecca 176
Caxton 6
Celebration of death 178
Celebration of life and death 174-183
Ceremony of Innocence (W.W. II) 154-156
"Changing World of the Social Sciences, The" 191
Charlotte's Web 22
   reactions to 40
Chatfield, Carol A. 219
Cheerleader, The (sexuality) 69
Cherniak, Donna and Allan Ferngold 74
Child Development 191
Child development 192
   cognitive structure 192
   egocentrism 192
   friendship 91-94
   intelligence, Piaget's theories on 194
   mental development 192
   peer associations 91-94
   prejudice in 193
   questioning stage 126
   search for meaning 136
   self acceptance 79
   social acceptance 92
   socialization 91-94
   stages of development 192
   testing hypothesis against fact 127
Child Development: Physical and Psychological Development Through Adolescence 191
Child from Five to Ten, The 191
Child from 9 to 13, The Psychology of Preadolescents and Early Puberty, The 191
Child Is Born, A [film series] (sexuality) 65
Child labor 9, 11, 12, 13, 16, 18, 20

Childhood, perceptions of (see also Early Childhood) 2, 196, 204
"Childhood's Island Receives Gift of Myrrh" 148-161
Children (see also Child development)
   and death 179
   and fears 179
   and parents 109
Children and Adolescents, Interpretive Essays on Piaget 192
Children and Books 194
Children and Literature: Views and Reviews 194
Children and Politics 195
Children and Their Literature 149
Children Are People 195
Children Are People: The Librarian in the Community 195
Children's book production 2, 20
Children's Book Week 19
Children's literature
   anti-war statements 151-152
   controversial issues 3, 191, 195
   death, list 199
   distinction from adult literature 5
   historical developments 1-24
   images of females, 82; list 199
   politics 138
   realism, 149, 225; list 205
   sexuality 52, 55, 56
   signals of war 148, 211-212
   survival themes 3
   use of in special situations 189
   values transmitted in 189
Children's Literature, an Issues Approach 109, 122, 195
Children's Literature in the Elementary School 195
Children's Monument in Peace Park 154
Children's questions 127
Child's Conception of the World, The 196
Child's Garden of Verses, A 17
Child's Right to Equal Reading, A 196
"Child's World of the Fictional Deaf, The" 189
Chisholm, Brock 223
Chocolate War, The (gangs, peers) 96-97
Cianciolo, Patricia 224
City in Winter (Black family) 122
City Rhythms (celebration, city) 175
Clarkson, Evan 132
Clearing in the Forest, A (man and environment) 129-130
Cleaver, Vera and Bill 43, 123, 181, 184, 224
Clifton, Lucille 176

Cohen, David 212
Cohen, Miriam 106
Cole, Sheila R. 101
Collier, James L. 64
Come Along (celebration) 176
Commager, Henry Steele 218
"Common schools" 13
"Communal Sex and Communal Survival: Individualism Busts the Commune Boom" 196
Cone, Molly 33, 146
Conspiracy Against Childhood, The 196
Constant, Helen 180-181
Constantine, Harry L. and Joan 70
Cooper, James Fenimore 14
Cooper's History of America 12
Corcoran, Barbara 98, 117
Cormier, Robert 96
Cotton, John 7
"Countering Old Myths" 197
Cowley, Joy 167
Cradle Hymn 9
Crawford, Charles P. 96
Cresswell, Helen 145
Critical Approach to Children's Literature, A (Fenwick) 197
Critical Approach to Children's Literature, A (Smith) 197
Critical Handbook of Children's Literature, A 197
Critical History of Children's Literature, A 151, 197
Crow Boy (aloneness) 37
Cunningham, Julia 42
Czaplinski, Suzanne M. 220

Dag Hammerskjold, People of Destiny Series (peace) 171
Daigon, Arthur 207
Daisy Chain, The 16
Daniels, Joan 186
Danny Rowley (families, second marriage) 110
Darkness over the Land (peace) 173
Dasmann, Raymond F. 198
Davies, Peter 56
Day, Thomas 12
"Decade of Teen Age Reading in Baltimore" 197
Defoe, Daniel 9
DeJong, Meindert 152
DeMause, Lloyd 202, 214
Democracy and Education 18
Dennison, George 211

234 / Survival Themes

Deschooling Society 198
Description of a Great Variety of Animals and Vegetables, A 10
"Developing the Adolescent's Self Concept with Literature" 33
Dewey, John 18, 19
Dialogue of Communicacyon 6
Diamond, Stephen 70
Diary of a Young Girl 172
"Didacticism in New Dress" 189
Different Kind of Country, A 198
Dinky Hocker Shoots Smack (peers, families) 77, 97-98
Disarmament: The Challenge of Civilization (peace) 169
Discussing Death: A Guide to Death Education 198
Divine Emblems 8
Divine Songs 9
Dixon, Paige 181
Dizenzo, Patricia 60, 69
Doctor's Guide to Having an Abortion 72
Dodge, Mary Mapes 16
Dollar Man, The (one parent family) 111
Donovan, John 45
Don't Slam the Door When You Go (peers) 98
Don't You Remember? (celebration) 176
Dorp Dead (feelings, violence) 42
Down the Rabbit Hole 149, 198
Dragonwings (images, Chinese) 82
Dream Watcher, The (loneliness) 30-31
Drug use 217
Duberman, Martin 74
DuBois, William Pène 21
Duck in the Gun (peace) 167
Dulles, Foster Rhea 206
Duvall, Evelyn 67
Dyves Pragmaticus 7

Eakin, Mary K. 191, 200
Early childhood 2, 46
    and education 17
Ecology and environmental problems 128
Eddie's Bear (man and environment) 131
Edge of Next Year, The (families, reaction to death) 112
Edge of Two Worlds (peace) 170
Education, compulsory 15
Eichler, Margrit 177
Elfman, Blossom 57, 72
Elkin, Judith 189

Elkund, David 126, 192
Ellen Grae (feelings) 43
Ellis, Ella Thorp 133
Emblem books 8
Emerging Humanity, Multi-Ethnic Literature for Children and Adolescents 199
Emotions, in literature 39
Endless Steppe: Growing Up in Siberia, The (W.W. II) 140-141, 155
English Fairy Tales 18
English Reformation 6
Enright, Elizabeth 21
"Essential Conditions in the Development of Self" 223
Estanbanico (Black images) 83
Estes, Eleanor 21
Ets, Marie Hall 37, 38
Evans, Marie 37
Explaining Death to Children 199
Eyerly, Jeannette 113
Eyre, Frank 191

Fabulous Histories 11
Factory Acts, England 12, 16
Families 107-124
   American development 108-109
   future 216
   runaways comment on 218
   "young people speak for themselves" about 107
Family Failing, A (families, divorce) 122
Family Game, The 77
Family Under the Bridge, The (families in poverty) 112-113
Farkas, Sara 207
Feelings, "young people speak for themselves" about 39
Fehrenbach, T. R. 169
"Feminist Look at Children's Books, A" 199
Feminist Resources for School and Colleges: A Guide to Curriculum Materials 200
Fenner, Phyllis 215
Fennimore, Flora 33
Fenwick, Sara Innis 197
Fiddler of High Lonesome (peace) 168
Field, Eugene 18
First Snow, The (death) 180-181
Fisher, Peter 75
Fitzhugh, Louise and Sandra Scoppetone 167
"Five Revolutions in American Life" 223

Fly Away Paul (peers, sexuality) 56-57
Fog Comes on Little Pig Feet, The (peers) 98-99
"For Every Child's Health" 223
"For Everything There Is a Season" 208
Forbes, Ester 20
Foreman, Michael 167
Forgotten Majority, The [sound-filmstrip] (women's liberation) 77
Forman, James 144-145, 152-157, 172
Foster, E. C. 130
Foster, Genevieve 20, 21
Fox, Paula 34-35, 99
Foxe, John 9
Frank, Anne 172
Frank, Josette 206, 225
Fratley, Jacqueline M. 200
Free to Be ... You and Me [recording] (sexism) 76
Freyberg, Jean T. 204
Friday Night Is Papa Night (families, Puerto Rican) 122-123
Friedrich (Jews in Nazi Germany) 141
Friend of the Singing One, The (man and environment) 130
Friends, The (peers, families) 99
Friendship, peer pressures 91-106
  "young people speak for themselves" about 95-96
From Primer to Pleasure in Reading 200
From the Mixed Up Files of Mrs. Basil E. Frankweiler 83
Future of the Family, The [filmstrip] 66

Gaeddert, Lou Ann 178
Gag, Wanda 20
Game, The [film] (sexuality) 68
Gandhi, People of Destiny Series (peace) 171
Gangs, behavior and formation 94
Gates, Doris 20
Gay Bibliography, A 74
Gay Crusaders, The 75
Gay Mystique, The 75
Gay World, The 75
Gentle Ben (man and environment) 130
George, Jean Craighead 131-133
George 83
George Washington's World 20
Georgiou, Constantine 149
Gersoni-Stavn, Diane 219
Gesell, Arnold 191
Gifford-Jones, W. 65

Gigantick Histories 10
"Gingerroot and Ginseng Tea: The World of the Asian Novel" 200
Girl Called Al, A 116
Girl Like Me, A (families, adoption, teenage pregnancy) 113
Girls of Huntington House, The (sexuality) 57, 72
Gladys Told Me to Meet Her Here (friendship) 104
Glass Room, The (families) 114
Glimpse of Tiger, A (sexuality) 69
Gloomy Gus (man and environment) 130
Go Ask Alice 121
Goff, Beth 123
"Golden Age" of publishing 19
Goldsmith, Oliver 11
Good Bird, The (peace) 168
Good Books for Children 200
Good Night, Prof. Dear (sexuality) 69
Good Times, Bad Times (homosexuality) 58, 61
Goodbye to the Jungle (families, abandoned children) 123
Goodegon, Laurel 189
Goodwin, Harold 169
Gordon, Sol 220
Gough, John 6
Graham, Lorenz 22
Grahame, Kenneth 19
Green, Diana 172
Green, Wade 169
Green and Burning Tree, The 200
Green and Something Else (feelings, fear) 46
Greene, Bette 157
Greene, Constance 116
Greenfield, Eloise 119, 175
Greenstein, Fred I. 195
Grettir the Strong (feelings, violence) 43
Grifalconi, Ann 175
Grimm's Fairy Tales 14
Groff, Patrick 187, 189, 213
Grollman, Earl R. 199
Gross, Seymour L. 203
Group Marriage 70
Group processes today 196
Grover, John and Dick Grace 74
Grover (death, suicide) 181
Grownups Cry Too (feelings) 48
Guests in the Promised Land (Black images) 84
Guide to Non-Sexist Children's Books, A 201

Guiding Your Child to a More Creative Life 201
Gulliver's Travels 1, 9
Guttmacher, Alan 64
Guy, Rosa 44, 99
Guy Lenny (families, second marriage) 114

Hachenburg, Hanus (Terezin poet) 158
Hale, Lucretia 17
Half Breed (prejudices) 84
Half Million Teenagers, A [film] (venereal disease) 73
Hall, Robert E. 72
Hamilton, Virginia 85-86, 89
Hans Brinker and the Silver Skates 16
Hanson, Joan 48
Happy Orpheline, The (families, orphans) 115
Harada, Violet 200
Hard Life of a Teenager, The (sexuality) 64
Hardy, John Edward 203
Harris, Benjamin 8, 9
Harris, Christie 86
Harris, Karen H. 188
Harrison, Delois 169
Hating Book, The (feelings) 47
Haugaard, Erik C. 150, 155
Hautzig, Esther 141, 155
Haviland, Virginia 194
Hawthorne, Nathaniel 16
Hazard, Paul 1, 149, 189
He Bear, She Bear (sex roles) 84
Head, Ann 69
Hedgepeth, William and Denis Stock 70
Help for Girls (alternatives to pregnancy) 71
"Helping the Child's Heart and World" 223
Henry, Jeanette 222
Henry 3 (families, values) 115, 170
Herbst, Laura 222
He's My Brother (feelings) 47
Higginson, Thomas 17
Hill, Janet 195
Hinton, Susan E. 101-103
"Hip Pocket Books--The Baya Reading Interest Report" 202
Hirsh, Marilyn and Maya Narayan 62
His Enemy, His Friend (war and peace) 153, 173
His Own Where (sexuality) 58-59, 69
History of Childhood, The 202
History of Sanford and Merton, The 12

History of the Fairchild Family 14
Historye of Reynard the Fox, The 6
Hoagie's Rifle Gun (man and environment) 130-131
Hobbit, The 20
Hoffman, Martin 75
Hoffman, Phyllis 106
Hofland, Mrs. 14
Holland, Isabelle 59, 77
Holmes, Margaret C. 219
Holy Bible in Verse 9
Home from Far (death, reactions to) 181
Home from the Hill (families, homeless) 115-116
"Homosexual Literature" 74
Homosexuality 54, 74-75, 204
Homosexuality: A Selective Bibliography 74
Homosexuals and Society [audio cassette] 75
Hook a Fish, Catch a Mountain (ecology) 131
Horn Book Reflections on Children's Books and Reading 202
Hornbook, The 6
Horses of Anger (W.W. II, Germany) 156, 172
Horvath, Betty 121
House of Dies Drear, The (Black images) 86
House of Sixty Fathers, The (W.W. II) 152
House of Tomorrow (sexuality) 72
House of Wings, The (feelings) 44
House That Jack Built, The 17
Houston, James 88, 169
How Children See Our World 203
How Children Stopped the Wars (peace) 171-172
How Do I Feel? (feelings) 47
How Many Miles to Babylon (gangs, families) 99-100
How to Get an Abortion [audio cassette] 71
Howe, Florence 220
Huck, Charlotte S. 195
Human Birth, Growth and Development [filmstrip set] 67
Humor in fiction 174
Hundred Penny Box, The (families, the aged) 120
Hunt, Irene 172
Hunter, Kristin 84, 122
Hurlock, Elizabeth 91, 108, 191
Huston, Anne 104
Hutchins, Pat 167
Hutchinson, Rose E. 134

I Know What I Like (feelings) 47
I Know You, Al (families, second marriage) 116

I Never Loved Your Mind (sexuality) 69
I Never Saw Another Butterfly (W.W. II) 53, 152, 170
I Was There (Hitler youth, Nazi era) 142
I Will Go Barefoot All Summer for You (sexuality) 77
I Wonder If Herbie's Home Yet (friendship) 104-105
I Would Rather Be a Turnip 123
If I Built a Village (ecology) 131
If I Die in a Combat Zone (war, Vietnam) 164
If I Had My Way (feelings) 47
Ilg, Frances L. 191
Illich, Ivan 198
I'll Protect You from the Jungle Beasts (feelings, fear) 47-48
I'm Glad I'm Me (celebration of life) 176
I'm 17, I'm Pregnant and I Don't Know What to Do [film] 71
Image forming materials, selection of 81-82
Image of the Black in Children's Fiction 203
Images 79-89
  effect of on children 80
  in biography 187
  of minorities in literature (see also Blacks; Native Americans) 80
Images of the Negro in American Literature 203
In Between Miya (images, Japanese family) 84
"In the Country of Teenage Fiction" 203
In the Night Kitchen (sexuality) 61-62
In the Shadow of the Falcon (ecology) 132
"Increasing Children's Fantasies: Hold High the Cardboard Sword" 204
Individual, and society 26
Industrial revolution 9
Information Center on Children's Cultures 204
Inhelder, B. 215
Inner World of Childhood, A Study in Analytical Psychology 204
Interracial Books for Children 205
Interracial Marriage: Expectations and Realities 64
Invisible Minority, The [filmstrip] (homosexuality) 75
"Is Tomorrow a Four Letter Word?" 205
Island of the Blue Dolphins (loneliness) 31-32
Issues in Children's Book Selection 205
It's Like This, Cat (peers, alienation, families) 100
It's Not What You Expect (venereal disease) 72
Iwasaki, Chihiro 104

J.D. (feelings) 37
Jacklin, Carol Nagy 213
Jacobs, Joseph 18
Jennifer, Hecate, MacBeth, William McKinley and Me,
    Elizabeth (images of children) 83
Jennings, Frank C. 208
Johnny Crow's Garden 19
Johnny Tremain 20
Johnson, Annabel and Edgar 140
Johnson, Eric W. 65
Johnston, Frances E. 223
Jones, Clinton R. 75
Jones, Weyman 170
Jordan, June 58, 69, 177
Jordan, Mildred 146
Joshua's Day (feelings, anger) 48
Journey to Topaz (Japanese internment, W.W. II) 142
Joy, in children 174
Juba This and Juba That (celebration) 176
Julie of the Wolves (man and environment) 132
Jungle Books, The 18
Junior novel, the 27, 208
Just Me 37

Kantrowitz, Mildred 104
Karl, Jean 205
Kate (Jewish family, culture conflict) 143
Kathy [film] (venereal disease) 73
Kavik, the Wolf Dog (man and environment) 130
Keating, Charlotte Matthews 190
Keating and Owen Act, The 18
Keats, Ezra Jack 175
Kelen, Emery 170
Kerr, Judith 155
Kerr, M. E. 77, 97
Kesselman, Wendy 82
Key, Mary Ritchie 217
Kind of Secret Weapon, A (W.W. II, Denmark) 143, 155,
    158
King of the Golden River, The 16
Kingman, Lee 69
Kingsbury, M. E. 189
Kingsley, Charles 16
Kingston, Carolyn 224
Kipling, Rudyard 18
Kirkpatrick, Oliver 168

Kirkwood, James 58
Klein, Hilary Dole 201
Klein, Norma 47, 78, 117, 118
Knowledge of the Heavens and Earth Made Easy, The 10
Kohen Raz, Reuven 52-54, 93-94, 108, 191
Konigsburg, E. L. 83, 199
Kosinski, Jerzy 140
Krasilovsky, Phyllis 49
Krumgold, Joseph 115, 170

LaLuz, National Review of LaLuz 206
Labor in America 206
LaFarge, Phyllis 175
LaFontaine, Jean de 167
Lampman, Evelyn Sibley 84
Lanes, Selma 149, 198
Lang, Andrew 18
Lanier, Sterling E. 170
Lapides, Linda 197
Lasker, Joe 47
Last of the Mohicans 14
Last of the Trumpeters (ecology) 134
Latimer, Bettye 220
Latin America: An Annotated List of Materials for Children 206
Lavender [film] (lesbianism) 75
Lawson, Don 172
Lawson, Robert 21
Laycock, George 170
Lederman, Janet 186
Leela and the Watermelon (sexuality) 62
Leichman, Seymour 171
"Leisure in Children's Literature" 189
Lepman, Jella 190, 203
Lerner, Max 223
Lesbian Woman 75
Leshan, Eda J. 196
Lessons for Children 11
"Lest We Forget: Books on the Holocaust" 207
Lester, Julius 85
Letcher, Katie 77
Let's Be Enemies (feelings, anger) 168
Lewis, C. S. 22
Lexau, John 46
Library Journal 17
Life of Keshav: A Family Story from India 116-117

Lifton, Betty Jean 154, 159, 173
Likely Place, A 34
Lilliard, Paula Polk 212
Lindenfield, Frank 215
Linevski, A. 145
Lion and the Rat, The 167
Lion, the Witch and the Wardrobe, The 22
Listen for the Fig Tree (Black family, blind girl) 120
"Literature and the Schools" 207
"Literature for Adolescents, Pap or Protein?" 208
Literature for Adolescents, Selection and Use 207
"Literature for the Average Student" 210
Little, Jean 35, 143, 181
Little Book for Little Children, A 9
Little Fishes (W.W. II, victims) 150, 155
Little Goody Two Shoes 11
Little House in the Big Woods 20
Little Lord Fauntleroy 18
Little Match Girl 16
Little Pretty Pocketbook, A 10
Little Prince (peace) 171
Little Riders, The (W.W. II) 152
Little Women 17
Lives of Children, The: The Story of the 1st Street School 211
Lobel, Anita 168
Locke, John, theories on education 9
Lollipop Party, The (celebration) 176
Lonely War of William Pinto (war and peace) 172
Loner, The (aloneness and loneliness) 32-33
Long Escape, The (children at Dunkerque) 164
Long Journey, The (families, alternative life styles) 117
Long Journey Home: Stories from Black History (images) 85
Lordy, Aunt Hattie (celebration of country living) 176
Lorenzini, Carlo 18
Love
  as a theme in literature 40
  as related to power 40
Love and Marriage [filmstrip] 66
"Love and Power, the Psychological Signals of War" 148, 211
Love and Sex in Plain Language 65
Love and the Facts of Life [filmstrip] 67
Love Is a Special Way of Feeling 48
"Loving Choices" 62-78
Lukens, Rebecca T. 197
Lunatic, The [film] (sexuality) 73

M. C. Higgins the Great (Black images) 86
MacCann, Donnarae 188
McClelland, David 148, 211
Maccoby, Eleanor Emmons 213
MacDonald, Dwight 138
McDonald, George 17
McDougall, Ruth Doan 69
McHargue, Georgess 197
Mack, Raymond 215
McSwigan, Marie 151
Maddock, Reginald 110
Madeline (celebration) 177
Madeline's Rescue 177
Magic Number (peace) 169
Magic Wall (peace) 168
Male and Female: A Study of the Sexes 76
Males, views of in literature 81
Man and environment 128-138
Ma'n Da La (celebration) 177
Man Without a Face, The (homosexuality) 59, 61, 77
Mann, Horace 13
Mann, Peggy 134
Martin, Del and Phyllis Lyon 75
Martin Luther King, Jr.: Man of Peace (peace) 171
Martin's Father (celebration) 177
Marty, Martin E. 137
Mary Jane 22
Mary Jo's Grandmother (aloneness) 37-38
Mary Poppins 20
"Match girls" 16
Mathis, Sharon Bell 102, 119, 120
Matter of Life and Death: How Wars Get Started (peace) 172
"Maturation of the Junior Novel from Gestation to the Pill, The" 206
"Maturing Effect of War, The" 156-159
Maurice's Room 35
May, Rollo 40, 215
May I Cross Your Golden River (celebration of death) 181-182
"Maybe This Will Help" 189
Maynard, Fredelle 201
Mazer, Harry 111, 114
Mead, Margaret 76
Meade, Richard A. 207
Meaning Well (peers) 101
Means, Florence 85

Meigs, Cornelia 197
Melcher, Frederic 19
Members of the Gang (peers) 105
Mennonite Martha (religion) 143-144
Mental Health 212
Merla, Patricia 225
Merriam, Eve 175
Merrill, Jean 164, 171
Mickinock, Ray 87, 214
Midnight Fox, The (man and environment) 133
Miles, Miska 130, 180
Miles, Robert 210
Miller, Merle 75
Millett, Kate 76
Millions of Cats 20
Mills, Gretchen 198
Milne, A. A. 20
Minarik, Else Holmelund 48
Minority images (see also Blacks; Native Americans) 80
"Minority Nobody Knows, A" 212
Minority Problems: A Textbook of Readings in Intergroup Relations 212
Minudri, Regina 202
Miracle of the Mountains (peace) 170
Mr. and Mrs. Bo Jo Jones (young marriage) 69
Mister Brown and Mister Gray (peace) 169
Mizumura, Kazue 131
Moberg, Verne 196
Mom, the Wolf Man and Me (one parent family) 78, 117-118
Momma [newspaper] 71
Monster's Nose Was Cold (feelings) 48
Montessori, Maria 219
  on child and family 108
Montessori, A Modern Approach 212
Moon Deer, The, Thirteen Moons Series (ecology) 133
Moon of the Alligators, The, Thirteen Moons Series 133
Moon of the Gray Wolves, The, Thirteen Moons Series 133
Moon of the Mountain Lions, The, Thirteen Moons Series 132-133
Moore, Barrington, Jr. 216
Moore, Clement 14
Moral Judgement of the Child, The 212
"Moral Values and Children's Literature" 206
More All of a Kind Family (Jewish family) 110
Morey, Walt 130
Morse, Jedediah 12

Morte d'Arthur   6
Mother Goose rhymes   1
Mountain, The (man and environment)   133
Mountain of Truth, The (mysticism, religion)   144
Moustakas, Charles   223
"Muckrakers"   18
Mulberry Music, The (celebration of death)   182
Multi-Ethnic Media, Selected Bibliographies in Print   212
Munves, Elizabeth D.   223
Murphy, Robert   135
My Darling, My Hamburger (sexuality)   59, 69
My Enemy, My Brother (post-W.W. II, Arab-Israeli conflict)
      144, 145, 156, 157
My Grandson Lew (death)   182
My Special Best Words (Black family, celebration)   177
"Myths, Reality and Shades of Gray: What We Know and
      Don't Know About Sex Differences"   213

Naja, the Snake and Mangus, the Mongoose (peace)   167
Naomi in the Middle (sibling rivalry)   118
National Educational Association   18
Native Americans   87-88
   in literature, list   214
   negative images of, list   222-223
   stereotypes and inaccuracies about   214
Never Trust a Cowbird (peace)   170
Neville, Emily   100, 105, 150
New England Primer, The   8, 13
New Life, New Room (Black family, celebration)   177
"New List of Books for Free Children, A"   213
New Look at Children's Literature, A   213
Newbery Award   19
Newman, Robert   43
Night Watchmen (politics, individual freedom)   145
No Fighting, No Biting (feelings)   48
No More Trains to Tottenville (sexuality)   77
No Trespassing (peers)   105
Noar, Gertrude   224
Noisy Nancy Norris (celebration of life)   178
Norris, Gunilla B.   46
Norton, Andre   133, 171
Norton, Mary   22
"Nutritional Well Being, Our Goal for All Children"   223

Obadiah the Bold (Quakers)   147

O'Dell, Scott 31-32
Oh, Sex Education 63
Old Glory and the Realtime Freaks (sexuality) 77
Old Tale Carved out of Stone, An (ancient religion) 145
On Being a Woman 65
On Being Different (homosexuality) 75
Once-a-Year Day, The (friendship) 105
Once Upon a Mountain (peace) 167
One Is One (aloneness and loneliness) 33
O'Neill, Nena and George 70
Open Marriage: A New Life Style for Couples 70
Oral tradition, the 1
Orgel, Doris 182
Original Poems for Infant Minds 13
Our Bodies, Ourselves 76
Our Cup Is Broken (Native Americans, prejudices against) 85
"Our Forebears Made Childhood a Nightmare" 214
Outside (man and environment) 133
Outsiders, The (gangs) 101-102

Painter, Helen 216
Pairings and groupings 90-124
Pancakes--Paris (W.W. II) 151
Parent-child relationships 109, 218
Parker, William 74
Parnell, Peter 133
Parrish, Helen 83
Party, The [film] (sexuality, peer pressures) 68, 69
Patterson, Lillie 171
Pauli, Hertha 173
Peace Is an Adventure 170
Peaceable Revolution 173
Pearce, Phillippa 22
Peck, Ellen 64
Peck, Richard 203
Peer associations and pressures 56-57, 91-94
Peet, Bill 135
Penny Wars (sexuality) 78
People of Destiny Series (peace) 171
Pepper and Salt 18
Perrault 9
Peter and Veronica (peers) 104
Peter Pan Bag, The (sexuality) 69
"Peter Pan Principle" 149-150
Peterkin Papers, The 17

248 / Survival Themes

Peterson, Christine C. 219
Pheiffer, Leo 137
Phoebe (teenage pregnancy) 60, 69
Phoebe [film] 68
Piaget, Jean 36, 46, 192, 193, 196, 212, 215
Picard, Barbara Leonie 33
Picture books, emphasis on fear 188
Pierce, Ruth 71
Pig War, The (war and peace) 166
Pigman, The (peers) 102
Pilgrim's Progress 8
Pinocchio 18
Plain Girl (Mennonites) 146
Planet of Junior Brown, The 85-86
Play with Me 38
"Plight of the Native American, The" 87, 214
Plink, Plink, Plink (feelings) 49
Pocket Full of Seeds, A (W.W. II, French Jews) 145-146
Poem on the Rising Glory of America, A 11
Poems of Childhood 18
Portrait of Ivan 35
Potatoes, Potatoes (peace) 168
Potter, Beatrix 19
Potter, Bronson 41
Power and Innocence 40, 215
Prather, Ray 105
Pre-adolescent development
  group relationships 192
  peer associations and relationships 92-93
  puberty, early onset of 54
  sexuality, male and female 52-54
Prejudice and Race Relations 215
Preston, Edna Mitchell 49-50
Primer of Salysbury Use, The 6
Prince and the Pauper, The 17
Prodigal Son Sifted, The 8
Progressive Education Association 18
Promise, a Promise, A (Judaism) 146
Proof of the Pudding, The 215
Proud to Be Amish 146
Psychology of the Child 215
"Publishers for Peace Bibliography" 166-173
Puritan theology 7
Pushcart War, The (war and peace) 164
Pyle, Howard 18

Quiet Place, A (Black family, foster children) 118

Rabbit Hill 21
Race and the child 80
Radical Perspectives on Social Problems: Readings in
    Critical Sociology 215
Rafferty, Max 221
Rain Rain Rivers (celebration) 178
Raucher, Herman 69
Raven's Cry, The (Native Americans, plight of) 86
Reaching Children and Young People Through Literature 216
Reading Ladders for Human Relations 216, 225
Realism 4, 150, 151
Rebecca of Sunnybrook Farm 19
Reform Movement, England 15
Reid, Virginia M. 216
Reiss, Johanna 157
Religion and politics 137-147
"Religion Today and Tomorrow" 137
Renaissance, The 6
Return to Hiroshima 154, 159, 173
"Reviewing in an Age of Change" 216
Rhodes, Hugh 7
Rhymes of Childhood 18
Richard, Norman 171
Richards, Kenneth 171
Richter, Hans Peter 141, 142
Riley, James Whitcomb 18
Ring the Judas Bell (post-W.W. II, Greece) 156
Rinkoff, Barbara 105
Roam the Wild Country (man and environment) 133
Robinson Crusoe 1, 9
Rock and Willow, The (Alabama farm family) 118-119
Rogers, Carl R. 70
"Role of the Female in Children's Books ..." 217
Roosevelt Grady 27
Roscoe, William 14
Rose, Arnold 212
Rose, Caroline B. 212
Rose, The [film] (sexuality) 65
Rosenbaum, Joan and Lutie McAuliffe 50
Rossetti, Christina 17
Rowan, Helen 212
Rubin, Isador 64
Ruby (feelings, love, homosexuality) 44, 45, 61
Rudman, Marsha Kabakow 109, 122, 195

250 / Survival Themes

Rumblefish (gangs) 103
Run Softly, Go Fast (sexuality) 69
Runaway Generation, The 26, 138, 217
Ruskin, John 16
Rustin, Bayard 215

Sachs, Marilyn 103, 110, 145
Saint-Exupéry, Antoine de 171
Salley, Coleen C. 187
Sandburg, Carl 20
Sandoz, Mari 87
Sappho Was a Right-On Woman (lesbianism) 75
Schecter, Betty 173
Schick, Eleanor 122
Scholt, Grayce 189
"School as Surrogate Conscience, The" 218
Schwarz-Bart, Andre 88
Scoppetone, Sandra 60
Search for a New Land (Black images) 85
Search for Delicious (peace) 169
Secret Garden, The 19
Secret of Childhood, The 219
Selected Bibliography on Homosexuality, A 74
Selected Media About the American Indian for Children 219
Self-awareness, development in adolescent 32-33
Self-esteem, problem of in children and adolescents 81
Sendak, Maurice 61
Seton, Ernest T. 18
Seventeen Book of Answers, The (sexuality) 64
Seventeenth Street Gang (peers) 105-106
Seventh Son: The Life and Writings of W. E. B. DuBois, The 85
Sewell, Anna 17
Sex and Birth Control 64
Sex in the Adolescent Years: New Directions 64
Sex roles, stereotypes and differences 213
"Sex, Society and the Female Dilemma: A Dialogue Between Simone DeBeauvoir and Betty Friedan" 219
Sex: Telling It Straight 65
Sexism and Youth 219
Sexism in Award Winning Picture Books 220
Sexual Adolescent, The: Communicating with Teenagers about Sex 220
Sexual Politics 76
"Sexual Stereotypes Start Early" 220

Sexuality
   in literature for children and young people 52, 55, 56
   pre-adolescent, Kohen Raz on 52-54
   "young people speak for themselves" on 51
   young people's attitudes toward 218
"Sexuality in Children's Books" 206
Shargel, Susan 224
Sharmat, Marjorie 104
<u>Sheep of the Lal Bagh, The</u> (man and environment) 133
Sherburne, Zoa 60
Sherwood, Mrs. 14
Shulevitz, Uri 178
Shutze, Marcia and M. Jean Greenlaw 149
<u>Shy Little Girl, The</u> (feelings) 49
<u>Silence over Dunkerque</u> (W.W. II) 152, 165
<u>Simon</u> (aloneness) 33-34
<u>Sing Song</u> 17
<u>Single and Pregnant</u> 71
<u>Sister</u> (Black family) 119
<u>Skies of Crete, The</u> (W.W. II, victims) 152, 153, 156
<u>Slaughterhouse-Five</u> (Dresden fire bombing) 165
<u>Slipping Down Life, A</u> (feelings, love) 45
Small, Robert C. 207
Smith, Doris Buchanan 183
Smith, James Steel 197
Smith, Lillian 224
<u>Snow Treasure</u> (Norse children, Nazi occupation) 151
Socialization, the child and 91-94
<u>Society and the Healthy Homosexual</u> 75
"Some Recent Concepts of the Physical Growth of Children" 223
<u>Something, The</u> (feelings, fear) 49
<u>Songs of Innocence</u> 12
Sonneborn, Ruth 122, 176
Sorensen, Robert C. 63
<u>Sorensen Report: Adolescent Sexuality, The</u> 63
Sorenson, Virginia 146
<u>South Town</u> 22
Spargo, John 18, 187
Speare, Elizabeth 147
Sperry, Armstrong 30
Spiro, Melford 216
<u>Squib</u> (death) 182-183
Squire, James 211
Stacey, Judith 186
<u>Starman's Son</u> (peace) 171

252 / Survival Themes

<u>Starting Out Right: Choosing Books About Black People for Young Children, Preschool Through Third Grade</u> 220
<u>Statistic Named Anne, A</u> [film] (sexuality) 72
<u>Steffie and Me</u> (friendship) 106
Steptoe, John 49, 87, 177
Sterling, Dorothy 22
Stevenson, Robert Louis 17
<u>Stevie</u> (feelings, jealousy, Black images) 49
<u>Sticks and Stones</u> (sexuality) 77
Stiles, Martha B. 173
Stirling, Nora 69
Stolz, Mary 112
Stone, Elbertha H. 176
<u>Stone Faced Boy, The</u> (feelings) 34
<u>Story Catcher, The</u> (Native American images) 87
<u>Story of a Bad Boy, The</u> 17
<u>Story of Eric</u> [film] (sexuality) 65
<u>Story of Mankind, The</u> 20
<u>Street of the Flower Boxes, The</u> (man and environment) 134
Stuart, Irving and Lawrence E. Abt 64
<u>Suffer Little Children: Reflections on American Education</u> 221
Suhl, Yuri 165
Suicide, loneliness and 29
Sullivan, Marjorie 190
Sullivan, Peggy 216
<u>Summer of '42</u> (sexuality) 69
<u>Summer of My German Soldier</u> (war, effects of) 157
Summerhill, A. S. 216, 218
Sunday schools 12
Surowieki, Sandra Lucas 48
Survival, defined 4
Sutherland, Zena 187, 194
Swarthout, Glendon 129
Swift, Jonathan 9
<u>Swiss Family Robinson</u> 14

<u>Take Wing</u> (loneliness, retarded child) 35
<u>Tale of Peter Rabbit, The</u> 19
<u>Tanglewood Tales</u> 16
Tashjian, Virginia A. 176
<u>Taste of Blackberries, A</u> (death) 183
Taylor, Anne and Jane 13
Taylor, Byrd 49
Taylor, Edgar 14
Taylor, Sydney 110

Index / 253

Teacup Full of Roses (Black family) 119-120
Teenage reading preferences 197
  lists 202, 203, 208
Television 3, 150
Temper Tantrum Book (feelings) 49-50
Tenth Good Thing about Barney, The (death) 183
Ter Haar, Jaap 162
Text books and the American Indian 222
That Was Then, This Is Now (gangs) 102-103
"That's One Good Indian: Unacceptable Images in Children's
    Novels" 222
Then Again, Maybe I Won't (family values) 123
There Is a Tide (aloneness) 35-36
Thomas, Ianthe 176
Thomas, Marlo 76
Thompson, Jean 72
Thoughts on the Education of Daughters 11
"Thoughts on the Future Family" 216
Three Letter Word for Love, A [film] (sexuality) 66
Through the Looking Glass 1
Thwaite, Mary F. 200
Thy Friend Obadiah (Quakers) 146-147
Tikla 'Liktak 88
Tillich, Paul 137
Tim All Alone (loneliness) 38
Time Ago Tales of Jahdu, The (Black images) 86
Time for Peace 173
To Be a Slave (Black images) 85
"To Every Man a Chance" 224
Today's World 223
Tolkien, J. R. R. 20
Tom and Sam (peace) 167
Tom Swift 2, 19
Tom's Midnight Garden 22
Tony's Hardwork Day (loneliness) 38
Too Bad About the Haines Girl (teenage pregnancy) 60
Tops (peace) 168
Torgensen, Don 171
Toward Peace: The Nobel Prize 173
Tower of Babel (peace) 168
Towne, Mary 114
Townsend, John 69, 123, 225
Tragic Mode in Children's Literature, The 224
Traitors, The (W.W. II) 157
Travers, Pamela 20
Treasure Island 17
Trimmer, Sarah 11

Trouble in the Jungle (families, abandoned children) 123
Trumpet of the Swan (man and environment) 134
Trying Hard to Hear You (homosexuality) 60-61
Tuned Out (families, drug problem) 120-121
Tunis, John 152, 153, 165, 173
Turkle, Brinton 146, 168
Twain, Mark 17
Twenty and Ten (Norse children, Nazi occupation) 151
Twenty One Balloons, The 21
Twenty Thousand Leagues Under the Sea 17
Twinkle, Twinkle Little Star 13
Two Giants (peace) 167
Tyler, Anne 45

Uchida, Yoshiko 84
Udry, Janice 37, 168
Umbrella (celebration) 178
Uncle Misha's Partisans (W.W. II, resistance) 165-166
Understand Sex: A Young Person's Guide 64
United Nations in War and Peace 169
Unreluctant Years, The 224
Untapped Generation (sexuality) 63
Untermeyer, Louis 173
Upstairs Room, The (W.W. II, Holland) 157-158
Uptown (Black images) 87

VD Attack Plan [film] 73
VD Blues 73
VD Blues [television film] 73
VD: Facts You Should Know 74
VD Handbook 74
VD Myth and Reality [filmstrip] 74
VD--Prevent It [film] 73
VD: The ABC's 74
Values 215-216
Van Loon, Hendrik Willem 20
Van Stockum, Hilda Van 152
Varga, Juda 168
Venereal Disease: A Present Dancer [film] 74
"Vera and Bill Cleaver Know Their Whys and Wherefores" 224
Verne, Jules 17
Veronica Ganz (peers) 103-104
Veysey, Laurence 196
Vincent, E. Lee 191

Vindication of the Rights of Women 11
Violence 40-42
Viorst, Judith 183
Visit from St. Nicholas, A 14
Vocations for Social Change: The People's Yellow Pages 70
Vonnegut, Kurt, Jr. 165

Wahl, Jan 171
Walsh, Joan 48
War and peace 148
War for the Lot (war and peace) 170
Water Babies, The 16
Watts, Isaac 9
We Can Change It 224
We Shall Live in Peace 169
Wein, Bibi 26, 138, 217
Weinberg, Dr. George 75
Weisner, William 168
Weistein, Irving 164
Wells, Rosemary 98
Wersba, Barbara 30, 57, 69
Wezel, Peter 168
What About Homosexuality? 75
"What Does Research Reveal About Attitudes Toward Reading?" 211
What Is Fear? An Introduction to Feelings 50
What Is Marriage? [filmstrip] 66
"What Is Real? Asked the Rabbit One Day" 225
What the Trees Said (sexuality) 70
When Hitler Stole Pink Rabbit (W.W. II, Jewish family) 155
When Love Needs Care [film] (venereal disease) 72
When the Legends Die (Native American images) 87
Where Is Daddy? The Story of a Divorce 123-124
Where the Lilies Bloom (death, families) 184
White, E. B. 22, 134
White Bird (man and environment) 134
Who Really Killed Cock Robin? (ecology) 134-135
Wickes, Frances G. 204
    on death 179
Wier, Ester 32
Wiggin, Kate Douglas 19
Wild Animals I Have Known 18
Wild Geese Calling (man and environment) 135
Wild in the World (loneliness, death) 45-46
Wilder, Laura Ingalls 20

Wilkerson, David and Don 63
Will I Have a Friend? (friendship) 106
Wind in the Willows, The 16
Winged Watchman, The (Holland, Nazi occupation) 152
Winnie the Pooh 20
Winship, Elizabeth C. 64
Witch of Blackbird Pond, The (religion and politics) 147
Wojciechowska, Maia 120
Wolf Run: A Caribou Eskimo Tale (Eskimo culture) 88
Wollstonecraft, Mary 11
Woman Named Solitude, A (Black images, slavery) 88-89
Women, views of in literature 81
Women's Movement 81
Women's Role in Society [audio cassette] 76
Wonder Book for Boys and Girls, A 16
Wondriska, William 169
Woodard, Gloria 188
Written for Children, An Outline of English-Language Children's Literature 225
Wump World, The (man and environment) 135
Wyss, Johann David 14

Yashima, Taro 37
Yep, Laurence 82
Yonge, Charlotte 16
You Would If You Loved Me (sexuality) 69
Young Folk's History of the U.S., A 17
Young People
   and politics 138, 217
   on freedom 218
   on parents, sex and families 218
   search for self 26
   sexual knowledge 63
   sexual self understanding 64
   social roles 75
Young, Single and Pregnant [filmstrip] 66
Your Child's Reading Today 225
Youth and War: World War One to Vietnam 172-173

Z for Zachariah (atomic war aftermath) 135-136
Zeb (aloneness and loneliness) 36
Zeely (Black images) 89
Zim, Herbert 21
Zindel, Paul 59, 69, 102
Zolotow, Charlotte 47, 182

DATE DUE